Sacrifice in the Modern World

Sacrifice in the Modern World

On the Particularity and Generality of Nazi Myth

David Pan

NORTHWESTERN UNIVERSITY PRESS
EVANSTON, ILLINOIS

Northwestern University Press
www.nupress.northwestern.edu

Copyright © 2012 by Northwestern University Press. Published 2012.
All rights reserved.

Printed in the United States of America

10 9 8 7 6 5 4 3 2 1

Library of Congress Cataloging-in-Publication Data

Pan, David, 1963–
  Sacrifice in the modern world : on the particularity and generality of Nazi myth / David Pan.
    p. cm.
  Includes bibliographical references and index.
  ISBN 978-0-8101-2816-3 (cloth : alk. paper)
  1. Sacrifice—Social aspects—Germany—History—20th century. 2. National socialism—Moral and ethical aspects. 3. Violence—Social aspects—Germany—History—20th century. 4. Mythology—Political aspects—Germany—History—20th century. I. Title.
  DD256.6.P36 2012
  306.6—dc23
                                                                    2012011865

♾ The paper used in this publication meets the minimum requirements of the American National Standard for Information Sciences—Permanence of Paper for Printed Library Materials, ANSI Z39.48-1992.

This book is dedicated to the memory of Paul Piccone

CONTENTS

Acknowledgments	*ix*
List of Abbreviations	*xi*
Introduction	*3*
Chapter One Violence and Culture: The Sublime from Kant to Adorno	*13*
Chapter Two The Politics of Myth in the Nazi Period: Alfred Baeumler and Carl Einstein	*45*
Chapter Three Theories of Sacrifice in the Modern World: Georges Bataille, René Girard, and Walter Burkert	*79*
Chapter Four The Genealogy of Nazi Morality	*113*
Conclusion	*149*
Notes	*153*
Index	*163*

ACKNOWLEDGMENTS

The ideas in this book have developed over a long time and with the help and encouragement of many. I am grateful to Russell Berman, Andreas Huyssen, Paul Michael Lützeler, and Hans Dieter Zimmermann for their indispensable assistance in bringing my thoughts to fruition. Brigitte Rossbacher and Robert Weninger provided suggestions for revisions to chapter 2. I would like to thank the Department of Comparative Literature and Foreign Languages at the University of California, Riverside, for allowing me to present an earlier version of chapter 3 and for their very helpful comments, particularly from John Kim, Robert Doran, and Sabine Doran. Muriel Achache, Ute Berns, Arianel Flores, Lutz Koepnick, Cecilia Novero, Maren Pan, Mary Piccone, Daniel Purdy, and William Rasch have provided advice and encouragement during various stages of this project. Some of the initial ideas were first developed during a period in which my work was supported by a Getty Grant, and the writing of this manuscript could not have been completed without the assistance of a fellowship from the Alexander von Humboldt Foundation. At Northwestern University Press, I would like to thank Heather Antti, Rudy Faust, Marianne Jankowski, Parneshia Jones, Gianna Mosser, and Peter Raccuglia for their outstanding work in all the different phases of the publication process. Finally, this book would not have appeared without the vision and dedication of Henry Carrigan.

An earlier version of chapter 1 was published as "Adorno's Failed Aesthetics of Myth," *Telos* 115 (1999): 7–35. Chapter 2 is based on material originally published as "Instrumentalizing the Sacred: From Alfred Baeumler to Manfred Frank," in *Wendezeiten, Zeitenwenden: Positionsbestimmungen zur deutschsprachigen Literatur, 1945–1995*, edited by Robert Weninger and Brigitte Rossbacher (Tübingen: Stauffenburg, 1997), 233–47; "The Struggle for Myth in the Nazi Period: Alfred Baeumler, Ernst Bloch, and Carl Einstein," *South Atlantic Review* 65, no. 1 (2000): 41–57; and "Revising the Dialectic of Enlightenment: Alfred Baeumler and the Nazi Appropriation of Myth," *New German Critique* 84 (2001): 37–54. I am grateful to the publishers for allowing this material to appear here.

ABBREVIATIONS

AH Adolf Hitler. "Grundsätzliche Betrachtungen über die Kunst." *Bausteine zum deutschen Nationaltheater* 1, no. 3. Munich: Franz Eher, 1933.

AS1 Georges Bataille. *The Accursed Share: An Essay on General Economy*. Vol. 1: *Consumption*, translated by Robert Hurley. New York: Zone Books, 1988.

AT Theodor W. Adorno. *Aesthetic Theory*, edited by Gretel Adorno and Rolf Tiedemann, translated by Robert Hullot-Kentor. Minneapolis: University of Minnesota Press, 1997.

B Alfred Baeumler. "Einleitung: Bachofen, der Mythologe der Romantik." In *Der Mythus von Orient und Okzident* by Johann Jakob Bachofen (1926). Munich: Beck, 1956.

BG Alfred Baeumler. *Bildung und Gemeinschaft*. Berlin: Junker und Dünnhaupt, 1942.

BT Friedrich Nietzsche. *The Birth of Tragedy and Other Writings*, edited by Raymond Geuss and Ronald Speirs, translated by Ronald Speirs. Cambridge: Cambridge University Press, 1999.

CJ Immanuel Kant. *Critique of Judgment*, translated by Werner S. Pluhar. Indianapolis: Hackett, 1987.

DE Max Horkheimer and Theodor W. Adorno. *Dialectic of Enlightenment*, translated by John Cumming. New York: Continuum, 1972.

E Carl Einstein. *Werke*. Vol. 3: *1929–1940*, edited by Marion Schmid and Liliane Meffre. Berlin: Medusa, 1985.

GE Manfred Frank. *Gott im Exil: Vorlesungen über die Neue Mythologie, II. Teil*. Frankfurt am Main: Suhrkamp, 1988.

HN Walter Burkert. *Homo Necans: The Anthropology of Ancient Greek Sacrificial Ritual and Myth*, translated by Peter Bing. Berkeley: University of California Press, 1983.

HS Giorgio Agamben. *Homo Sacer: Sovereign Power and Bare Life*, translated by Daniel Heller-Roazen. Stanford, Calif.: Stanford University Press, 1998.

JF Johann Gottlieb Fichte. *Addresses to the German Nation*, translated by R. F. Jones and G. H. Turnbull, edited by George Armstrong Kelly (1808). New York: Harper and Row, 1968.

KG	Manfred Frank. *Der kommende Gott: Vorlesungen über die Neue Mythologie, I. Teil.* Frankfurt am Main: Suhrkamp, 1982.
MW	Alfred Baeumler. *Männerbund und Wissenschaft.* Berlin: Junker und Dünnhaupt, 1934.
OT	Hannah Arendt. *The Origins of Totalitarianism.* New York: Harcourt, Brace and World, 1966.
PD	Jürgen Habermas. *The Philosophical Discourse of Modernity,* translated by Frederick Lawrence. Cambridge, Mass.: MIT Press, 1987.
PS	Georg Wilhelm Friedrich Hegel. *Phenomenology of Spirit,* translated by Arnold V. Miller. New York: Oxford University Press, 1977.
TH	René Girard. *Things Hidden Since the Foundation of the World,* translated by Stephen Bann and Michael Metteer. London: Athlone Press, 1987.
VS	René Girard. *Violence and the Sacred,* translated by Patrick Gregory. Baltimore, Md.: Johns Hopkins University Press, 1977.

SACRIFICE IN THE
MODERN WORLD

Introduction

> Hermes asked Zeus how he should distribute shame and justice to humans. "Should I distribute them as the other arts were? This is how the others were distributed: one person practicing the art of medicine suffices for many ordinary people; and so forth with the other practitioners. Should I establish justice and shame among humans in this way, or distribute it to all?" "To all," said Zeus, "and let all have a share. For cities would never come to be if only a few possessed these, as is the case with the other arts. And establish this law as coming from me: Death to him who cannot partake of shame and justice, for he is a pestilence to the city."
> —Plato, *Protagoras*

When considered in terms of the notion of sacrifice, the modern world has been overshadowed by the experience of Nazism and the Holocaust, and these events have often been read as the climax in terms of which other examples of sacrifice gain urgency and historical significance. Although the notion of progress led early ethnographic studies of sacrifice to focus on ritual animal or human sacrifices in "primitive" cultures,[1] the experience of Nazism suggests that sacrifice as a ritual and as a behavioral trope is not limited to some past era or "backward" cultures, but is a modern phenomenon as well. Present-day examples of self-sacrifice, martyrdom, and victimization continue to oblige us to reflect on the continuing importance of sacrifice as a human phenomenon.

A primary tenet of recent theories of sacrifice is that Nazism and the Holocaust are paradigms of a form of modern sacrifice, and several approaches have used the Nazis as an instance of sacrifice in general. These theories are split between a pessimistic view that sees a continual repetition of aggression and violence in sacrifice and an optimistic view that claims that sacrifice is based on an ideology that can be overcome by the ability to see through its falsity. The pessimistic view underlies Sigmund Freud's treatment of aggression as a basic human instinct, one whose increasing power threatens to release a wave of destruction that becomes more horrible with more technologically sophisticated civilizations.[2] In a variation on this approach, Georges Bataille's analysis of sacrifice leads to an understanding of World War II as an example of a necessary destruction of excess that can only be avoided in the future to the extent that the destructive impulse can find alternative channels, such as sacrifice, gift giving, or consumerism.[3] By contrast, the more optimistic approaches attempt to imagine a world without sacrifice. Somber though their account is, Max Horkheimer and Theodor Adorno maintain the possibility of utopia when they argue that sacrifice is a form of exchange and reification. If Nazi sacrifice is simply a consistently applied form of the instrumentalizing reason that accompanies all sacrifice, then the man-made character of this reason suggests that its development can be altered for the better.[4] In another such approach, René Girard argues that Nazi sacrifice is an example of a scapegoat mechanism, whereby group aggression is directed at innocent victims who are falsely branded as the guilty fomenters of trouble in society.[5] To the extent that Girard imagines that we might come to understand the irrationality of the scapegoat mechanism, his theory also provides for the possibility of overcoming sacrifice. Also attempting to imagine an alternative to sacrifice, Giorgio Agamben argues that Nazi sacrifice followed the structure of the ancient Roman *homo sacer*, in which a particular class of people is reduced to the status of bare life and designated as both unfit for sacrifice and available to be killed without any consequences for the killer.[6]

Instead of seeing sacrifice as a pathology that either is permanent or may one day be overcome, this book will treat sacrifice as an essential element of a particular culture's ethical system. Whether or not they can imagine a future without sacrifice, there is a tendency in all of these theories to present a single, uniform explanation for sacrifice that applies not only to the Nazis but to all the different manifestations of sacrifice across time and cultural traditions. By contrast, the idea to be explored here is that the phenomenon of sacrifice should be considered in its cultural variety and not as an invariant structure or process. Accordingly, the present study will attempt to understand Nazi sacrifice in its particularity and as merely one variation on the structuring of sacrifice. Rather than holding up the Nazis as an example for how sacrifice functions in general, this study will approach sacrifice as a pervasive phenomenon that has a distinct manifestation in every particular time and place.

The treatment of sacrifice as a culturally specific phenomenon faces the double theoretical task of first determining what generic characteristics all examples of sacrifices have in common and then understanding how a particular version of sacrifice is specific to its culture. The primary premise here is that a particular structure of sacrifice will have a formative and distinguishing influence on the way that a surrounding culture is organized. Although every culture presupposes some notion of sacrifice in its value system, every specific manifestation of sacrifice will be unique. The universality of sacrifice consists precisely in the tendency to create cultural variety. While the particular "economy of sacrifice" that is dominant in a culture will generally have a crucial role in defining that culture's values and ethics, each specific instance of sacrifice will present a unique model for how it might function in practice. The thesis about the formative character of sacrifice on every culture depends upon the idea, which will be elucidated briefly here and more thoroughly in the following chapters, that sacrifice is organized as an interplay between aesthetic structures and a process of decision making that culminates in the fulfillment of a promise.

An Aesthetics of Sacrifice

The first step for this discussion is to determine the understanding of the relationship between violence and culture by which different manifestations of sacrifice might be judged. The optimistic account of this relationship, exemplified in Theodor Adorno's work on aesthetics, maintains that culture opposes violence and that the advancement of human culture is accompanied by a progression away from violence and toward discussion and agreement as the means for resolving conflicts. In rejecting this account in chapter 1, this study takes an anti-utopian stance; it also assumes that continuing progress is not the goal of human endeavor. The anti-utopian position, in fact, arises from the pragmatic decision to remain agnostic about the possibility of such a utopia of nonviolence. This pragmatism allows for a review of the history of forms of sacrifice up to the present day as indicative of the ways in which violence and culture might continue to relate to each other in the future. At the same time, the neutrality concerning human society's final goals is an almost necessary condition for a study of sacrifice as a historical practice. For if, as will be argued here, sacrifice is in its essence a technique for determining and establishing final goals for a particular community, then a predetermination of final goals would prejudice the study of sacrifice in such a way that the details and mechanisms of the technique itself would be obscured. Such a prejudice toward a particular set of final goals is not just a characteristic of Adorno's utopian attempt to explain sacrifice as a technique to be overcome and replaced by nonviolence. Considerations of sacrifice as an ongoing human activity have also been unduly influenced by either a Christian ethic, as in the case of René Girard, or a kind of an individualist ethic, as in the case of Georges Bataille.

The idea of aesthetics to be developed here derives from Adorno's attempt to recover in aesthetic experience the possibility of "non-identity"—a situation of freedom, or, in Adorno's terms, a liberation from the domination of the concepts imposed by reason. But while Adorno's goal is to defend non-identity—that is, nature in its freedom—against domination by rational concepts, he is unwilling to accept the full measure of violence that true non-identity implies. In order for non-identity to exist, nature must be conceived of as a realm of contradiction to human desires and a source of violence. It is not simply the "natural world" of plants, animals, and insects, but any situation of chaos, including the development of human history, in which no reliable predictions can be made about future developments and in which these developments might at any time, from a human perspective, turn painful and destructive. Because he assumes that nature should no longer be an object of fear in the modern world but a place of reconciliation, Adorno's aesthetics are built around the subject's domination of the world that would be the basis of harmony with nature. The centrality of the individual for Adorno's aesthetics leads him to conclude that aesthetic truth cannot manifest itself without the help of philosophical analysis. This merging of aesthetic with philosophical truth destroys the possibility of non-identity by subordinating it to a conceptual determination.

While retaining Adorno's insights about the idea of an aesthetic truth, this study will use a methodology that accepts violence as an element that every culture must face. The source of this violence is nature, understood not as a stable set of objects but as the Freudian reality principle—that is, everything that opposes a specific set of human goals, including both the power of external nature and the unpredictability of social relations that leads to social and political violence. These limitations on human goals require us to constantly make sacrifices in which certain values are to be upheld over others. While the aesthetic depiction of sacrifice presents particular examples of how these choices can be made, in a ritual of sacrifice we make a commitment to adhere to a particular conception of sacrifice.

A focus on violence as itself the source of a reality missing from everyday life becomes the basis of the theory of myth and ritual sacrifice developed by the Nazi philosopher Alfred Baeumler. He thereby develops an idea of reality that J. P. Stern identifies as pervasive among European modernist writers after Nietzsche and that consists of a discernment of a "true" reality grounded in violence that exists behind a superficial, ordinary reality.[7] While Stern sees this "quest for 'reality'" as an important step toward the development of National Socialism,[8] Baeumler's example shows how it may be possible to distinguish a National Socialist version of this quest from alternative ones. Baeumler's specific view of sacrifice designates the blood ritual as material and therefore more real than the myth, a perspective that discounts the aesthetic meaning of the sacrifice and focuses on its materiality. In the deliberate spilling of blood, the sacrifice for Baeumler creates a violence that immediately escalates the gravity of an event. For him, violence itself produces a truer kind of reality that can serve as the basis of culture. This move away from the aesthetics of sacrifice and toward its materiality ends up denying the importance of considering the specific structure of sacrifice that a ritual would affirm.

The aesthetic confrontation with violence occurs neither as a power struggle nor as a fascination with the pure materiality of death and destruction. Rather, an aesthetic understanding of sacrifice both recognizes the centrality of violence as a limit on human action and yet sees sacrifice as part of a judgment process that establishes the human goals that define the society's relationship to violence. There are two impulses to this process: a mimetic one and a willful one. If nature can never really be conquered by human understanding and continues to exist, in whatever guise, as an antagonist to human endeavor, then the individual subject must remain subordinate to outside forces, and the subject's power cannot be the basis of the construction of aesthetic experience. Not reason, but mimesis—that is, the imitation of outside forces functioning as a recognition of the power of nature—is the source of the inspiration that creates works of art. Mimesis and aesthetic experience function to create an aesthetic truth that becomes the cultural basis for judging individual human actions.

Yet, this mimesis does not consist of a total subordination of the subject to the violence of nature. The aesthetic reaction to nature is neither a passive horror nor a futile attempt at mastery, but a willful sacrifice of the subject for the benefit of a higher ideal. This structure of sacrifice, which Immanuel Kant describes in his analytic of the sublime, is not based on the subordination of nature to the domination of the subject, but of a submission of the subject to the dictates of a metaphysical authority that exceeds both nature and the individual subject. This subordination of individual desires to a higher ideal is the movement that defines moral action. But because this sacrifice is an aesthetic experience rather than a rational conclusion, the practice of morality is not based in reason but in aesthetic judgment, and morality must ground itself in an authority higher than the individual subject. At the same time, the construction of this metaphysical ideal does not precede the aesthetic experience but is a negative projection from out of the form of the aesthetic experience.

Because metaphysical truth depends here on aesthetic processes, morality and the ideals upon which it is based are culturally specific, linked to the particular experiences of a community. The community provides the necessary context for the development of the subject, and the subject is dependent upon the larger community for its existence and structure. The basic cultural unit cannot be the individual subject, as Adorno assumes, but the group that constructs the subject. Accordingly, the defense of particularity cannot be a defense of the individual subject, but of cultural specificity, and the idea of freedom must be reconfigured so that it is understood, not as an emancipation of the individual, but as a self-determination of a community.

The Narrative Structure of Sacrifice

In Henri Hubert and Marcel Mauss's definition, "sacrifice is a religious act which, through the consecration of a victim, modifies the condition of the moral person who accomplishes it or that of certain objects with which he is concerned."[9] This idea of sacrifice, in which the victim is consecrated for the sake of a transformation into something else, has an aesthetic structure. The relation implied by the act of consecration is a narrative movement that links an action to a consequence. This movement from action to consequence is not just a relation of causal necessity, as in the case when one would say that plunging a knife in the heart causes a person to die. Rather, an example of sacrifice would understand this death as being carried out willfully *for the sake of* something else. In the example of the Nazi conception, it might be said that, for them, sacrifice is carried out for the sake of the redemption of the German nation. While this example of sacrifice implies some measure of cause and effect between the sacrifice of a life and the good of the German nation, there are three distinguishing aspects of the phrase *for the sake of* that take it beyond the cause-and-effect relation.

First, the phrase implies that the action and the consequence stand in a relation of conflict, so that the action involves the destruction or restriction of one thing in order to further the well-being of another thing. Second, in considering this relation of conflict, there is a statement about values in which the two sides of the balance, in this case individual life and the nation, are weighed against each other, and one is declared to be more valuable than the other. The movement of sacrifice is one that presents a conflict that must then be resolved by making a decision. This sequence of events—conflict, decision, resolution—is the basic structure of a dramatic narrative. Because sacrifice contains a dramatic structure, it must also be considered in terms of its aesthetic effect on those who witness (see or hear of) the sacrifice. The third point, then, is that this aesthetic effect is constitutive for subjectivity. As Hubert and Mauss note, the consecration of the victim "modifies the condition of the moral person who accomplishes it." This transformation is a fundamental one that establishes the moral structure of behavior, not just for the performer of the sacrifice but for all those who aesthetically participate in the process. In this analysis of the sacrifice, it is not a kind of blind repetition, but an aesthetic event whose repetition always involves a situation of choice and a renewed decision. This decision does not precede the ideal for which the sacrifice is made. Rather, the ideal emerges as a consequence of the sacrifice.

In the example of Nazism, the German nation comes into being as an object and ideal only through the enactment of the sacrifice. Without the sacrifice, the German nation does not exist as a real entity. This point about the dependence of the ideal on the sacrifice is perhaps the most far-reaching and also the most in need of support, as it defines all ideals as dependent on a sacrificial dynamic. The enactment of sacrifice in a particular situation would in this case be the movement that establishes a particular ideal as the final goal of human existence for those involved.

This aesthetic effect cannot be taken for granted, however. Rather, the key to understanding the enduring significance of sacrifice is to understand the process whereby a particular example of sacrifice succeeds or fails to gain legitimacy and adherence in a culture. The ability of a particular sacrificial narrative to establish itself depends upon the extent to which this narrative is perceived as an accurate means of summing up the ways in which violence and culture relate to each other in a particular case. If the sacrifice presents what people feel to be a false depiction of the particular violent forces impacting a culture or of their understanding of the key goals of their culture, then it will no longer be taken seriously. On the other hand, the particular construction of ideals that a sacrifice implies will also have a determining effect on what people will consider to be dangerous or not dangerous to their way of life.

This weighing of values against each other that is involved in a sacrifice means that sacrifice is also intimately linked to mechanisms of morality, and Claudia Koonz has convincingly argued that Nazism included a strong sense of moral purpose on the part of many of its main actors.[10] If this weighing of values occurs as part of an aesthetic experience rather than one conducted in a process of rational debate or within a context of religious revelation, then the link between sacrifice and morality can be investigated as part of an analysis of the trope of sacrifice as it occurs in a culture. Morality, understood as a set of rules that places limits on individual actions for some greater good, is enacted in the process of sacrifice, in which values are weighed against each other and a decision is made. The sacrifice embodies the mental process involved in any moral decision. Such a consideration of sacrifice that links it to morality presumes that aesthetic experience is crucial for establishing morality and that dramatic narrative lies at the center of this experience. This understanding of sacrifice as an aesthetic experience and as part of a moral mechanism already biases the analysis toward a specific model of sacrifice in which the aesthetic experience of the sacrifice is taken seriously as a constitutive part of the moral meaning.

As mentioned, one of the main consequences of this aesthetic structure of sacrifice is that it must be treated as a culturally specific phenomenon. Since every reception community will establish its own notion of sacrifice differently, sacrifice cannot be considered as a single phenomenon with a unified structure. To the extent that every narrative of sacrifice exhibits a distinct structure, each culture will have its own way of conceiving and approaching sacrifice. The specificity of sacrifice leads to two consequences for the analysis. First, the individual instances of sacrifice are not related to a universal notion of sacrifice and violence but only to previous instances of sacrifice in a cultural tradition. Second, each sacrifice is taken to be a specification of an ethical system at a particular time and place. Because the enactment of every sacrifice must consist of a weighing of different values and a decision for one value, every instance of sacrifice establishes an ethic for that particular situation. It does not establish a universal ethic, but only one that holds for that particular decision. To the extent that the decision manifested in that sacrifice becomes exemplary for other instances of sacrifice, however, the ethical ideal manifested in the sacrifice will be extended into a sequence of sacrifices that relate each instance to another previous instance. Although this interlocking chain of sacrifices does not establish any universal authority that would transcend those particular instances, the chain of instances also constitutes a tradition that, in offering both limitations and possibilities for future actions, cannot be described as a kind of easy relativism. Instead, each particular sacrifice becomes the focal point where tradition and a present situation meet, a decision is made, and the consequences are interpreted in a succeeding sacrificial moment, this chain then building the basis for the goals and ideals of a culture, for better or for worse.

Nazi Sacrifice

Because the consideration of sacrifice as an aesthetic phenomenon precludes the attempt to provide an exhaustive account, the study of Nazi sacrifice can only be one small piece of the larger theme of sacrifice in human culture. Just as the varieties of aesthetic forms lead to differing notions of cultural identity, the analysis of sacrifice in a particular situation describes just one way in which the phenomenon of sacrifice manifests itself.

The example of Nazi sacrifice distinguishes itself by its reliance on a merging of a focus on individual sovereignty with its apotheosis in the nation. While it has been commonly assumed that the Nazi movement supported a suppression of individual development by the structures of the state, this book will argue that the Nazi vision was in fact an individualist one in which the free development of individuals, without the interference of the state, should lead naturally to the growth of the nation as the collective embodiment of individual development. This construction of the nation as the fluid and ever-developing manifestation of the development of individual Germans harmonizes the interests of the individual with those of the nation and also sets up the link between Hitler the individual and the German nation as a whole. *like bildungsroman?*

These characteristics of the Nazi vision of individual and nation demonstrate its ties to the idea of *Bildung* developed in the nineteenth century. This connection is supported in chapter 4, first, by the historical inability of the *Bildungsbürgertum* to oppose the Nazis, and, second, by references in Nazi pedagogical theory to the idea of *Bildung,* and, third, to the similarity of goals between the ideas of Wilhelm von Humboldt and of Johann Gottlieb Fichte on the one hand and those of the Nazis on the other hand. They all insist, first, on the primacy of affinity (i.e., an inner passion) for determining the development of the individual and, second, on the strong connection between the development of the individual and the world-historical development of the nation.

The specific Nazi addition to the notion of *Bildung* was the use of racism as the idea underlying the progress of the German nation as a world-historical event. The Nazi promotion of German individual and national development as a culmination of human development defines the National Socialist project as one in which the focus is on the single-minded pursuit of such development rather than on setting limits on the individual and the nation. The Nazi structure of sacrifice brought together the focus on world-historical development inherited from German idealism with an insistence on the importance of sacrifice. Although the insistence on sacrifice may be read as a departure from this idealist tradition, the Nazis reveal the structure of sacrifice that is implicit in this tradition. As Hannah Arendt has argued, constant movement and unending development rather than stasis and stability were the key characteristics of the Nazi movement. The idea of continuing movement established the context for both the specific structure of Nazi sacrifice as well as its antagonism to traditional constraints.

At the same time as the Nazis developed a notion of sacrifice to accompany the emancipatory impulse of the *Bildung* tradition, their racism created a class of scapegoats that Agamben links to the ancient Roman category of the *homo sacer*. Consequently, the Nazi model of sacrifice consisted of a double dynamic in which the soldierly heroes of the nation are celebrated as sacrifices for a world-historical development, and in which those, such as Jews and Communists, that have been defined as unsuitable for sacrifice within the German national project, are violently eliminated. The Nazis can be distinguished by their attempt to separate sacrifice from violence in such a way that they become two distinct phenomena, sacrifice being celebrated in public rituals and violence being applied in secret as a way of eliminating certain groups.

Consequently, resistance to Nazi violence does not consist of a rejection of sacrifice, but an embracing of it. As Arnold Schoenberg's *A Survivor from Warsaw* demonstrates, the dehumanization carried out by the Nazis in the camps depended on an elimination of the symbolic processes of sacrifice and their replacement with arbitrary violence. The only possibility of resistance to this dehumanizing violence consisted in a process of rehumanization that only occurs with the subjugation of the individual to a set of rules for sacrifice that affirm an ideal, in this case in the chanting of the Jewish Prayer of the Dead. By placing their deaths within the context of the prayer, the prisoners' chanting transforms their deaths from extermination into sacrifice for an ideal embodied in the Jewish religion. Sacrifice then becomes the opposite, not to life, but to death without sacrifice, a death without meaning and without a ritual that could integrate it into a cultural tradition.

Because the Nazi conception of sacrifice exemplifies processes that are an essential part of every culture, though not in that particular form, the example of the Nazis continues to haunt modern society. The challenge of any approach to the question of sacrifice, and the project of this book, is to accept it as a continually recurring phenomenon while still being able to criticize those manifestations of sacrifice that lead to a multiplication of violence rather than to its neutralization.

Chapter One

Violence and Culture

The Sublime from Kant to Adorno

This book treats sacrifice as an aesthetic phenomenon that functions like works of art to the extent that specific sacrificial narratives and rituals are established and endure based on their ability to appeal to the subjects who make up their audience. The goal of this chapter is to demonstrate that this appeal is based on disinterested, aesthetic criteria and that an analysis of the particular sacrificial narratives and rituals found in a cultural tradition will yield insights about the structures of subjectivity dominant in that culture. According to this account, sacrifice is built upon a process of aesthetic judgment whose goal is to enact a particular interpretation of the relationship of a people to its ideals.

This chapter demonstrates this aesthetic aspect of sacrifice through an analysis and critique of Theodor Adorno's aesthetic theory. His approach to aesthetics is useful here because he posits a specifically aesthetic form of truth that is separate from conceptual truth. He is thus able to grant to works of art a certain mimetic capacity in which they are able to mediate to us insights about our fundamental relationship to nature. In adapting his theories to a theory of sacrifice, I employ his notion of aesthetic truth while at the same time arguing that he did not apply it as consistently as he might have. I offer two main critiques of Adorno's aesthetics. First, his understanding of the mimesis of nature that the work of art carries out is useful as a way of understanding art as a conduit for experience about the world outside of human constructs. But Adorno's theory is limited in that he assumes that nature is a space of harmony; in fact, a notion of nature that sees it as outside of human constructs must conceive of nature as a place of violence. Second, because he considers violence as coming from "the concept," that is, human control and manipulation, rather than from nature, he has a notion of a universal subject that preexists violence and that conforms to a supposed harmony of nature. For Adorno, the subject exists naturally in a state of freedom and only suffers violence as a result of rational manipulation.

In arguing against Adorno on these two points, this chapter seeks to establish sacrifice as a fundamental aesthetic structure that functions, first, to set up a culture's relationship to the violence of nature and, second, to define the constraints on subjectivity in that culture in a way that specifically adapts subjects to the violent forces that they confront in their biological and social environment. In what follows, I first defend Max Horkheimer and Theodor Adorno's notion of aesthetic truth. In doing so, however, I argue that Horkheimer and Adorno unnecessarily limit aesthetic truth to works of art when in fact the rituals and sacrifices that they consider to fall under the category of myth also function according to aesthetic rules. I then justify the aesthetic quality of "myth" by showing that mimesis of nature must be a mimesis of violence in nature and that this mimesis has the structure of the sublime, which is in turn a sacrificial structure. I follow this idea in order to then describe sacrifice and the sublime as the aesthetic structures that establish the basic parameters for subjectivity in a particular cultural tradition.

Aesthetic Truth

Unless it is possible to speak of a specifically aesthetic mode of truth that functions according to its own logic, sacrifice can only be seen as either arbitrary superstition or an ideological instrument used to legitimate unjust hierarchies. One of the greatest achievements of Max Horkheimer and Theodor Adorno's *Dialectic of Enlightenment,* and the prerequisite for a serious consideration of sacrifice as constitutive for culture, is the distinction of a rational mode of truth, which is purely instrumental, from an aesthetic mode of truth, which is the only means of establishing moral values.[1] Unfortunately, the subsequent history of the Frankfurt School's Critical Theory has consisted of a variety of attempts to either deny the validity of this distinction or avoid facing its consequences.

Jürgen Habermas has been one of the most outspoken opponents of the idea of aesthetic truth, arguing that aestheticization destroys the very concept of truth, leaving behind only a theory of power in which the world falls "back into myth, in which powers influence one another and no element remains that could transcend the battle of the powers."[2] According to Habermas, Horkheimer and Adorno remain bound within a paradoxical situation of continual, determinate negation in which all theoretical solutions are rejected. Consequently, Adorno's late philosophy becomes a hermetic and circular movement between paradox and artistic mimesis, negative dialectics and aesthetic theory, his rejection of theoretical solutions amounting to a surrender to the rule of power (*PD* 128–29).

Habermas's alternative is to develop an idea of communicative rationality in which values are separate from empirical considerations and thus free of power dynamics. They are determined only by "the unforced force of the better argument" (*PD* 130). Borrowing from Max Weber, Habermas assumes that modernity has divided truth into three different spheres—science, morality, and art—and that "expert cultures" within each are able to arrive collectively at intersubjectively valid judgments. In making this argument, Habermas on the one hand separates art from morality and on the other hand posits a single form of truth governed by reason, which dominates decision making in all three spheres. Because truth is attained only within expert cultures, there is a danger that the isolation of truth within research communities will lead truth claims, even in his own account, to become "esoteric in character and endangered in being split off from ordinary communicative practice" (*PD* 113).

This separation of truth from everyday life is precisely the problem that Horkheimer and Adorno's aesthetic understanding of truth attempts to address. Whereas Habermas links art in the modern world to the emancipation of the subject "from the imperatives of purposive action and from the conventions of quotidian perception" (*PD* 113), for Horkheimer and Adorno, art must remain involved in everyday life in order to maintain a strong connection between truth and experience. The link between the experience of art and everyday experience is essential, because they conceive of moral truth, not as the special preserve of researchers and philosophers who speak as representatives of the rest of society, but as embedded in the personal experiences of all individuals. Since they assume that moral truth grounded in experience cannot be based on reason, which is objective and abstract, Horkheimer and Adorno turn to art as the carrier of a specifically aesthetic form of truth that maintains an intimate link to subjectivity and particularity. Because beauty and the sublime cannot be constructed intersubjectively by means of arguments and dialogue, but must be received through a process of inspiration, art provides an opening to a type of truth that is given, rather than constructed; intuited, rather than proven.

Yet, this aesthetic form of truth is not arbitrary, that is, dominated by power and manipulation, as Habermas suspects (*PD* 124–25). Instead, as Peter Uwe Hohendahl has demonstrated, Horkheimer and Adorno envision an aesthetic mode of truth that, though not based on reason, has its own basis for legitimacy: mimesis.[3] They describe mimesis as the specific method of myth as opposed to science. In contrast to reason, which reduces all of nature to an undifferentiated raw material, "the world of magic retained distinctions whose traces have disappeared even in linguistic form. . . . Like science, magic pursues aims, but seeks to achieve them by mimesis—not by progressively distancing itself from the object" (*DE* 10–11). Whereas Habermas understands myth only as violence and domination, Horkheimer and Adorno's view of magic as mimesis emphasizes the positive aspect of myth. Not only does magic still maintain the qualitative differences in nature that have been eradicated by science, it provides a way of relating to nature and experience that is based on imitation rather than manipulation. From this viewpoint, the modern separation of value spheres—which Habermas contends is the basis for intersubjective truth—destroys the totality of experience created by myth. The mythic unity of cognition and mimesis has become fragmented into the mutually exclusive spheres of science and art in the modern world, where neither is able to mediate to the individual an experience of totality. Instead, truth has been separated from sensual experience, and everyday experience no longer has truth value (*DE* 17–18).

Horkheimer and Adorno's outline of an aesthetic understanding of truth attempts to overcome this alienation and to reconstruct the totality within the particular: "It is in the nature of the work of art, or aesthetic semblance, to be what the new, terrifying occurrence became in the primitive's magic: the appearance of the whole in the particular" (*DE* 19). By leading art back toward the mythic function of magic, they seek to recover a totality for subjective experience and with it an experience of the absolute, and of ultimate values, that has been lost with the domination of reason. The mythic totality they envision is not a rational totality, in which "disqualified nature becomes the chaotic matter of mere classification, and the all-powerful self becomes mere possession—abstract identity," but an aesthetic totality based on "specific representation" and the particularity (rather than the exchangeability) of human experience (*DE* 10). This distinction between a rational totality and an aesthetic totality is crucial for conceiving of a culture free of reification, in which the specificity of individual experience is not eliminated to make way for the universal domination of reason.[4]

Art Versus Myth

For Horkheimer and Adorno, twentieth-century works of art attempt to create the mythic experience of totality in a modern situation, where myths have lost their validity. The contradiction between mythic totality and modern alienation becomes the defining one for modern art. Yet, the differentiation between a modern art of alienation and a mythic experience of totality raises a fundamental problem concerning the status of myth. Because Horkheimer and Adorno assume a fatal dialectic of culture, in which myth is overtaken by enlightenment but in which simultaneously enlightenment turns back into myth (*DE* 11–14), they are unable to imagine the possibility of a positive return to myth. Modern art, because it is predicated on a situation of alienation, cannot be a model for a return to a mythic totality. Instead, it is burdened with the same contradictions that have created the modern experience of alienation of truth from experience (and thus its transformation into falsehood) in the first place. An overcoming of this alienation would suggest either a replacement of modern art with myth as a mediator of truth and experience or a reevaluation of modern art as a contemporary form of myth. But the idea of a dialectic, in which myth is already enlightenment and enlightenment turns into myth, undermines the possibility of establishing a stable mythic totality.

Horkheimer and Adorno are left in a predicament similar to Habermas's when it comes to an evaluation of the status of art and myth. Art must remain isolated from life in order to maintain its negative character in relation to the alienation that pervades everyday experience. In the end, a mythic totality is impossible in the modern world for both Habermas and Horkheimer and Adorno. For the former, the loss of totality is a sign of progress in the creation of expert cultures capable of determining intersubjective validity. For the latter, this loss is the cause of a permanent alienation of truth from individual experience. Because art can no longer function in the same way as myth once did, myth is relegated to an irretrievable past.

Although *Dialectic of Enlightenment* provides a critique of enlightenment that leaves the metaphysical dimension of myth and religion as the only alternative to the alienation of modernity, Adorno is unable to build upon this critique of modernity. In his subsequent work, he attempts to conceive of art as a secularized version of the metaphysical experiences found in religion and myth. His dialectical method henceforth becomes a sophisticated means of equivocating between two incompatible projects: affirming the transcendent qualities of myth and religion, on the one hand, and maintaining the primacy of secular art in the establishment of a cultural tradition, on the other.

Adorno can manage to do both only by conceiving of a form of art that includes the sublime as a transcendent factor yet does not upset the primacy of the individual as the basis of order in modernity. Because it can only reduce culture to art by retaining the individual as the center around which the totality of the world constructs itself, Adorno's concept of art is intimately linked to the individual's domination of nature—the very mechanism that he and Horkheimer criticize so effectively in *Dialectic of Enlightenment*. Adorno repudiates the antimodern argument of *Dialectic of Enlightenment* that would lead toward myth and ritual as the basis of social order; instead, he develops a theory of art that can never move beyond the illusion of the modern subject as the self-sufficient creator of its own identity.

The dependence of Adorno's theory of art on the individual's domination of nature becomes apparent when one compares his ideas with Nietzsche's outline of an aesthetics of myth in *The Birth of Tragedy*. Adorno borrows from Nietzsche in order to develop the principal categories of his aesthetics, with the distinction between Apollo and Dionysus furnishing the template with which Adorno constructs his fundamental opposition between semblance and expression as the imperatives determining the work of art.[5] Both Nietzsche and Adorno insist on the importance of the semblance character of art as the element that maintains art's distinctiveness. Nietzsche explains how the task of the chorus in Greek tragedy is to transform the theatrical experience into an event divorced from the mundane world around it.[6] Similarly, for Adorno, if the work of art does not retain some element of semblance, and thus its distinction from the world of things, it becomes an everyday object that has been functionalized and objectified like all other objects (*AT* 103).

While the work of art for both Nietzsche and Adorno must maintain its distinction from the world of objects around it, it must also transcend this isolation in order to avoid becoming mere illusion. Just as Nietzsche's concept of the Apollonian reappears in Adorno's work as "semblance," Adorno's concept "expression" exhibits the same characteristics as Nietzsche's concept of the Dionysian. Both expression for Adorno and the Dionysian for Nietzsche function to bring reality into the illusory sphere of art, thereby transcending the Apollonian semblance. As with Nietzsche, the reality of aesthetic images for Adorno does not lie in their representational value or in their direct presentation of an image from history or from the experiences of the artist. Instead of entering the work of art as representation (e.g., as happens in a "historical novel"), reality enters the work of art through its inner form. The structure of conflicting forces within the work of art creates a specific type of "imitation" that is to be distinguished from direct representation. "[Art's] expression is the antithesis of expressing something" (*AT* 112). Rather than representing pathos, art imitates it through a mimetic process that must be understood as a kind of reenactment. Adorno differentiates a communicative from a mimetic aspect of language and relates expression to mimetic language: "The new art tries to bring about the transformation of communicative into mimetic language" (*AT* 112). While communicative language is representational and depends on the relation between sign and referent, mimetic language emphasizes the constellation of signs in which the referent of each sign is less important than how the constellation as a whole creates a familiar experience for the recipient.[7]

The close tie between Adorno's concept of mimesis and Nietzsche's concept of the Dionysian derives from their common return to a concept of mimesis that "originated with the rituals and mysteries of the Dionysian cult" and signified expression rather than reproduction.[8] Resembling the transformation of reality created by Dionysian rituals, the task of both mimesis for Adorno and the Dionysian for Nietzsche is to return the world to a state of nonobjectification. In order to designate this state, Nietzsche speaks of the Dionysian artist's communion with the primordial unity, while Adorno refers to the thing-in-itself. In both cases, art does not copy nature but rather presents things as they exist before objectification into discrete entities and concepts (*AT* 63).

Because art refers to this nonobjectified dimension, in *The Birth of Tragedy* Nietzsche depicts it as a metaphysical activity. The reenactment of processes outside the work of art occurs as individual artists transcend their own subjectivity by merging with a primordial unity: "In the first instance the lyric poet, a Dionysiac artist, has become entirely at one with the primordial unity, with its pain and contradiction, and he produces a copy of this primordial unity as music, which has been described elsewhere, quite rightly, as a repetition of the world and a second copy of it" (*BT* 30). The artist's subjectivity merges with processes occurring outside the work of art. In transforming the world into this preconceptual state, mimesis and the Dionysian open the work of art to a metaphysical reality. But because the primordial unity expresses itself as irresolvable pain and contradiction, Nietzsche refers to this mythic mimesis as an inescapable conflict between the individuation and the dissolution of the subject.

For Nietzsche, such a mimesis of nature implies the destruction and pain of a total dissolution of all individuation. As a consequence, "the entire opposition between the subjective and the objective . . . is absolutely inappropriate in aesthetics since the subject, the willing individual in pursuit of his own egotistical goals, can only be considered the opponent of art and not its origin" (*BT* 32). In contrast to Nietzsche, Adorno attempts to confine nature within the opposition between subject and object (and thus to the limits of the subject) by referring, not to primordial unity, but to a "primacy of the object in subjective experience" (*AT* 71). Because Adorno's formulation retains the categories of subject and object—rather than referring to a Dionysian dissolution of individuation and the opening to a metaphysical dimension, such as the primordial unity—his concept of art remains beholden to the subject/object split he attempts to negate. In maintaining this tie to subjectivity, he turns the work of art into a construction that can come into being only through the subject's domination over the object (*AT* 77). He retains this tie to subjectivity because his concept of nature is based on a notion of reconciliation that cleanses nature of the horrifying aspects threatening both the individual's survival and the unity of individual consciousness.

Aesthetic Theory attempts to take over Nietzsche's aesthetics while eliminating nature as a source of violence. Nietzsche postulates a fundamental conflict between human endeavor and the forces of nature, that is, his lyricist reenacts the pain and contradiction of the primordial unity. Adorno attempts to deny the necessity of such conflict by assuming that aesthetic images do not set up a relation to nature, that "their reality is their historical content" (*AT* 85). Although Adorno's mimesis has the same aesthetic structure as Nietzsche's Dionysian, he replaces the idea of a primordial unity of nature as that which transcends art with history.[9] While Nietzsche explains the double Apollonian/Dionysian character of myth by referring to nature as contradiction, Adorno derives the double character of art as semblance and expression by emphasizing first that art relates to history in setting itself off from empirical reality and second that it reenacts historical processes in the relation of aesthetic images to each other rather than to empirical reality (*AT* 86). Rather than establishing a relation to nature, the immanent historicity that creates expression in the work of art is a mimesis of history: "The latent processes in artworks, which break through in the instant, are their inner historicity, sedimented external history" (*AT* 85–86). The inner historicity and formal processes of the work of art are a reenactment on its own terms of experiences that take place outside the work of art. In linking this "outside" to history rather than to nature, Adorno is able to emphasize the avoidable character of the contradiction to human endeavor.

Frederic Jameson has argued that Adorno's chief contribution to philosophy and aesthetics consists of this "transcoding" of both philosophical and aesthetic questions into "substantive socioeconomic ones."[10] But in claiming "that aesthetics always leads back to history itself, and that for art the 'non-identical' is society,"[11] Jameson reproduces Adorno's suppression of any fundamental contradiction between man and nature. In replacing nature with history as the place of the nonidentical, Adorno and Jameson domesticate the nonidentical, destroying the possibility of recognizing either alterity or transcendence, both of which depend on violence and suffering. By insisting on the historical and thus fundamentally avoidable character of suffering, Adorno projects a possible utopian state in which suffering has been eradicated and desires have been fulfilled. Yet, he fails to see that this state of harmony between man and nature could only be established by eliminating the nonidentical moment in both art and reality that he wishes to save. Mimesis becomes for him an experience of reconciliation rather than contradiction and violence.[12] He reinterprets contradiction as historical and thereby argues that contradiction is ultimately avoidable and correctable. Similarly, he understands the nonidentical not as violence, but as freedom, in order to maintain the possibility of reconciliation and utopia. Because his theory is built on the possibility of harmony between man and nature, he undermines the idea of aesthetic truth by subsuming it under the identity logic of reason rather than under the contradictions of non-identity. "The oneness of aesthetic constituents with those of cognition is, however, the unity of spirit and thus the unity of reason" (*AT* 138). Through this elimination of the nonidentical, Adorno's aesthetics lead to the dissolution of art as mimesis.

Beauty and the Sublime

The first step in Adorno's dismantling of aesthetic truth is the turn away from the sublime and toward beauty as the fundamental category of art. Rather than emphasizing the sublime, which exceeds subjective capacities and thereby provides an experience of the nonidentical, Adorno's aesthetics are organized around the idea of beauty, which is based on harmony with the subject. He is able to dispense with the sublime while still retaining a notion of the nonidentical by basing his aesthetics on Kant's idea of natural beauty, but then altering it slightly in order to give it a tinge of the incomprehensibility of the sublime. In Kant's analysis, beauty in nature derives from the experience of a harmony of objects with the faculties used for perceiving them: "(Independent) natural beauty carries with it a purposiveness in its form, by which the object seems as it were predetermined for our power of judgment, so that this beauty constitutes in itself an object of our liking."[13] While Kant insists on the "apparent harmony" between subject and object in the experience of beauty, Adorno notes a certain incomprehensibility in the object: "Natural beauty points to the primacy of the object in subjective experience. Natural beauty is perceived both as authoritatively binding and as something incomprehensible that questioningly awaits its solution" (*AT* 71). Although this passage seems to defend the primacy of the object and of the nonidentical, and Lambert Zuidervaart reads it as such,[14] Adorno's reference to beauty rather than to the sublime to designate that which exceeds the subject confines nonidentity within the bounds of the object.

Incomprehensible though beauty might be in Adorno's depiction, the question it poses still "awaits a solution" that would affirm once again the subject's mastery. Adorno's revision of Kant's notion of beauty allows him to base his aesthetics on the harmony of beauty, even though Adorno insists that he has included a consideration of the nonidentical that threatens this harmony. By enclosing the nonidentical within a revised notion of beauty, rather than allowing it to remain connected with the sublime, Adorno renders harmless those forces in nature that exceed the individual's capacities.

In Kant's analysis the centrality of the individual's need for constructing beauty allows a separate consideration, within the analysis of the sublime, of those aspects of nature completely incommensurable with the individual. In differentiating beauty from the sublime, Kant is free to describe the sublime as an experience of a contradiction between human faculties and nature, in which nature completely exceeds the individual and its desires: "However, in what we usually call sublime in nature there is such an utter lack of anything leading to particular objective principles and to forms of nature conforming to them, that it is rather in its chaos that nature most arouses our ideas of the sublime, or in its wildest and most ruleless disarray and devastation, provided it displays magnitude and might" (*CJ* 99–100). For Kant, the sublime is the designation for an experience in which the human subject must face its own incommensurability with nature.

In basing his aesthetics on beauty, Adorno avoids a serious consideration of the "disarray and devastation" that threaten human desires. This is not to say that he ignores the sublime. He recognizes that it contains the nonidentical element that his theory of art strives to recover for human experience. Despite his focus on beauty, Adorno maintains an important role for the sublime, emphasizing that modern art has attempted to take over the spiritual function that Kant attributes to it. "The sublime, which Kant reserved exclusively for nature, later became the historical constituent of art itself" (*AT* 196). The experience of the sublime, which for Kant was reserved for the reception of natural phenomena, becomes for Adorno the basis for the transcendence of art. "Works in which the aesthetic form, under pressure of the truth content, transcends itself occupy the position that was once held by the concept of the sublime" (*AT* 196). He insists here on the centrality of the sublime for the work of art, but, as we will see, he imports it into the work of art while trying to maintain the avoidability of the violence to which it refers.

The sublime is important for Adorno because the relation to it points to the moment of suffering in the work of art. Just as Nietzsche's Dionysian art force is rooted in primal pain and contradiction, expression for Adorno presents objective historical suffering as that which transcends the semblance of the work of art. "Expression is the suffering countenance of artworks" (*AT* 111). The centrality of suffering for expression leads Adorno to the same musical model for art that Nietzsche uses in *The Birth of Tragedy*. In both cases, "dissonance" is the key term. While Nietzsche speaks of "musical dissonance" with reference to the Dionysian (*BT* 113–14), for Adorno "dissonance is effectively expression; the consonant and harmonious want to soften and eliminate it" (*AT* 110). Although Adorno's discussion of suffering and the sublime as constitutive for the work of art brings him close to Nietzsche's views, Adorno breaks with Nietzsche in attempting to separate pain from nature. Even if Adorno agrees that dissonance, rather than harmony, is the source of art's transcendence, he attempts to mitigate the implications of this insight by contending that this suffering is avoidable. As we have seen, for him it is not a part of nature but of history. Because, for Nietzsche, art refers to "the primordial unity, with its pain and contradiction," it mediates an experience of the chaos of nature, which is the undefined and unpredictable opposite to the human construction of laws. For Adorno, however, the suffering brought into the work of art through expression must be something man-made and correctable (originating in history), rather than being natural and inevitable (and emanating from the primordial unity).

Adorno's assumption that nature is a cipher for reconciliation, rather than for contradiction, leads him to criticize Kant's linking of the sublime to nature's power. "However, by situating the sublime in overpowering grandeur and setting up the antithesis of power and powerlessness, Kant directly affirmed his unquestioning complicity with domination" (*AT* 199). Adorno can only accuse Kant of complicity with domination by assuming that the violence of nature is avoidable and that human endeavor can eventually force nature into unity with human desires. Adorno considers it impossible that the primordial unity might be the source of the expression and dissonance found in art because nature is mute. It cannot exist as a true antagonist of human endeavor because there is no fundamental conflict between man and nature. Adorno denies nature's power and affirms the human ability not just to subjugate nature, but also to determine the overarching totality within which nature can be assigned a peaceful role.

This denial of nature's excessive power in comparison with human capacities is the crucial assumption that separates Adorno's from Kant's and Nietzsche's concept of the sublime. Just as he refashions Kant's notion of beauty so that it includes aspects of the sublime, Adorno redefines the sublime to make it a form of beauty and, in doing so, undermines Kant's attempt to distinguish those aspects of nature that are commensurate with human faculties from those that are not. As opposed to both Kant's and Nietzsche's emphasis on the threatening aspect of nature as the crucial element in the experience of the sublime, Adorno's separation of nature from power and restriction forces him to argue, in contrast to Kant, that the sublime presents nature as a return to an original state before the oppression of spirit: "Nature, no longer oppressed by spirit, frees itself from the miserable nexus of rank second nature and subjective sovereignty. Such emancipation would be the return of nature, and it—the counterimage of mere existence—is the sublime" (*AT* 197). Unable to accept the connection between nature and violence in the Kantian sublime, Adorno redefines this connection as an emancipation from and protest against the domination of the spirit. Nature is only threatening in Adorno's idea of the sublime to the extent that the sublime uses the threat of domination in order to project a realm of freedom from constraint: "Towering mountains are eloquent not as what crushes overwhelmingly but as images of a space liberated from fetters and strictures, a liberation in which it is possible to participate" (*AT* 199). For Adorno, the sublimity of mountains lies not in their oppressive power but in the promise of a freedom from bounds and restrictions, and so it follows that he can understand the sublime not as an indication of the indomitable violence of nature but of the human capacity to attain freedom by subduing this violence.

Kant also designates the spiritual as a realm of freedom. But in doing so, he understands freedom as constituted by the experience of domination and sacrifice. The sublime consists of an acceptance of the restrictions set by nature and a consequent sacrifice of material for spiritual well-being. In conceiving of nature as an overwhelming power, the experience of the sublime depends on man's fear in the face of this power. "Hence nature can count as a might, and so as dynamically sublime, for aesthetic judgment only insofar as we consider it as an object of fear" (*CJ* 119). Although Tom Huhn argues, in defense of Adorno, that Kant's understanding of the sublime effaces nature,[15] the contrast between Kant's recognition of nature's power and Adorno's attempt to create a reconciliation between man and nature demonstrates that it is not Kant but Adorno who eliminates nature as an independent force from his theory.

By affirming human impotence in the face of nature's violence, Kant insists on the persistence of nature as a force beyond human control. This stance does not necessarily result in complicity with domination, as Adorno assumes. For in arguing that the experience of the power of nature in fear is the prerequisite for the experience of the sublime, Kant points out that the sublime depends primarily on the human ability to overcome subjection to the power of nature through the sacrifice of material comfort for the sake of spiritual ideals:

> Hence if in judging nature aesthetically we call it sublime, we do so not because nature arouses fear, but because it calls forth our strength (which does not belong to nature [within us]), to regard as small the [objects] of our [natural] concerns: property, health, and life, and because of this we regard nature's might (to which we are indeed subjected in these [natural] concerns) as yet not having such dominance over us, as persons, that we should have to bow to it if our highest principles were at stake and we had to choose between upholding or abandoning them. Hence nature is here called sublime [*erhaben*] merely because it elevates [*erhebt*] our imagination, [making] it exhibit those cases where the mind can come to feel its own sublimity, which lies in its vocation and elevates it even above nature. (*CJ* 121)

For Kant, the sublime is at once a recognition of the power of nature and a reaction to this power: the individual sacrifices material well-being in order to demonstrate resistance to the physical world over which nature has control. Yet, this superiority over the physical and thus over nature is only made evident to the extent that there is a willingness to sacrifice the physical for the sake of the ideal. This sacrifice demonstrates both an acceptance of and a freedom from the physical constraints of nature. But, because this vision of sacrifice depends on "its own sublimity, which lies in its vocation" (*die eigene Erhabenheit seiner Bestimmung*), the rejection of the power of nature serves to support the sublimity, not of the subject itself, but of its "vocation."

Freedom from the power of nature is impossible without a sacrifice that functions as a submission to a set of rules.

> By the same token, a liking for the sublime in nature is only negative (whereas a liking for the beautiful is positive); it is a feeling that the imagination by its own action is depriving itself of its freedom, in being deter-

mined purposively according to a law different from that of its empirical use. The imagination thereby acquires an expansion and a might that surpasses the one it sacrifices; but the basis of this might is concealed from it; instead the imagination feels the sacrifice or deprivation and at the same time the cause to which it is being subjugated. (*CJ* 129)

Kant describes here the construction of a spiritual reality as the direct consequence of a confrontation with the power of nature, prefiguring Nietzsche's own derivation of an aesthetic truth from this opposition between man and nature. The material impotence of the human subject leads to its dissolution as an autonomous entity. It can only escape total annihilation by submitting to a law that becomes greater than materiality. This process is embodied in sacrifice, and sacrifice functions as an aesthetic process that links materiality to a spiritual determination. Like the work of art as Adorno sees it, the experience of sacrifice in the sublime, in creating a mimesis of nature, is for Kant concrete and spiritual at the same time. Unlike beauty, however, the sublime involves a confrontation with violence as an inevitable part of the human experience of nature.

Kant's description of the sublime provides the justification for linking ethics with aesthetics. The experience of the sublime creates precisely the movement of consciousness that must occur with any ethical act. The sublime is not only significant because it recreates this movement, but because it provides the model for it. In order to create ethical actions, rather than merely a set of abstract ethical laws, a culture must impress upon its members a visceral and intimate experience of the sublimity of their actions, that is, the dependence of their actions on an overarching spiritual framework that transcends the material world in the process of working through that world. Ethical behavior can only become a norm if all individuals feel the metaphysical cause to which their actions and aspirations are to be subordinated. While Kant's aesthetics attempt to link the sublime to the idea of practical reason as the subject's "vocation," the structure of the sublime that he lays out is in fact essential for every functioning ethical system, and he later refers to religious experiences as examples of the sublime (*CJ* 135).

Unable to accept nature as incommensurate with desires, Adorno does not recognize the necessity of the individual's sacrifice for the construction of transcendence. Instead, he attempts to transform the Kantian sacrificial structure of the sublime into a utopian structure. As with Kant, art's negation of the material world is a spiritual event: "Only as spirit is art the antithesis of empirical reality as the determinate negation of the existing order of the world" (*AT* 89). This negation is not a denial of materiality itself, but only a protest against "the existing order of the world"—a historical situation in which unnecessary suffering takes place. This protest presents the possibility of an alternate world more congenial to subjective desires. Spirit in the work of art points to utopia rather than to a divine order as the transcendent moment: "Through the irreconcilable renunciation of the semblance of reconciliation, art holds fast to the promise of reconciliation in the midst of the unreconciled: This is the true consciousness of an age in which the real possibility of utopia—that given the level of productive forces the earth could here and now be paradise—converges with the possibility of total catastrophe" (*AT* 33). Since Adorno is unwilling to give up on utopia and maintains it as an essential part of his system, his realization of the impossibility of utopia is phrased as a temporary historical aberration rather than an existential situation of opposition between man and nature.

By turning this opposition into a historical situation, Adorno develops a historical rather than a metaphysical understanding of transcendence. Adorno shifts the origins of suffering into history in order to avoid a dependence on nature and the divine as the transcendent elements of the work of art. By considering freedom to be a historical alternative to restriction, Adorno turns it into a historical space of utopian harmony rather than a negative projection of a fundamental dissonance between human aspiration and natural forces. Adorno's use of utopia, rather than the primordial unity, to describe that which transcends the immanent form of the work of art is an attempt to create transcendence without referring to anything outside of history. But this alternative mode of transcendence ends up eliminating the possibility of non-identity as that which results from a fundamental opposition between man and nature.

Insofar as he must limit the extent to which nature opposes human endeavor in order to establish utopia as his own form of secular transcendence, Adorno destroys the possibility of non-identity. If nature is not seen as a source of discord, but of unity, it has been eliminated as an antagonist to human desires, and violence and domination must originate not in nature but in human mistakes that can eventually be set right. In locating violence in history, rather than in nature, Adorno is able to explain the pain and suffering expressed in the work of art as socially determined, rather than as a part of nature. As a result, the reaction to suffering is not sacrifice, but social change, that is, a conscious manipulation of history. Yet, such manipulation (i.e., creating paradise through production) depends on the presumption that true nature has been eradicated and that reification is total. The idea of utopia is not merely a reaction to reification, but actually depends upon reification in order to constitute itself. The establishment of utopia as the basis of transcendence enforces reification in society because it replaces a transcendence of both materiality and the individual with a subjugation of nature to the individual's desires. Despite all his attempts at creating a negative dialectics that would avoid this problem, Adorno's philosophy remains based on identity and the concept, rather than on non-identity and mimesis.

Adorno is able to hide the dependence of utopia on the fact of reification by arguing that nature in the modern world has been replaced by the domination of the concept. For him, the nonidentical is something that nature once must have been, but now is no longer. "Natural beauty is the trace of the nonidentical in things under the spell of universal identity. As long as this spell prevails, the nonidentical has no positive existence" (*AT* 73). As much as Adorno seeks to recover the nonidentical, these sentences are an example of his underlying assumption that nature as nonidentical has been eradicated. But this argument is merely a historical way of denying the power of nature. It posits the total eradication of nature that the theory needs in order to cohere.

Since mimesis can only make sense as a mimesis of nature (as the non-identical and unpredictable), Adorno's presumption that nature has been totally subjugated to the concept and that only human manipulation exists as a force in reality destroys the possibility of mimesis. If mimesis is nonetheless a crucial aspect of modern art, this can only be a clue that non-identity still exists and that the idea of a total eradication of nature as non-identity is a modern delusion. If nature had really been eradicated as something that goes beyond human concepts, then all of reality could be manipulated to fulfill human desires, and a state of utopia in which there is no conflict between man and nature and man rules over nature like a god would in fact exist. But as long as nature presents a threat to the fulfillment of human desires, it cannot be reduced to human concepts; it still remains unreified, and thus a source of fear and the basis for mimesis.

In assuming that in the modern world nature has been subjugated to the concept, Adorno develops an aesthetics organized around a subject-based totality with no place for aspects of nature that potentially exceed the subject. To the extent that he views nature as reconciliation, rather than contradiction, it remains trapped within identity logic and the domination of the subject. "Artworks have this much in common with idealistic philosophy: They locate reconciliation in identity with the subject" (*AT* 77). Because it focuses on reconciliation as identity with the subject, Adorno's aesthetics has no mechanism for understanding the sublime as a situation in which this identity breaks down. As a result, the sublime, which in Kant is the place of this incommensurability of nature with the subject, becomes for Adorno a form of beauty, and beauty becomes the defining category for Adorno's aesthetics.[16]

Alternative Understandings of the Sublime

The centrality of the individual subject in the understanding of art has become the major point of critique in subsequent analyses of the sublime. Thus, Jean-François Lyotard agrees with Kant in recognizing that the experience of the sublime is linked to the subject's sacrifice. "By sacrificing itself [in the experience of the sublime], the imagination sacrifices nature, which is aesthetically sacred, in order to exalt holy law."[17] By interpreting the sublime as "the sacrifice of the imagination," he can claim that the sublime is based on a sacrilegious destruction of the aesthetic of the imagination in favor of the rationality of moral law.[18] But by setting the moral faculty of the mind in opposition to the aesthetic imagination, Lyotard transforms the aesthetic into a natural force. Because he insists that nature is itself "aesthetically sacred," even before the sacrifice and independent of a moral law, Lyotard's reading reduces the sublime to the moment of horror and denies the possibility of any subjective reaction that could oppose this horror. If nature is itself sacred, then horror in the face of nature becomes the crucial moment in the experience of the sublime. Such a reading cannot explain the uplifting aspect of the sublime and its connection to the creation and maintenance of ethical values.

In equating the sublime with the sacred, Kant offers a different approach by emphasizing that no object is ever sublime or sacred in itself. Sacred objects do not exist in his analysis, only the experience of the sacred, which occurs through the sacrifice of material objects according to the dictates of a moral law. The imagination does indeed sacrifice nature in order to exalt holy law, but it is only in this act of sacrifice that the experience of the sacred ever occurs. Moreover, this sacrifice of nature is not a sacrifice of the imagination itself, as Lyotard claims, but only of its "empirical use" (*CJ* 129). Imagination, in sacrificing its use in the empirical realm, "acquires an expansion and might" in the supersensual realm (*CJ* 129).

As opposed to Lyotard, Kant insists on the essential role of moral law in creating the aesthetic experience of the sacred. In his account spiritual values cannot exist if the sublime is reduced to the moment of fear. Although fear is essential for the construction of the sublime, it is not experienced directly, but disinterestedly. "We can, however, consider an object fearful without being afraid of it, namely, if we judge it in such a way that we merely think of the case where we might possibly want to put up resistance against it, and that any resistance would in that case be utterly futile" (CJ 119–20). Rather than residing in the direct feeling of fear, the crucial moment of the sublime occurs when the subject is able to gain distance from this fear in order to be able to defy material circumstances in spite of their power and thereby to affirm a spiritual reality that transcends the physical world. A reduction of the sublime to the moment of horror eliminates a transcendent ideal, and with it any set of values according to which an individual could organize her or his experience and actions. The antimetaphysical stance that only recognizes the moment of horror in the sublime can explain neither ethical behavior nor the construction of meaning that would allow consciousness to exist. Without the ability to assert some ideal against the immediacy of physical terror, consciousness disintegrates. For the transcendence of the physical world is simultaneously the act that gives meaning to the physical, fitting it within the parameters of a set of values that organizes experience. Without values to integrate experience into a meaningful framework, human experience would not be able to constitute itself.

Yet, the establishment of values is not just a constructive task that can be carried out rationally as the expansion of the realm of the subject into the empty space of nature, as if the subject could simply expand the dominion of reason over previously untamed wilderness. In his alternative discussion of the sublime, Albrecht Wellmer contends that Adorno's focus on the subject leads to the metaphysical idea of utopia. This idea must be eliminated in order to allow a world of pure immanence that Wellmer celebrates as an emancipation from metaphysical referents. In order to create this world, Wellmer must eliminate the overwhelming power of nature from his theory by considering the sublime to be an opposition between the abyss of meaninglessness and the ideal of reason. For him, "the opposition, the polarity, the irresolvable tension which gives rise to the feeling of the sublime would be one in the intelligible subject itself: namely the tension between the experience of an abyss of meaninglessness or non-sense, through which the subject of speech becomes aware of its own fragility, on the one hand, and on the other hand the subject's resistance to the superior force of negativity, through which the subject is able to sublate the experience of its own negligibility within the world of communicatively shared meaning and, in this manner, lifts itself out of its negligibility."[19]

In order to lift "itself out of its negligibility," the individual posits a linguistic community of rational subjects as the creator of meaning. The world is not given to the individual but created out of human communication. The rational construction of meaning in language becomes the source of both values and of the world itself. As a consequence, nature as it exists outside of human understanding is an "abyss," rather than an active force. Nature does not precede human attempts to understand it, and art's task is not to create a mimesis of nature but to push back the boundaries of meaninglessness by making the unintelligible into something pleasurable. "However, that other side of discursive reason, the abyss of meaning, is not only the unintelligible as the horrible, but also nature as a source of delight beyond all meaning."[20] By identifying nature with the abyss and as a source of delight, Wellmer discounts the active power of nature and assumes that it is simply a void that can eventually be colonized by human understanding. Nature as an active force that might oppose human endeavor does not exist.

As a result, art does not have any function independent of reason. It is simply the cutting edge of reason as it creates meaning out of the meaninglessness of nature: "By transforming the terror of what is unintelligible into aesthetic delight, [art] widens, at the same time, the space of communicatively shared meaning."[21] In imagining that art transforms the unintelligible into aesthetic delight, Wellmer turns the distinction between the sublime and the beautiful in Kant into a process of moving from the former to the latter. But in establishing this move as the fundamental activity of art, Wellmer is rejecting the idea that there are limits to human endeavor and understanding that are marked out by the experience of the sublime and that limit the reach of reason to instrumental tasks rather than value-producing ones. As *Dialectic of Enlightenment* convincingly demonstrates, reason is not a value, but a method (*DE* 85–88). Consequently, it is possible to speak of instrumental reason as a means of achieving particular ends, but impossible to speak of substantive reason as an end in itself or as a foundation for meaning.

To affirm communicative rationality as the highest value that transcends the subject is only to say that the individual cannot exist alone, but depends on a larger community for its constitution. Although this point is important for understanding the basis of subjectivity, it is inadequate for explaining the construction of the values that define the totality of subjective experience and that give it meaning. Because the construction of values must occur within the consciousness of every individual if ethical behavior is to remain real and everyday, rather than abstract and exceptional, values cannot be separated into distinct "value spheres" governed by experts and communicative rationality, as Habermas and Wellmer propose, but must be established within a single unified, aesthetically based totality that can be grasped immediately by an individual consciousness in the sublime moment.

In positing the rational construction of collective meaning in language as the ideal that opposes materiality in the experience of the sublime, Wellmer fails to recognize the true horror of nature that the individual faces and the consequent necessity of an aesthetic, rather than a rational, foundation for values. Nature creates a supreme fear in the individual precisely because all of one's human capacities, including reason and linguistic constructs, prove useless in the face of nature's power. Kant emphasizes that nature is not simply a void to be colonized by language but a "chaos" that displays "magnitude and might." Nature exceeds human capacities, not simply by lying beyond the reach of language, but by actively destroying human constructions. The possibility of values must therefore be built on the individual's acceptance of the material power of nature and an accompanying projection of an ideal that exceeds both human capacities and the indomitable power of nature. The sublime cannot exist in a world of pure immanence, but presupposes and enacts the movement toward a supersensual realm that transcends this immanence.

Adorno also fails to recognize this necessity of the transcendent for the construction of the sublime, considering nature as reconcilable with human desires and positing a utopian reconciliation as the ideal that transcends material reality. Yet, Adorno's aesthetics are still superior to Wellmer's in that he describes art as a mimesis of subjective experience that can only take place to the extent that processes in the work of art are a reenactment of processes that are essential to the experiences of the subject: "as if artworks, by molding themselves to the subject through their organization, recapitulated the way the subject originated, how it wrested itself free. Artworks bear expression not where they communicate the subject, but rather where they reverberate with the protohistory of subjectivity, of ensoulment, for which tremolo of any sort is a miserable surrogate" (*AT* 112–13). In focusing on the "protohistory of subjectivity," Adorno holds onto an experiential moment that can mediate between physical reality and spiritual values, allowing for the transformation of pure materiality into a meaningful world.

Subjectivity and Collectivity

The mimetic structure that links the primal history of subjectivity to its recapitulation in the work of art is similar to Nietzsche's linking of the

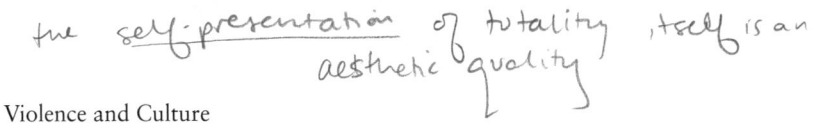

Dionysian to collective experience in the parable of conflict between man and nature. Both Adorno's notion of mimesis and Nietzsche's Dionysian use the individual as the measure of experience and of values. But, in contrast to Nietzsche, for whom the Dionysian aspect of the work of art is able to relate mimetically to a reality beyond the work of art by merging with a primordial unity that goes beyond the individual, expression for Adorno does not point beyond the individual but is a mimesis of the process by which individual subjectivity develops. Rather than seeing nature as that which transcends both the human subject and the work of art, Adorno invokes the history of the subject as itself the dominating factor. "This is the affinity of the artwork to the subject and it endures because this protohistory survives in the subject and recommences in every moment of history" (*AT* 113). Expression for Adorno gains its force from the affinity between the processual character of the work of art and the process of individuation that he assumes must occur in the same way in every subject.

But instead of starting afresh at every historical moment, as Adorno asserts, the individual is determined by the collective within which he or she develops. If the history of the individual does not lie at the beginning of mankind, but rather is the fundamental story of every subject, constantly repeated in the development of every individual in history, the work of art's recapitulation of the emergence of the individual would not illuminate a primal history of subjectivity and the distortions that result from alienation, but would record the culturally specific forces that determine a particular individual's emergence. In creating a mimesis of subjective processes rather than a representation of images, the work of art does not provide a history of how an abstract, universal subject is deformed by repression but outlines how a specific community forms its members through its particular modes of discipline. This discipline is not a form of irrational violence, but the precondition for the development of subjectivity.

By referring the immanent processes of the work of art to an abstract history of the subject, Adorno only manages to relate the development of one subjectivity (that of the artist) to that of another (that of the audience member). But if there is a similarity between the two that is not coincidental, then there must be another transcendent aspect that links both.[22] For Nietzsche, this aspect is the primordial unity, that is, an unknowable metaphysical force that permeates an otherwise immanent history in the same way that it presides over the development of the subject. The agent of this primordial unity is the collective, as it establishes and carries on the traditions and rituals that enable subjectivity. But, because every community will have its own specific relation to the primordial unity, and thus its own version of that which transcends immanent being, subjectivity will always be an outgrowth of a specific culture.

Adorno's inability to recognize this dependence of subjective experience on the traditions and conventions of a community leads him to assume a universal validity for his aesthetic judgments that they do not and cannot possess. This deficiency in his thinking has consequences that become evident in Shierry Nicholsen's analysis of the role of subjective aesthetic experience in Adorno's judgments on art. She demonstrates that his musical judgments, though subsequently buttressed by theoretical elaborations, originated in his first impressions of music.[23] The subjectivity out of which Adorno writes belongs to a specific community of individuals who have shared a similar upbringing, and the validity of his insights depends on this shared context, rather than on an objective and universal judgment. As a consequence, his aesthetic judgments are often based, not on logical arguments, but on association and innuendo understandable only to a group of initiates sharing Adorno's assumptions. But Adorno's commitment to a unified and universal history of subjectivity prevents him from comprehending how conventions and styles in art are essential to preserving art's particularity, which can never be particular as such but is always particular to a specific group. He interprets the return to convention in the late work of Beethoven, for example, not as a realization of the community-bound and thus convention-based character of art, but as regression and cliché, as a sign of damage and "a kind of poison."[24]

Adorno replaces collective with subjective experience as the locus of cultural particularity. In his view, history rather than the primordial unity links one subjectivity to another, and both nature and the divine are considered either benign or irrelevant factors. Rather than conceiving of a particular collective with its rituals and traditions as the precondition for the development of subjective experience, Adorno derives the collective from the individual subject. The collective that he constructs is, consequently, an abstract entity based on the assumption of a universal subject, rather than on a particular culture with noninterchangeable subjects.

Although he recognizes the collective as the source of the legitimacy of works of art (*AT* 86), he denies the relation to the collective in his aesthetics by focusing on art as the product of the individual rather than on myth as a collective event. He asserts the superiority of art to myth by arguing that, in the modern world, nature has been tamed and no longer presents a true opposition to human desires. This view of myth differentiates Adorno's progressivist outlook from Nietzsche's and even

Kant's primitivist ones. Adorno historicizes the relation between man and nature, while Nietzsche and Kant assume a basic similarity between the ancient and the modern worlds in their relations to nature.

Despite his general assumption of progress from the savage to the civilized, Kant's concept of the relation between man and nature in the experience of the sublime does not distinguish between primitive and civilized society. Both situations are defined by the antagonism between the power of nature and the weakness of man. In neither case is reconciliation with nature possible, but only the human adherence to an ideal. In replying to the objection that his analysis of the sublime is too sophisticated to underlie the judgments of all men, including the simple and the uneducated, he provides the following response:

> I admit that this principle seems farfetched and the result of some subtle reasoning, and hence high-flown [*überschwenglich*] for an aesthetic judgment. And yet our observation of man proves the opposite, and proves that even the commonest judging can be based on this principle, even though we are not always conscious of it. For what is it that is an object of the highest admiration even to the savage? It is a person who is not terrified, not afraid, and hence does not yield to danger but promptly sets to work with vigor and full deliberation. Even in a fully civilized society there remains this superior esteem for the warrior, except that we demand more of him: that he also demonstrate all the virtues of peace—gentleness, sympathy, and even appropriate care for his own person—precisely because they reveal to us that his mind cannot be subdued by danger. (*CJ* 121)

Because nature's power always exceeds human capabilities, the sacrifice of physical existence for ideals is the characteristic of the warrior that Kant designates as ideal behavior for both the modern and the savage.

By contrast, Adorno assumes that the modern world dominates nature, while the primitive world is dominated by a fear of nature's power. "Times in which nature confronts man overpoweringly allow no room for natural beauty. . . . Wherever nature was not actually mastered, the image of its untamed condition terrified" (*AT* 65). Adorno connects nature in the modern world to reconciliation, while Nietzsche and Kant see nature as presenting limitations on human aspiration and emphasize a fundamental conflict between the two in both the modern and the primitive world. These differences from Kant's and Nietzsche's conceptions lead Adorno to assume a gradual progression of art away from myth, and thus from the spell of nature. "As its prose character intensifies, art extricates itself completely from myth and thus from the spell of nature, which nevertheless continues in the subjective domination of nature" (*AT* 66). The progression from nature's predominance to the subject's domination of nature creates the distinction between art and myth in Adorno's theory.

Despite the fact that his theory of form ultimately derives from Nietzsche's explanation of myth as a Dionysian formal structure, Adorno denies that art and myth might function according to similar structures. In claiming that formal consistency is only a property of secular art and not of myth, he assumes that inner form can result only from the subject's domination of the contents of the work of art. "Artworks extend the realm of human domination to the extreme, not literally, though, but rather by the strength of the establishment of a sphere existing for itself, which just through its posited immanence divides itself from real domination and thus negates the heteronomy of domination" (*AT* 77). Since, for Adorno, the subjective domination of nature has only been accomplished in the modern world, only modern art can create inner form. By contrast, myth exists only in a situation where nature is still uncontrolled. Adorno denies that myth could contain the formal consistency that would constitute its expressive character. "The aesthetic images, however, emancipate themselves from mythical images by subordinating themselves to their own unreality; that is what the law of form means" (*AT* 86). He reserves mimesis through form for art and imputes to myth a mode of representation that seeks to depict the absolute.

Locating the source of discord in the concept and not in the limits set by nature, Adorno distinguishes between art, which maintains the possibility of reconciliation by negatively depicting it as that which is beyond the concept, and myth, which rejects this possibility by emphasizing the inescapability of natural limits. Although Adorno correctly attributes to magic and myth an archaic violence that originates in the indomitable power of nature, he does not accept that the mimesis of this power is what creates inner form in both art and myth. He attempts to appropriate exclusively for art the Dionysian structures of myth by assuming that formal structure arises as the result of the subject's domination both of nature and of the contents of the work of art. However, in order for inner form to create expression, it must arise as the result, not of the subject's domination, but of its sacrifice in favor of a higher ideal in the confrontation with the power of nature. By failing to note the importance of formal structure for myth, Adorno also overlooks the essentially sacrificial structure of mimesis in art. But because sacrifice links the aesthetic mimesis to social structure, Adorno must find an alternative way of linking art to society.

Merging Art with Philosophy

Because Adorno rejects the collective construction of values in myth in favor of the individualist construction in art, the collective postulated by his aesthetics is abstract; it is not founded on traditions and rituals, but on critique and reflection. The agent of aesthetic reception is not a collective with shared metaphysical assumptions, but a discursive subject that creates the supposedly indispensable philosophical critique of art.[25] Adorno's denial of the inescapability of sacrifice pushes his form of art in the direction of philosophy. In his aesthetics, critique must create the overarching context within which the work of art can speak to others. "The spirit of artworks is not a concept, yet through spirit artworks become commensurable to the concept. By reading the spirit of artworks out of their configurations and confronting the elements with each other and with the spirit that appears in them, critique passes over into the truth of the spirit, which is located beyond the aesthetic configuration. This is why critique is necessary to the works" (*AT* 88). Adorno imagines a process whereby the work of art needs critique and concepts in order to fully express itself. In privileging the formal criticism that Adorno engages in, this process discounts the importance of the kind of intuitive relation to art that Kant describes as being part of an aesthetic judgment, "even to the savage."

As Hohendahl describes, *Negative Dialectics, Aesthetic Theory,* and "Essay as Form," embody various attempts to "postulate a rapprochement between art's immanent logic and discursive thought."[26] Instead of allowing art to remain an independent realm of experience separate from conceptual structures, Adorno attempts to integrate the aesthetic dimension into the mechanisms of philosophy. He achieves this by creating a type of conceptual criticism in the essay form that goes beyond traditional philosophical discourse and its discursive logic.[27] In describing this aestheticized mode of criticism, Hohendahl notes that, for Adorno, "the essay's defiance of discursive logic, its keen interest in associations and equivocations (*Äquivokationen*), brings it close to aesthetic language," and negative dialectics as a mode of critique "can be separated from aesthetic forms; its dialectical procedure remains discursive, although not bound by rigorous rules of rational argumentation."[28] Nicholsen describes this style of discourse in detail by showing how a passage from Adorno's essay, "Titles," is designed to give the impression of discursive argumentation while avoiding a clear and decisive argument in order that the reader might be provoked into further reflection.[29] But, while Nicholsen claims that this reflection creates a space of "freedom and lack of restriction," the autonomy of the reader is strictly delimited. The reader is not free to draw her or his own conclusions based on the configurations presented. Rather, as Nicholsen must also admit, "this mass of reflection-provoking configurations of concrete elements is ultimately drawn back within the discursive form as a conceptual conclusion is drawn on the basis of it."[30] Instead of allowing aesthetic judgments to develop on their own, Adorno's merging of art and philosophy in aesthetic theory ultimately draws aesthetic experience back to a predetermined conceptual conclusion. In his attempt to free theory from the constraints of the concept, he only manages to delegitimate aesthetic experience and to transform "art into an agent of critical theory's interests."[31] Theory will always be built on concepts, and, to the extent that Adorno theorizes with equivocations, rather than with clear theses, and with associations rather than with arguments, he is either engaging in prevarication and "casuistry"[32] or constructing an artwork that is calculated to lead the reader to a specific conceptual conclusion, as Nicholsen's analysis suggests.

Adorno attempts this dubious merging of philosophy and art, because, on the one hand, he seeks to translate the insights of art into the social realm, and on the other, does not allow himself to conceive of a type of art that establishes social structures based on aesthetic intuition alone—that is, the type of art that manifests itself as the rituals and traditions of a community whose aesthetic judgments establish a basis for ethical behavior. Rather than seeing aesthetic judgment itself as the basis of the communal aspect of art, he connects art to community by means of philosophy. He argues that art, like beauty in nature, relates to its contents negatively. But instead of recognizing that this negative relation can only be properly constructed with a transcendent aspect that is conceptually undefinable, he seeks to create a conceptual determination of it, looking to philosophy to say that which art is not permitted to express. "Just as in music what is beautiful flashes up in nature only to disappear in the instant one tries to grasp it. Art does not imitate nature, not even individual instances of natural beauty, but natural beauty as such. This denominates not only the aporia of natural beauty but the aporia of aesthetics as a whole. Its object is determined negatively, as indeterminable. It is for this reason that art requires philosophy, which interprets it in order to say what it is unable to say, whereas art is only able to say it by not saying it" (*AT* 72). The indeterminability of the transcendent object of art's mimesis does not lead Adorno to affirm the aesthetic judgment as the only approach to such an object, but to reintegrate art into philosophy as the conceptual determination of that transcendence.

In connecting art to philosophy, Adorno expresses the dependence of art on reception. Yet, the restriction of this reception to philosophy also separates society from the experiential dimension that is supposed to be mediated by the moment of reception in art. Adorno hides his prejudice in favor of concepts and philosophers by saying that philosophy can never really say what is to be communicated in art. This last pseudo-dialectical flourish, which both affirms and denies the importance of philosophy, is determined by Adorno's refusal to rely on the direct judgment of art's audience. The rejection of this popular dimension is also the denial of cultural specificity. Although art needs reception, this reception is, contra Adorno, not typically philosophical and universal, but intuitive and culturally specific. The collective reception of art or of myth does not attempt to establish the absolute conceptually, but allows it to remain a negative projection from the formal aesthetic structure. Because they avoid a conceptual determination, artworks as well as traditions and rituals maintain the only adequate mediation of truth with experience.

Adorno's merging of art with transcendence, while maintaining a subject-based totality, turns out to be impossible because transcendence in art necessarily involves a transcendence of the individual in favor of something beyond the individual subject. In positing utopia, rather than some form of supersensual reality, as the place of a transcendent dimension that constitutes the subject, Adorno creates an elaborate tautology wherein that which transcends the subject in art is the subject itself as delineated by its desires.

Yet, his project of gaining an understanding of a specifically aesthetic mode of truth as opposed to a rational one remains valid. While rational arguments can serve as a method of achieving previously defined goals, they cannot function as a basis for moral judgments. Instead, it may be that judgment can only be based in structures of transcendence mediated by aesthetic truth. As opposed to reason's abstraction and universality, transcendence and art are situational and culturally specific. As such, they may form the basis for the functioning of ethics, which must always be adapted to a particular situation. At the same time, the cultural specificity of aesthetic judgments does not destroy their truth value and turn them into pure considerations of power. Although aesthetic truth is not based on rational argument, it nevertheless retains legitimacy based on the sacrifice of materiality in favor of transcendent ideals. Reason, because it is not based on sacrifice but on the attainment of material goals, cannot serve as a substitute for aesthetic truth as a basis of morality. When the attempt is made to carry out this substitution, the result is an instrumentalization of sacrifice because there is no rational way to decide final goals, and the aesthetically mediated traditions and rituals for this determination have been rejected.

The Aesthetics of Sacrifice

As opposed to Adorno's use of philosophy to integrate aesthetic truth into a social order, mythic structures based on sacrifice directly link the aesthetic form to specific social actions in a disinterested process without a recourse to philosophy. Kant emphasizes that the disinterestedness of the spectator is a prerequisite for the functioning of the sublime as an aesthetic experience. "When in an aesthetic judgment we consider nature as a might that has no dominance over us, then it is *dynamically sublime*" (*CJ* 119). The sublime is felt only when nature's might is seen in a situation in which nature has no direct power over the witness at that moment. Kant recognizes here that aesthetic pleasure can only arise out of a state of individual disinterestedness in which we can "consider an object *fearful* without being afraid of it, namely if we judge it in such a way that we merely *think* of the case where we might possibly want to put up resistance against it, and that any resistance would in that case be utterly futile" (*CJ* 119–20). Although the experience of the sublime is a recognition of the overwhelming power of nature, this recognition is not a direct fear but a disinterested judgment from the point of view of the individual, and only those who are disinterested can make valid judgments about the sublime. "Just as we cannot pass judgment on the beautiful if we are seized by inclination and appetite, so we cannot pass judgment at all on the sublime in nature if we are afraid" (*CJ* 120). As opposed to conceptual determinations that can and will be interested conclusions oriented around specific needs and goals, judgments on the sublime that are required for a structure of sacrifice to be repeated and passed on are disinterested ones from the point of view of the individual making the judgment.

At the same time, judgments on the sublime are not merely receptive. They also establish a specific structure of transcendence that is a negative projection from out of the experience of the material power of nature. Sacrifice creates a vision of the absolute, not as a willful construction nor merely as a blind faith, but as an individually disinterested extrapolation from out of a current constellation of violent forces of nature. In creating a vision of the sacred, sacrifice does not represent the absolute as an Apollonian symbol, but as a Dionysian formal structure. The orientation to the sacred depends on aesthetic mechanisms (which Adorno attributes solely to art), because the sacred aspect of the sublime does not inhere within the sublime object itself, but rather, like the nonidentical in the work of art, is established by a mimetic relation to the forces of nature that then results in a definition of the sacred from out of the specific negation of the material. "We need not worry that the feeling of the sublime will lose [something] if it is exhibited in such an abstract way as this, which is wholly negative as regards the sensible. For though the imagination finds nothing beyond the sensible that could support it, this very removal of its barriers also makes it feel unbounded, so that its separation [from the sensible] is an exhibition of the infinite; and though an exhibition of the infinite can as such never be more than merely negative, it still expands the soul" (*CJ* 135). This understanding of the negative projection of the infinite from out of the sublime relates closely to Adorno's description of the work of art as a negative mimesis rather than a positive representation.

But though Kant describes the sublime as an aesthetic experience, his examples do not refer to works of art, but to religious rules that establish a system of sacrifice. His explanation of religious enthusiasm is similar to Nietzsche's understanding of the manifestation of the Dionysian in art and Adorno's model for expression in the work of art. The infinite can only be expressed negatively, and the negative structure of the sublime is the reason for the Old Testament ban on images.

> Perhaps the most sublime passage in the Jewish Law is the commandment: Thou shalt not make unto thee any graven image, or any likeness of any thing that is in heaven or on earth, or under the earth, etc. This commandment alone can explain the enthusiasm that the Jewish people in its civilized era felt for its religion when it compared itself with other peoples, or can explain the pride that Islam inspires. The same holds also for our presentation of the moral law, and for the predisposition within us for morality. It is indeed a mistake to worry that depriving this presentation of whatever could commend it to the senses will result in its carrying with it no more than a cold and lifeless approval without any moving force or emotion. It is exactly the other way round. For once the senses no longer see anything before them, while yet the unmistakable and indelible idea of morality remains, one would sooner need to temper the momentum of an unbounded imagination so as to keep it from rising to the level of enthusiasm, than to seek to support these ideas with images and childish devices for fear that they would otherwise be powerless. (*CJ* 135)

Although Kant is only seeking here to illustrate the power of an "idea of morality" and thus of a mental faculty as opposed to a presentation to the senses, he also describes how the enthusiasm that arises out of the experience of the sublime is a result of a negative projection. Consequently, though his larger project involves the investigation of the moral law as an element of reason, his examples come from the way Judaism and Islam establish the relationship between sacrifice and the absolute.

The renunciation of images leads to a vision of the absolute as something intangible and a conviction that morality has no need of "images and childish devices." His affirmation of the superfluousness of images is an attempt to deny the importance of aesthetic effects and the sufficiency of moral law for the establishment of morality. Yet, this denial of images is at the same time an affirmation of the sublime as an aesthetic effect. The Jewish morality he describes, though it dispenses with an Apollonian representation based on direct images, still depends upon an aesthetic movement of the sublime in which the ban on images itself creates a sacrificial renunciation that establishes the specific aesthetic form of the Jewish religion. In this passage, Kant tries to defend the moral law as an abstract principle while at the same time emphasizing the importance of an aesthetic movement as the basis of morality. He is led to this contradiction by his failure to differentiate between images as an Apollonian type of art based on representation and the movement of the sublime as an example of a Dionysian type of art based on expression through form. He consequently turns his argument about the sublime into an argument for moral law rather than for the centrality of the sacrificial structure of the sublime as a basis for morality.

But as Kant's own analysis of the sublime demonstrates, it is in overwhelming the subject's capacities that the power of nature establishes the outlines of the absolute. It may be that it is only in this overwhelming of the subject that the capacity for morality is produced. If this is true, then the basis of morality is not in an affirmation of the subject, but in the experience of sacrifice, whose functioning is inseparable from the aesthetic experience of the sublime.[33] Such an indispensability of an aesthetic experience for the construction of morality would lead to the conclusion that the formal structure of sacrifice is similar to Adorno's concept of the work of art. Sacrifice does not create a copy of the absolute, but acts mimetically in order to develop a vision of the sacred that is specifically tied to a disinterested judgment about the violence of nature. Kant's examples from various religious traditions show that although the absolute does not exist in the myth or ritual itself as a direct depiction, the experience of the sublime is still indispensable as the basis of a negative projection emanating from its form as sacrifice.

Kant's analysis of the sublime provides the foundations for an aesthetics of sacrifice. Because the binding quality of a sacrificial myth lives and dies according to its aesthetic effect, its construction of morality cannot be universal or abstract but remains in an intimate relation to the experience of a specific community. The power of sacrifice, as of art, depends on its ability to adjust to changes in the character of collective experience, and the truth of a sacrificial story or ritual is not a given, but depends upon the extent to which the structures of experience embedded in its form still retain validity for a particular collective. Since moral truth is constructed aesthetically in the experience of the sublime, the cultural realm of traditions and rituals is the key site for the determination of values. Such a culture is not constructed universally on the basis of reason, however, but through the sublime, whose validity is justified aesthetically in a continuing reception process whereby past narratives and rituals must continue to fulfill an aesthetic need in order to be repeated in the future.

In a way that will be described in more detail in later chapters, the specific movement of sacrifice that creates the experience of the sublime and makes the sacrifice into a pleasurable experience establishes the parameters for the sacred and for the construction of subjectivity in the group that institutionalizes the sacrifice. The establishment of ideals and of a vision of the sacred occurs through a struggle against nature and against enemies in which specific decisions on sacrifice lead to ideals as an extrapolation from the terms of the sacrifice. This process links an experience of violence with a vision of collective ideals. The disinterestedness of the individual in the sacrifice leads to an establishment of the specific qualities of a collective interest that then becomes the goal of the sacrifice. Although this collective interest may take many forms, both disruptive and benign, and in some ways belies the *individual* disinterestedness of the sublime judgment, this collective interest is not based on a conceptual construction of goals but on a specific vision of the sacred that arises out of aesthetic judgments rather than rational determinations.

Chapter Two

The Politics of Myth in the Nazi Period

Alfred Baeumler and Carl Einstein

The approach to sacrifice in this book proceeds from the assumption that, while both can mediate the human relation to the world, *myth* can be distinguished from *reason* based on the former's aesthetic functioning as opposed to the latter's dependence on concepts. In *Dialectic of Enlightenment* Horkheimer and Adorno demonstrate that reason establishes an instrumental relationship to the world, but the authors then seek to arrive at a substantive notion of reason that could ground a rational ethics. In contrast, the present study explores the idea that ethics might depend upon the aesthetic judgments that underlie an understanding of sacrifice. According to this perspective, sacrifice is not just an ideology or a result of an aggressive instinct. Instead, it establishes the parameters of an ethical system for a particular culture that is based on shared judgments about ultimate values and the ways in which those values are to be affirmed against opposing forces.

This understanding of sacrifice implies a notion of myth in which its narratives are not just a form of ideology or delusional projections; here, myth establishes a relation between humans and the world that takes into account the totality of a culture's specific experience as mediated through its ethical conceptions. Because its conception of the world links experience to ethics, myth's narratives function within an ethical perspective that is to be distinguished from the instrumental focus of rationality. The goal of this chapter is to distinguish this notion of myth from the rationalist denigration of myth in order to clear the conceptual space for an understanding of sacrifice in which it would mediate between values and ethical practices.

Because the argument for the centrality of sacrifice for culture runs the risk of justifying violence for its own sake, it is important to show that the aesthetic approach to sacrifice presents a clear alternative to the

45

ideological or materialist approaches to sacrifice taken by Nazi theorists. As this chapter attempts to show, the Nazi example does not put into question the idea of an aesthetic functioning of myth and sacrifice but only demonstrates the consequences of a nonaesthetic approach to these phenomena. The equating of Nazi understandings of myth and sacrifice with a general conception of these categories only serves to obscure the aesthetic processes that underlie sacrifice.

Unfortunately, an anti-aesthetic approach to myth has become dominant, not only in recent German attempts to salvage the concept of myth, but also in attempts to denigrate myth and sacrifice as inherently dangerous phenomena. For example, Philippe Lacoue-Labarthe and Jean-Luc Nancy emphasize that the problem of fascism is a contemporary one because "our present is far from done with its recent Nazi and fascist past." They go on to identify the dangerous elements of our times in "those already numerous contemporary discourses that refer to *myth,* to the necessity of a new myth or of a new mythic consciousness, or the reactivation of old myths."[1] Their connection of all discourse on myth with fascism stems from their definition of myth as mere ideology. This definition limits the category of myth to a conceptual strategy, "an explanation of history ... through a single concept: the concept of race, for example."[2] This understanding of myth as a set of ideas based on unthinking prejudices is certainly valid as a critique of ideologies, such as racism, which claim to have a scientific basis but in fact have no such foundations and can only be defended irrationally. But this reduction of myth to ideology fails to account for the persistence of myth in our modern, supposedly rational, world precisely because it does not recognize the aesthetic aspect of myth, in which myth functions not as an ideology to be enforced, but as a set of narratives that have an aesthetic legitimacy. Since this aesthetic functioning is not easily amenable to manipulation and correction, it is also as unpredictable in its development and consequences as any aesthetic genre, such as drama or painting.

The point here is not to downplay myth due to its "merely" aesthetic character but to recognize that this character is the source of myth's persistence and power in the face of any rationalist attempts to control it. An understanding of this aesthetic functioning will not provide us with the means to eradicate myth once and for all. Such a project would be akin to trying to eliminate all music or all poetry from the world. Instead, the point would be to approach myth, and narratives of sacrifice as a form of myth, as an aesthetic sphere whose processes can have both beneficial and malevolent effects. The goal cannot be to manipulate these processes rationally. At best, the goals of a particular mythology might be opposed based on an alternative set of values, but only after a basic appreciation of the aesthetics underlying these processes has been achieved.

This aesthetic approach to myth is not undermined by the Nazi example, precisely because the Nazi strategy was to equate myth with ideology in order to delegitimate traditional myths and establish a "new" mythology subject to rational manipulation. As Lacoue-Labarthe and Nancy themselves point out,[3] Alfred Rosenberg rejected traditional myths, and Hitler never accepted even the idea of myth but spoke the language of modern rationality and enlightenment.[4] Yet, in labeling all attempts to rethink the category of myth as fascist, Lacoue-Labarthe and Nancy unnecessarily limit our understanding of myth by assuming that myth can only be understood as ideology. They thereby continue a postwar identification of fascist aesthetics with the aesthetics of myth that has been based on the spurious view that fascist theories of myth advocated a return to mythic structures and that the idea of myth is thus fascist ideological terrain.

The difficulty of this identification becomes evident when one considers the ubiquity of the concept of myth in early twentieth-century intellectual debates. The role of myth in modern culture was a topic of intense interest, not just for Nazis, but for German writers and scholars with widely diverging political inclinations. J. P. Stern describes the pervasiveness of this discourse by relating it to the issue of "reality" as an idea that takes on a new meaning in the nineteenth and twentieth centuries. In a development that Stern traces to Hegel's and Nietzsche's privileging of art over empirical reality as the locus of a genuine reality, modernist writers in Europe began to refer to reality as either a mere empirical reality or as a true reality that exceeded the merely empirical. Once empirical reality became a problematic idea, the view developed that "truth and 'reality' were to be found everywhere except 'in proposition,'"[5] and therefore writers began to look to art as the source of a true reality no longer to be found in the empirical world or in scientific explanations. Once art is accorded the status of a source of true reality, it can be referred to as a kind of myth that, in recounting stories, provides insight into a true reality beyond what is empirically experienced.

While Stern finds the notion that truth cannot be found "in proposition" (i.e., in concepts) to be nonsensical, noting that "it is difficult to understand how it could have been seriously defended for so long,"[6] this attitude is in fact the basis of many theories of art and experience proposed since Hegel. Adorno's aesthetics present one such theory in which aesthetic truth becomes the precursor to philosophical truth, even though the latter is necessary for the completion of the former. Adorno carefully distinguishes art from myth by banishing the elements of sacrifice and violence in order to imagine an art based on beauty and harmony. As we have seen, Adorno's project excludes from consideration the violence of nature and the resulting subordination of the individual to this violence. Accordingly, we can consider myth to be a kind of art that provides access to its own kind of truth and does so with reference to violence when it stages a narrative of sacrifice. The goal of this chapter is to distinguish this aesthetic approach to myth, in which myth functions as part of an overall relationship to the world based on judgment, from the kind of Nazi-oriented perspective that Stern seeks to criticize; that is, in which myth is a kind of materiality or "true reality" behind everyday appearances that suppresses judgment.

Liberal and Fascist Theories of Myth

The point of Adorno's attempt to imagine an art that is free of violence is to counter the Nazi attempt to maintain myth as a contemporary phenomenon. This chapter argues, however, that the primary impulse of Nazi theories of myth was to recognize the importance of myth not in order to promote it, but to suppress its free aesthetic development. Nazi theories of sacrifice consequently treated myth as a manipulable ideology rather than an aesthetic form. In this respect, Nazi theories of myth are consistent with liberal theories to the extent that both share a goal of establishing a rationalist rather than a traditionalist approach to culture.

We can see the similarity when comparing the 1920s reflections on myth by Thomas Mann (1875–1955) with those by Alfred Baeumler (1887–1968). We would expect a difference of opinion between these two figures on the question of myth based on the divergence of their political trajectories. Though Mann took a conservative nationalist stance in his 1918 essay, "Reflections of an Unpolitical Man," he soon after became one of the most respected and vocal supporters of the Weimar Republic, defending it against its right-wing detractors in addresses such as "On the German Republic" (1922) and "German Address: An Appeal to Reason" (1930). As a Nobel Prize winner in 1929, he became one of the most prominent critics of the Nazis, and his stance forced him into exile in 1933 to other parts of Europe; he eventually fled to the United States during the Nazi years. Though he at first hesitated to take a strong public stand against the Nazis once they were in power, he finally did so in 1936, upon which the German government revoked his citizenship. During the war, he broadcast a series of anti-Nazi radio addresses to Germany over the BBC entitled *German Listeners!* and after 1945 he continued his critique of both the Nazis and of the German people's complicity in the rise of the party. He would never again live in Germany.[7]

By contrast, Baeumler was, in the words of Hans Sluga, "more than any other German philosopher, the typical fascist intellectual."[8] Though Baeumler's career begins with a book on the problem of irrationality in eighteenth-century aesthetics that is still used today by scholars of eighteenth-century intellectual history,[9] his work turned in the course of the 1920s more and more toward the Nazis. He developed his ideas on myth in a 1926 introduction to a volume of writings by Johann Jakob Bachofen, and this text strongly influenced Alfred Rosenberg's understanding of myth in *The Myth of the 20th Century*, with Rosenberg citing Baeumler's work early on in his book.[10] After Hitler's rise to power, Baeumler received an appointment as chair of Philosophy and Political Pedagogy at the University of Berlin, where he worked closely with Rosenberg until 1945, heading the academic division (*Amt Wissenschaft*) of Rosenberg's Office for the Surveillance of the Whole Intellectual and Ideological Education and Training of the National Socialist Party and organizing conferences designed to develop a Nazi philosophy.[11] Though Rosenberg's increasing marginalization within the Nazi hierarchy limited the broader dissemination of Baeumler's ideas, they still represented the best example of a Nazi theory of myth. Not only did Baeumler consolidate into a coherent theory of culture current ideas on the power of ritual, the philosopher as politician, and the nation as a symbolic form, he developed these ideas into a theoretical justification for racism and a practical program for Nazi pedagogy.[12]

While Baeumler's early work attracted Mann's praise, in 1926 Mann accused Baeumler of promoting in his Bachofen introduction a Nazi agenda in defending the "great Return to the mystical-historical-romantic womb of the mother." Against such a reactionary return to romanticism and mysticism, Mann defended idealism and humanism and sought the victory of Apollonian rules and concepts over mythic forces, writing that "instead of praying to the myth, one would do better today to help one's people to achieve such [Apollonian] victories."[13] Suspecting that the interest in myth would lead to fascism, Mann tried to establish a rational, antimythic alternative.

Although Helmut Koopmann has argued that Mann's antifascist, enlightenment position can be differentiated from Baeumler's fascist one because Mann supported the victory of the father principle while Baeumler sought a regression back toward the cult of the mother,[14] a comparison of Mann's critique with Baeumler's text demonstrates not only that the two were working with the same Bachofen-based understanding of myth and human history but also that they were in full agreement in supporting the victory of "paternal" form over "maternal" chaos.[15] Mann's conjectures about Baeumler's Nazi tendencies were eventually confirmed by Baeumler's later political development, but he was in error on the issue of Baeumler's support of archaic, mythic forces. Baeumler did not seek a return to a primitive maternal culture but instead attempted to justify the paternal victory of "form" over an earlier maternal materiality without form.[16] In a passage demonstrating the proximity of Baeumler's position to Mann's, Baeumler wrote in support of "the radiant consciousness of a constantly victorious struggle against the power of older, darker views."[17] The triumph of both epic and tragedy was for Baeumler a triumph of the Apollonian paternal religious perspective over the power of older, darker forces. Like Mann, Baeumler subordinated the mythic and the primitive to the rule of an "Apollonian" law.

The similarity between Baeumler's and Mann's support of Apollonian form over mythic chaos has led to recent attempts in Germany to recover aspects of Baeumler's thought for contemporary, liberal discussions of myth. Hubert Brunträger, for example, uses the similarity between Baeumler's and Mann's ideas as an argument for Baeumler's possible liberal affinities and as a means of distinguishing the early work from his explicitly fascist work after 1933. He even suggests that in the Bachofen introduction his views are so similar to Mann's that there might have been a chance of pulling Baeumler "into the democratic camp."[18] Brunträger thereby follows Manfred Frank's attempts to distill a liberal element out of Baeumler's early work that might be used for a contemporary discussion of myth. A German philosopher and professor at the University of Tübingen since 1987, Frank established himself as the introducer of French poststructuralism to a German audience and published extensively on German romanticism and related theories of myth, taking up Friedrich Schelling's notion of a "new mythology." In his theories of myth, Frank combines Jürgen Habermas's idea of communicative rationality with theories of aesthetics and myth developed by romantics such as Schelling and Friedrich Creuzer and then extended in Baeumler's work of the 1920s. In using Baeumler's ideas, Frank is careful to emphasize a break in Baeumler's thought after 1933. This allows him to recover for his own thinking the understanding of myth developed by Baeumler in the 1926 Bachofen introduction while condemning Baeumler's later "turn" toward fascism. In his interpretation of Baeumler's work, Frank attempts to demonstrate a shift in Baeumler's thought from an early "cultic" theory of myth to a later racial one, allowing Frank to "save" the former while condemning the latter.[19]

But, as I will attempt to show, Baeumler's ideas demonstrate a continuity in which the early material is not only entirely consistent with but also logically leads to the racist conclusions of the later work. This continuity sheds new light on the reconcilability of Baeumler's position with Thomas Mann's. Instead of demonstrating the validity of Baeumler's early views, as Frank would contend, the close relationship to Mann indicates the proximity between a Nazi and a liberal understanding of the role of myth in society.

This proximity arises out of the connections between enlightenment and fascism. Horkheimer and Adorno interpret this connection as evidence for a dialectic of enlightenment and myth, in which each turns into the other: "Just as the myths already realize enlightenment, so enlightenment with every step becomes more deeply engulfed in mythology" (*DE* 11–12). But while Horkheimer and Adorno recognize the complicity of enlightenment with fascism that is demonstrated by the similarity between Mann's and Baeumler's positions on myth, the idea of a dialectic of myth and enlightenment tends to obscure the fact that, instead of carrying out a regression toward myth, both Baeumler and Mann oppose the return of myth. Their parallel attempts on the one hand to recognize the power of myth and on the other hand to suppress this power led in the case of Baeumler not to a regeneration of myth but to its suppression.

Horkheimer and Adorno themselves outline the terms of such a stricter differentiation of myth from enlightenment when they contrast the methods of myth with those of reason. While reason reduces all of nature to an undifferentiated raw material, "magic pursues aims, but seeks to achieve them by mimesis—not by progressively distancing itself from the object" (*DE* 11). This view of magic as mimesis emphasizes the anti-enlightenment aspect of myth as a positive characteristic. Not only does magic still maintain the qualitative differences in nature that have been eradicated by science, it also provides a way of relating to nature and experience that is based on imitation rather than rational manipulation. As mimesis, myth accurately perceives the power of nature as stronger than man and describes the parameters of this domination: "*mana,* the moving spirit, is no projection, but the echo of the real supremacy of nature in the weak souls of primitive men" (*DE* 15). Reason, by contrast, is based on manipulation. "Enlightenment behaves toward things as a dictator toward men. He knows them insofar as he can manipulate them. The man of science knows things in so far as he can make them" (*DE* 9). As a form of manipulation, reason maintains an antimythic attitude to the extent that it presupposes the subject's domination over nature rather than its subordination to it. By delineating a conception of myth as mimesis that they oppose to the rational domination of nature, Horkheimer and Adorno outline how myth and enlightenment are to be differentiated in a way that vindicates myth over enlightenment. If one takes seriously the distinction between mimesis and manipulation, one would have to revise the thesis of the dialectic of enlightenment in order to suggest, not a dialectic, but an opposition between myth and enlightenment in which the former might be defended against the latter.

Although they would not seriously consider such a possibility, Horkheimer and Adorno did differentiate between a genuine myth and a false one, preparing the way for a reconsideration of myth's role in contemporary society. Genuine myth perceives the power of nature as stronger than man and describes the parameters of this "real supremacy of nature." False myth, by contrast, does not merely register the violence of nature but attempts to extend this violence to new victims. "The phony Fascist mythology is shown to be the genuine myth of antiquity, insofar as the genuine one saw retribution, whereas the false one blindly doles it out to the victims" (*DE* 13; my translation). By differentiating between genuine and false myth, Horkheimer and Adorno seek to maintain mythic forms of relating to nature while condemning myth when used as an alibi for violence. Yet, this differentiation does not actually distinguish between two types of myth but between a mythic mimesis, which aesthetically divines the violence of nature, and manipulation, which is not mythic at all but is simply a pursuit of rationalist ends.

Such a revision of Horkheimer and Adorno's thesis offers a solution to the question of how the Nazis were able to combine their scientism with a revival of mythic forms. The Nazis never actually sought to revive myth as an aesthetic process. Rather, the Nazi cultural project was in fact much closer to an enlightenment attempt to overcome myth.[20] If this is true, then the move that ties enlightenment to Nazism is not the return to myth, as Mann's *Pariser Rechenschaft* as well as Horkheimer and Adorno's *Dialectic of Enlightenment* argue, but a suppression of myth as an aesthetic mode. As such, the Nazi relation to myth follows the same trajectory as the liberal attempt to dispense with it. The key difference is, of course, that the Nazis eradicated myth as part of their repression of free aesthetic activity in general, while liberal opponents carry out their attack through rhetoric, without repressive measures. This is obviously a crucial difference, but in both cases the explicit project is to replace myth with rational structures.

Left-Wing Theories of Myth

The antimythic perspective of the Nazis becomes obvious in a comparison of fascist with alternative ideas on myth. If Nazis such as Baeumler and Rosenberg carried out a repression of myth rather than a revival, their intense interest in myth notwithstanding, then it may be that alternative theories of myth can be considered antifascist to the extent that they sought to emancipate myth from such repression. But the left-wing critique of the Nazis was itself divided by a dispute between rationalists and irrationalists. On one end of the spectrum Georg Lukács argues that there is a single unbroken trajectory in German thought that leads from Schelling's irrationalism through the *Lebensphilosophie* of Friedrich Nietzsche, Wilhelm Dilthey, and Georg Simmel and then directly into the fascist myth-making of Ludwig Klages, Ernst Jünger, Baeumler, and Rosenberg. For Lukács there are no essential distinctions to be made within this trajectory, and all the different conceptions of myth and irrationalism must be uniformly condemned as protofascist.[21] Horkheimer and Adorno maintain a more differentiated view of irrationalism, arguing that myth and rationality are intertwined and criticizing enlightenment for its complicity with mythic regression. Similarly, Walter Benjamin discusses the mythic possibilities of "aura" in art, not only to demonstrate aura's obsolescence in a modern world in which new nonauratic modes of spectatorship become dominant,[22] but also to devise new forms of myth and ritual such as profane illumination and involuntary memory.[23] Yet despite their more flexible attitudes, Benjamin, Horkheimer, and Adorno generally accord with Lukács in denying that myth and ritual might function as positive aspects of culture rather than solely as negative and violent forces.

By contrast, Thomas Mann, Carl Einstein (1885–1940), and Ernst Bloch (1885–1977) were the thinkers-in-exile who engaged most seriously with myth and thus developed theories that were the closest to Baeumler's. While recent scholarship has focused on the relationship between Mann and Baeumler, there has been less investigation into the work of those working outside Germany who attempted a more straightforward return to myth in modern society. Yet, Bloch's and Einstein's promythic views make their work well suited for a comparison with Baeumler's similar evaluation of myth, not only because all three are of the same generation, but because their ideas in fact derive from the same intellectual sources.

In contrast to the other left-wing intellectuals mentioned above, both Bloch and Einstein were intimately connected with Expressionism—Bloch's *Geist der Utopie* (1918) having been received as a philosophical manifesto for Expressionism, and Einstein's early novel, *Bebuquin* (1912), considered a seminal example of literary Expressionism. Moreover, they were both particularly interested in Expressionism's primitivist aspects. While Einstein was the author of *Negerplastik*, the first European study of African sculpture, Bloch wrote one of the first positive reviews of Einstein's book when it appeared in 1915. Both writers maintained their interest in both Expressionism and primitivism throughout the 1920s and 1930s: Einstein went on to write several other major works on "primitive" art, and Bloch continued to defend both Expressionism and "folk art," most notably during the "Expressionism debate" of the 1930s.[24]

Baeumler's intellectual background intersected with those of Bloch and Einstein at various points. For all three, Nietzsche was a primary philosophical influence on their thinking. Bloch's earliest known publication, from his student days, takes Nietzsche as its topic, and Nietzsche plays a key role in Einstein's *Bebuquin*. Baeumler, for his part, published a number of books and essays on Nietzsche throughout his career and was the editor of the 1930 Kröner edition of Nietzsche's collected works. In addition, they all happened to have attended Georg Simmel's lectures and seminars at the University of Berlin in the same period around 1908, though Einstein's and Baeumler's interests were probably the most intimately related, both also having worked with the art historian, Heinrich Wölfflin, and both borrowing heavily from Wölfflin's ideas on aesthetic form in order to develop their separate theories of myth in the 1920s and 1930s. Thus, all three were strongly influenced by the "irrationalist" thinkers such as Nietzsche and Simmel whom Lukács cites as the sources of Nazi thought.

But in spite of the correspondences in their early intellectual backgrounds, Baeumler, Bloch, and Einstein pursued widely divergent political agendas. Bloch moved toward socialism in the course of his opposition to World War I, joining the German Communist Party after the war and criticizing the Nazis from a Marxist perspective. Like Mann, he was forced into exile by the Nazis, not only on the basis of his Jewish heritage but also due to his Marxist critiques. Like Mann, he wandered through Europe in the 1930s, staying for brief periods in Vienna, Zurich, and Prague, and he was a prominent participant in Marxist debates on Expressionism and Stalinism. While he defended Expressionism against Georg Lukács's attacks, he also infamously defended Stalin's purges and the Moscow show trials. After a stay in the United States during the Second World War, Bloch renewed his ties to socialism by moving to East Germany and taking a position at the University of Leipzig. Although he achieved a prominent position in postwar East Germany, he eventually came into conflict with its government and defected to West Germany in 1961.

Like Bloch, Einstein moved toward socialism during the course of World War I, working with the Soldiers' Councils in Brussels at the end of the war and then with socialist revolutionaries Karl Liebknecht and Rosa Luxembourg in Berlin. In the 1920s, Einstein retreated from political activities and worked as a writer and art historian, publishing on both African art and the newest currents of twentieth-century European art. His 1926 *Kunst des 20. Jahrhunderts (20th Century Art)* was well received and went through three editions. By the time the Nazis came to power, he was already living in Paris and remained in exile due to both his prior socialist connections and his Jewish heritage. The Spanish Civil War brought him back into political activity, and he fought in the war with the anarchists under Buenaventura Durruti, presenting Durruti's eulogy on Spanish Republican radio in 1936.[25] After the Spanish Republican defeat, Einstein returned to Paris. When the Nazis invaded and occupied France, Einstein fled Paris and died, apparently by his own hand, in the French countryside.

The stark contrasts in Baeumler's, Bloch's, and Einstein's political biographies not only led to key differences in their theories but also to the circumstance that their ideas, though addressing the same issues of myth, community, and aesthetics, have not been considered together. While Baeumler's work on myth was first published in his 1926 Bachofen introduction, some of his most thoroughly elaborated work on myth appeared in the 1930s and 1940s under the Nazis. For example, his 1933 "Inaugural Address in Berlin" appeared at a time when it could not be compared with the work of the exile writers.[26] Both Bloch's *Heritage of Our Time* (Zurich, 1935), which dealt specifically with issues of fascism and myth, and Einstein's *Georges Braque* (Paris, 1934), which contained his ideas on myth, were published outside Germany. Einstein's study appeared only in French translation and was unavailable in German until 1985. Consequently, the varying perspectives on myth embodied in the work of these figures did not confront each other until the late 1980s and 1990s in Germany. Bloch's work, in which the mythic element is less pronounced than with Einstein and Baeumler, has remained the most popular of the three up to the present day. Nevertheless, interest in both Baeumler and Einstein has been slowly rising, though Baeumler's theories have been more prominent in recent discussions of myth. Whereas Einstein's ideas on myth are still looked upon with suspicion, Klaus Kiefer referring to them as part of a protofascist "neoprimitivism,"[27] Baeumler's theories of myth have perhaps gained the most attention through Manfred Frank's work (*GE* 33–35).

The issue of myth is posed by all three thinkers as a question of the intellectual's relation to a popular or folk culture; all turned to popular culture as a source of the immediacy and lived experience that philosophical debates lack. Yet, because of the *völkisch* political implications of this project, only Baeumler is willing to explicitly defend the struggle "of the healthy folk against the unpopular type of the purely theoretical man."[28] Instead of referring to the *Volk,* Bloch speaks of "noncontemporaneous contradictions" when referring to traditions and rituals that persist in modern culture,[29] and Einstein refers to "the elemental forces" that he seeks "to rediscover and mobilize," though he also at one point speaks of myth as an expression of the "collectively folk-oriented" (E 210, 314–15). In spite of differences in terminology, all three are drawn to popular culture as a source of insight and power that is missing in purely theoretical debates.

Yet, this common project should not be taken as a demonstration that Bloch and Einstein were somehow cryptofascist. Such a conclusion stems from the idea, most convincingly developed by George Mosse, that all attempts to vindicate a *völkisch* popular dimension of culture are simply variations on an ultimately fascist political project.[30] Though Einstein's and Bloch's invocations of "mythic archaic levels of time" (E 212) and "noncontemporaneity" link their ideas to Nazis such as Baeumler, their political sympathies were decidedly Marxist in Bloch's case and anarchist for Einstein, whose writings were directed by turns against liberalism, Marxism, and fascism (E 200, 213, 341). In order to understand the logic of their positions, it is necessary to consider their championing of myth and collective levels of experience to be part of a larger Expressionist project that in many ways overlapped with a *völkisch* one. Within this broader project, differing political stances (Nazism, liberalism, Marxism, anarchism) can be distinguished according to their particular approaches to the common goal of a culture grounded in the people. Rather than demonizing the entire German cultural tradition dealing with such issues and immediately labeling discussions of myth and the folk as protofascist, the following consideration of the differences between these thinkers, in spite of the commonalities in their projects, will provide not only a more nuanced understanding of the relationship between Nazi ideology and the broader German culture but also shed new light on a neglected discussion of the role of myth and tradition in modern society.

The primary issue that separates these thinkers is their willingness to accept the popular dimension of myth and ritual as a true source of authority and insight rather than simply a raw material to be mobilized for political ends. Einstein's unique perspective is based on his anarchist idea that popular culture, and not a national bureaucracy or class-based party, must be the location of political and social decision making. He defends this conviction by arguing that the popular dimension of a culture, operating on the basis of myths, rituals, and traditions, is itself a valid source of insights and not a barbarous void when compared to an academic and intellectual culture based on arguments and debate. The popular culture of myths and traditions is the sphere in which a specifically aesthetic mode of intuition is allowed to develop independently of philosophical debate and within a context of ethical decision making.

In Einstein's approach, myth and art are parallel forms. The power of myth derives from its aesthetic success, and the significance of art for life depends upon art's mythic function as an organizer of experience for the audience. Because he considers myth aesthetically, it cannot be defined as a historically "noncontemporaneous" phenomenon as in Bloch's work; rather it must be based in contemporary psychic structures and processes. Einstein considers the contradictions within the individual subject to be the basis for myth and ritual. Consequently, for him the permanence of the work of art or religious object itself is not important. He is primarily interested in the extent to which the myth or sacred object mediates a human experience. He notes for example "that the 'image' as an object is only an appearance; that which is important is only the corresponding actualization of a human process" (E 237). Because the vitality and essence of the sacred object lies in the experience of the recipient and does not reside within the object itself, the material image or object is secondary to the process of myth but at the same time essential to it. The goal of both the traditional myth and the modern work of art for Einstein is to be the point of departure for the spectator's experience of the sacred. The aesthetic form does not try to replace experience. Instead it enables experience by setting up a specific structure within which it can unfold in the consciousness of the spectator.

Mythic experience for Einstein consists of a constant construction and dissolution of images as they gain and lose their ability to resonate with the experiences of the receiver. One of the prerequisites for this dynamic process is a free space in which art and myth are allowed to develop independently of direct ideological control. The moment of reception becomes constitutive for the myth because the recipient does not merely receive but plays the crucial editorial role in determining which works survive and which do not. For Einstein, myth is aesthetic because it is defined by the relationship between the spectator and the work of art. The aesthetic freedom of this continuing relationship creates the basis for a process of continual revision of mythic experience, and Einstein's discussion of myth does not isolate it in the past but attempts to locate it in the present, for example in the cubist work of Georges Braque (E 294–96).[31]

Baeumler and Nietzsche on Myth and Art

Baeumler shares Einstein's interest in myth as a contemporary event. But whereas Einstein contends that the sacred quality of myth is a consequence of its aesthetic ability to enable a collective mediation of subjective experience within an open public space, Baeumler rejects aesthetic understandings of myth in order to relate myth to cult rituals. Because rituals are enacted practices, Baeumler feels that they offer a more "objective" foundation for myth than art. But this scientistic attempt to understand myth as a consequence of material facts eventually leads Baeumler to the argument that blood and race are the determiners of culture. His understanding of myth is based on a materialist, scientific explanation and manipulation of myth that eliminates the aesthetic freedom that would allow for a regeneration of mythic structures grounded in aesthetic processes.

Baeumler's philosophy depends heavily on Nietzsche's ideas, his main argument concerning myth developing as a reaction against ideas set forth by Nietzsche in *The Birth of Tragedy*. Consequently, Baeumler's approach at first seems similar to Nietzsche's to the extent that they both point out the importance of myth for Greek culture (B XXXI; *BT* 108–11). But whereas Nietzsche goes on to explain the connections between myth and art, thereby emphasizing myth's status as a cultural phenomenon,[32] Baeumler insists on a strict separation between religious and aesthetic phenomena in order to interpret myth as a fixed structure that *precedes* culture.[33]

This difference between Baeumler's and Nietzsche's readings of myth derives from their separate understandings of the symbolic character of myth. Baeumler presents a reading of the symbol as an original symbol of existence whose contents remain constant over time and precede art, criticizing in the process Nietzsche's failure to share this reading. For Baeumler, myth is an "original symbol of existence" and "an intuitive prehistoric construct with an eternal, all-inclusive, inexhaustible content" (B CCXLVIII–CCXLIX). As opposed to Baeumler's definition of the symbol, which freezes myth into a static construct, for Nietzsche the myth's symbolic character derives from its exemplary status, its ability to accurately relate to the experiences of the people to which it speaks. Because this aesthetic efficacy of the myth ultimately derives from its cultural reception, the inner form and contents of the myth are put to the test when the myth is measured against experience in the mind of the spectator. Consequently, the religious power of the myth derives from an aesthetic efficacy that is defined both in terms of inner form and reception.[34] The individual subject becomes the mediator of the primal forces out of which the particular forms of myth and ritual are constructed, and so this process presumes a free space of aesthetic production and reception.[35]

By contrast, Baeumler emphasizes the religious force of myth as nonaesthetic and thus real: "Nietzsche starts out with the *will* to life, which is identical with the instinct for the *future*. Bachofen by contrast places *life* at center, *real* nature" (B CCLIV). While Nietzsche understands myth and symbol as parts of an ongoing cultural process of becoming, grounded in the constantly changing character of subjective experience, Baeumler prefers Bachofen's work because of its postulation of a "real nature" that has a constant structure of "being." Baeumler turns to this static understanding of symbol because he seeks to find an objective and material rather than a subjective and aesthetic foundation for myth and symbol. He rejects all aesthetic-psychological explanations due to their individual subjective character (B CCLXXXIII), and he also challenges Nietzsche's explanation of tragedy from an individual experience of ecstasy for the same reason (B CCXLII). Instead of a concentration on a subjective aesthetic experience, Baeumler seeks to explain myth and tragedy by referring to an "objective" material reality.

After rejecting Nietzsche's subjective, aesthetic explanations of myth and religion, Baeumler argues for the objective, nonarbitrary quality of myth, locating the basis of this objectivity first in ritual and then in blood. In the Bachofen introduction, Baeumler proposes cult rituals as the "objective" foundation of myth because he sees in material practices a greater objectivity than can be found in a purely aesthetic event. He sets out this argument in his criticism of Nietzsche's subjective explanation of the Dionysian.

> A simple reflection demonstrates the impossibility that tragedy might have originated out of a Dionysian enthusiasm. The trance in which the dancer feels himself transformed into the god is the climax of the Dionysian orgy. As a climax this inner process is however also an *ending*. It is completely unclear how an objective structure might develop out of this ecstasy, a subjective process that will always remain subjective. The enthusiastic experience not only lacks all form but even any trace of a formative power. The ecstatic entranced dancer who feels the presence of the god sinks exhausted to the ground. His experience has a clearly delimited trajectory. Nothing refers beyond the inner development. (B LXXII)

The crucial issue here is whether an aesthetic experience of ecstasy has any structural form. Baeumler does not see any connection between form and ecstatic moments in the subject because these moments remain confined to a passive inner process that does not refer to anything outside itself. This view opposes Nietzsche's idea that it is precisely such an inner process that gives rise to form as the recapitulation of contradictions that extend from the experience of the subject into the "heart of the world."[36] Baeumler sees this Dionysian-mimetic understanding of form as purely subjective, and thus divorced from reality, and seeks in contrast to ground tragedy and myth in a "material" reality of cult ritual. He replaces Nietzsche's aesthetic explanation of tragedy with a "cultic" one.

For Nietzsche, the myth is always a story and thus a linguistic and aesthetic construction that recapitulates experience. The myth or the ritual, as Dionysian art, is simultaneously an aesthetic and a sacred event that mediates between subjective experience and a cultural tradition. Refusing to make any metaphysical statements about the sacred itself, Nietzsche only discusses the human *experience* of the sacred, analyzing this experience in order to determine how it functions within human consciousness. Nietzsche then concludes that the rules of sacred experience are in fact aesthetic rules.

In contrast to this linking of aesthetic to religious experience in both myth and ritual, Baeumler draws a fundamental distinction between ritual, which is sacred, and myth, which is merely aesthetic, in order to concentrate on ritual as the true source of the tragic. For him, myth is too idealized and thus too abstract to provide the kind of metaphysical foundation that he seeks for tragedy. The essence of tragedy for Baeumler does not lie in its stories, but in its rituals, the facts of its presentation and performance within a ritual setting. The tragedy is a myth only to the extent that the ritual speaks through it, grounding the tragedy in the sacred realm of ritual, and thus turning it into myth.

Myth or ritual as a mediator between subjective experience and communal experience in the sacred does not exist for Baeumler. Instead, he claims that the sacred can only exist as an outgrowth of cult rituals. He differentiates the reality of ritual from the ephemerality of myth and argues that ritual is closer to subjective experience because it consists of a set of actions rather than mere words. As action, ritual, according to Baeumler, functions more effectively as an individual affirmation of a sacred experience:

> The tragedy was undoubtedly experienced by the ancient Greeks as a heroic epic with a gripping form unheard of until that time. The novelty

consisted in the fact that the events were not narrated but presented in a *dramatic* form. The heroic epic presented itself, then, not as *myth*, but as *cult*. With this transition from myth to cult there is simultaneously a move toward the subjectivity of the presentation in the most general sense. To be sure, there is nothing more objective, more rigid, more archaic than cultic rituals, but the cult itself is always subjective insofar as it consists of actions, and actions always originate out of the affect. It must be carried out by living subjects, practiced and preserved as a custom, if it is not to die. Meanwhile the phantom form of the word, even without a subjectively directed effort, can float effortlessly through the centuries. (B LXXVI)

Baeumler rejects the stories of myth, not just because of their aesthetic as opposed to ritual character, but also because of their idealistic character as language as opposed to actions. Myth for Baeumler can detach itself from the subjectivity of a community because it consists of words that can be preserved without subjective effort. Rituals on the other hand must constantly be affirmed by those carrying them out in order to continue to exist. Though Baeumler affirms the importance of subjective experience here, he does not suggest that such experience could define the structure of myth or ritual, as Nietzsche argues. Rather, for Baeumler the ritual takes hold of subjective experience, molding it according to a "more objective, more rigid, more archaic" structure. Baeumler assumes that a ritual (such as a real animal or human sacrifice) is closer to the sacred than the recounting of myths because the former is material while the latter is merely aesthetic. When myth is distinguished from ritual, the subjective side of both is discarded in favor of a presumed materiality and objectivity of ritual practices. Even though Baeumler argues that the ritual depends on subjective affirmation for its survival, he does not view this affirmation as the basis of ritual, but as an effect. Because for him the true source of the symbol's power lies in a sphere that precedes subjective experience, the only basis for this power that Baeumler can provide is one that is predetermined by the dictates of either a supernatural or a biological reality. Frank argues that the supernatural explanation for the sacred would be preferable to the biological (and racist) one (*GE* 125–30). But in fact both of these explanations have the same structure, and in Baeumler's thought, they both function as a source of the sacred.

Baeumler develops the supernatural explanation for the sacred in his discussion of epic and tragedy. In the Bachofen introduction he depicts the world of the dead as the "primal" reality that provides the foundation for the sacred. He differentiates epic and tragedy, not on the basis of genre characteristics such as formal structure or style, but by referring to the character of the rituals connected to each. In the epic the rituals are conducted as incense offerings to the dead, while in the tragedy the rituals consist of blood offerings, and the difference between the two is based on varying relations to the dead. While the incense offering is abstract because it considers the dead as faraway spirits, the blood offering of tragedy maintains the consciousness of the proximity of the dead underneath the ground: "The hero in honor of whom one sings is not far, but hears and enjoys the presentation that is accompanied by a sacrifice. The whole is not a concert, a musical presentation, but fearfully serious. It is not presented for the benefit of the listeners, but of a spirit inhabiting the grave" (B LXXVI).

The tragedy's religious component does not derive from its aesthetic effect on the spectators, but from its cult status as a sacrificial ritual honoring the spirits of the dead. Instead of considering how sacrifice determines the spectator's experience of the dead, Baeumler argues that the world of the dead creates the structure of the tragedy. The tragic effect does not derive from its aesthetic characteristics but from its evocation of the dead. "The horror that surrounds the tragic work of art is the horror of the grave. The stifled silence of the participants, that mixture of terror and mortification that, according to Aristotle, is transmitted to the spectator arises out of a respect for the dead" (B LXXVIII). This supernatural explanation of tragic effects, focusing on the horror of the grave, is inadequate to the extent that it presupposes the respect for the dead that it needs to explain. Rather than a given, such a respect must itself be a consequence of a sacrifice's structuring of the experience of death. Whereas Nietzsche develops this psychological explanation for the sacredness of ritual and myth (*BT* 108), Baeumler considers the dead as supernatural beings whose inherently sacred status grounds the sacrificial ritual. In Baeumler's understanding, the cult ritual has a supernatural meaning that precedes and defines the sacrifice's significance as an experience of horror.

Baeumler in the Nazi Period

Baeumler retains the metaphysical structure of his supernatural explanation of the sacred when he moves toward a natural scientific explanation after 1933. Rather than referring to the spirits of the dead, however, he attempts to explain intellectual and cultural phenomena through a recourse to the supposed objectivity of material reality understood in a natural scientific sense. In both the supernatural and the biological interpretations, ritual is an expression of basic character traits of a particular people. These traits depend neither on the experiences of individuals nor on the cultural traditions of a community. Rather they are based upon the material "objectivity" of sacrificial rituals that preexist any psychologically justifying or culturally specific experience. The priority of the "material" in the Bachofen introduction thus opens the way for an argument based on the fixed "character" of a people founded in blood and race.

In his May 10, 1933, inaugural address for his appointment as Professor of Philosophy and Political Pedagogy in Berlin immediately after Hitler's rise to power, Baeumler uses the opposition between symbol and word in order to exhort the students of the university to participate in the book burning that would occur immediately after his lecture. As in his argument in the Bachofen introduction, he prefers the symbol because of its nonaesthetic character as something that is prior to the "aesthetic" word. "Service to the word leads in the end to a soft and delicate, to an 'aesthetic' attitude and finally to a situation in which man loses a sense for that which has not yet taken form, that which has not yet been articulated, but which is perhaps capable of form, a situation in which he loses a sense for the primal, for the chaos that will give birth to a star" (*MW* 131–32). While the word is "aesthetic," the symbol for Baeumler is real. Because the symbol's reality is not a result of an aesthetic experience, it must define its "originality" in terms of a direct and immediate connection between the symbol and a people. While Baeumler criticizes the old word, he does not seek to encourage an aesthetic process whereby such old myths would be replaced with new ones. Rather, he claims that the symbol *is* this reality and that no effort must be made in order to adjust it to fit a contemporary context. "The symbol is silent, and comprehension is direct." The immediacy of the symbol makes it into a source of unity that is prior to the conflicts connected with the word. "*We are unified in the symbols—we are not yet unified in the word.* That which hinders us is not an evil will, but the *old word*, the word that is no longer commensurate with the contemporary symbols" (*MW* 132).

Baeumler's separation of symbol from word isolates the former from the constant transformation that is part of the latter. Because the unity of the symbol is prior to all social interaction, it can only be based on "material" characteristics such as a set of existing ritual practices or the biological determinants of blood and race. For Baeumler, the fixed materiality of blood lends it its objective, historical quality as a foundation for myth: "Every true myth is a myth of blood. Blood is the most final historical reality that we know."[37] This turn to blood and hence to race as the underlying mechanism of myth is a modernizing move that delegitimates myth even as it attempts to affirm its significance. The turn to blood as the creator of myth, though not made explicit in Baeumler's work until the Nazi period, was already developed as a possibility in the Bachofen introduction. This text insists on a cultic rather than a psychological or aesthetic reading of myth, and Baeumler must only make a slight adjustment in order to transform the cult of dead heroes into the myth of blood. Baeumler never develops a theory of the sacred in which it acquires its own independent source of legitimation. Rather, he separates myth from ritual in order to argue that sacrificial ritual provides a sacred foundation for myth. Baeumler's understanding of blood and race is consistent with his earlier separation of ritual from myth because both sacrificial ritual and blood are presented as outside foundations for myth that precede culture and tradition. This search for material foundations begins only when the aesthetic function of both myth and ritual is disregarded as a means of mediating subjective experience. But in repudiating the aesthetic character of myth, Baeumler in fact suppresses myth as a realm of experience in favor of what he sees as either the supernatural or the biological foundations of culture. These foundations can then be enforced as ideological imperatives from above without regard for individual freedom of expression because their validity precedes all forms of individual judgment that underlie aesthetic production and reception.

Because for Baeumler the meaning of the cult is both fixed and predefined through the symbol, yet undefined in terms of specific contents, he must ultimately return to the word in order to give it "form." Neither blood nor the symbol has any specific content, and neither can directly determine the structures that define a community. As a consequence, Baeumler does not insist on a return to the purity of symbols at the end of his inaugural address, but on the need for an "interpretation of symbols" (*MW* 138). Baeumler sees this analytical attitude as the necessary philosophical determination of the meaning of the mythic symbol.

Baeumler's insistence on the necessity of philosophical interpretation for symbols to unfold leads to a suppression of myth and tradition by a rationalizing authority. When philosophy is necessary for myth to develop, then mythic consciousness is no longer a process that develops in each individual member of the community and remains dependent upon a collective reception process. Instead, myth's meaning becomes something that is to be orchestrated by thinkers from above. As Baeumler points out, the task of interpreting and determining the symbol falls to a philosophical-political leader. According to Baeumler, philosophers "are actors, lonely and bold men, chosen by fate to replace the dying myth with a new worldview. The philosopher is the creator of the image of the world that takes the place of the popular, mythic one."[38] Because myth has no source of legitimacy on its own and the legitimacy of ritual is mute, the mythic community must give way to a philosophical leader, and myth must defer to philosophy. Instead of using myth as a basis for community life, Baeumler instrumentalizes the idea of myth for a rationalist philosophical and political project whose goal is the victory of the philosopher over popular myth. This subordination of myth is made possible by his denial of the aesthetic character of the sacred. The sacred becomes an inflexible and static constant rather than the locus of the constantly changing forces in human experience that Einstein envisions. As a consequence, Baeumler never considers myth an independent sphere of human creativity and a source of aesthetic (as opposed to philosophical) insight. Instead, he attempts to instrumentalize myth as a legitimator of political projects whose final justification is based on philosophical and rational arguments. Once these arguments have been established, their conclusions can be enforced with an absolute conviction about their legitimacy, which is not based on any kind of popular consent but purely in terms of "material" justifications such as biology, blood, or the power of the cultic ritual.

Baeumler suppresses the mythic in the Bachofen introduction by treating form as a philosophical means of domination rather than the result of an aesthetic mimesis of experience that would require freedom of expression. The formal element in tragedy is not aesthetic (i.e., it is not an immanent process within the tragedy), and it is not passive. Rather, form for Baeumler is something that captures the spiritual and contains it. "In the moment where the unspeakable, the mysterious, the other, the *spirit* begins to speak, the tragedy is born. The unpresentable becomes image, the formless attains form. In the tragedy the formative power of the Greeks proves itself upon the most extraordinary object. It is consequently the most profoundly *Greek* achievement of the Greek spirit" (B LXXXII). The characters of tragedy gain their power through the fact that they are the manifestations of dead spirits. The "unspeakable, the mysterious, the other, the spirit" is the raw material that is formed into the tragedy. The presentation of spirits of the dead as characters on the stage is for Baeumler the accomplishment of tragedy and the result of the forming power of a people. Form is for Baeumler a means of harnessing the unspeakable and the mysterious in order to link tragedy to ritual. But, as he notes, "the catharsis is not an aesthetic process" (B LXXXI). Instead of an aesthetic process presenting a mimesis of experience, form is for Baeumler a conceptual, philosophical harnessing of an original cultic material.

This triumph of "form" over "chaos" becomes the model for Baeumler's philosophy of history. The tragedy's transformation of ritual into concepts represents "the turning point of the ages" (B LXXXVII). The distinction between epic and tragic religion becomes a difference between a paternal myth and a maternal cult and between an occidental and an oriental mythology. Maternal-based religious forms come from the East and belong to a prehistoric period in human history. This early Asiatic period in human history is gradually overcome in Greece and then in Rome by paternal Western religions that create the rule of law and of the state. The fundamental shift is from a religious cult based on a formless material to a system based on conceptual forms and laws (B CCLXVIII). This opposition defines a world historical conflict for Baeumler in which the formless maternal force continually tries to rise up against the form-giving paternal force. The victory of form becomes a suppression of one people, defined as Asiatic, by another, defined as Western. "The period of time during which the tragedy originated presents many characteristics of an epoch that is sinking from the brilliant heights of an epic 'enlightenment' into the night of superstition. All the demons were unleashed by the outburst of the religion of Dionysus. . . . In this hour of need the Greek genius succeeded in achieving the tragedy, which spiritually protected the West from the powers of Asia in the same way that the victory over the Persians protected them militarily" (B LXXXV). By understanding form as that which orders chaos and a characteristic of particular peoples, Baeumler prepares the concepts with which Rosenberg justifies his condemnation of non-Aryan cultures. In referring to their lack of formative power, Rosenberg cites Baeumler's arguments in order to advance his theory about the Aryan world-historical task of giving form to other cultures.[39] Baeumler himself later uses this argumentation to argue that the Jewish people "should not be tolerated" because they lack such formative power.[40]

The centrality of form as a conceptual harnessing of a mythic material provides Baeumler with a justification for the rule of a philosophical leader. Because the meaning of the cult is on the one hand fixed and predefined through the physicality of sacrificial rituals (in the Bachofen introduction) or blood ties (in *Alfred Rosenberg und der Mythus des 20. Jahrhunderts*) and on the other hand undefined in terms of specific contents, Baeumler must ultimately return to the word in order to give it "form." Since he bases myth on a material unity of cult ritual or of blood, neither of which have any form that could determine the structures defining a community, the specific meaning of sacrificial ritual and blood must consequently remain undefined until the philosophical-political leader imposes this meaning.[41] Without any independent basis for legitimacy, the mythic community must give way to a philosophical leader, and myth must defer to philosophy. The victory of the philosopher-leader over the mythic-popular is for Baeumler the victory of form.

Although Manfred Frank argues that Baeumler's early work in the Bachofen introduction must be distinguished from the later, explicitly fascist work, this later work is in fact based on the same basic structure of thought as the earlier theories. The victory of form is not just a twentieth-century event, as Baeumler implies in the passage from *Studien* quoted above and written in 1930, but already occurs in the 1926 Bachofen introduction as art's triumph over ritual in Greek tragedy: "The phenomenon of the tragic does not only originate out of a climax in the belief in demons and in the consciousness of death, but also out of their supercession. The creation of the tragedy is the most important stage in the process of Hellenizing the Dionysian religion and thereby the decisive step for the Hellenic world in its relation to the cult of the chthonic powers" (B LXXXVI). In Baeumler's account, tragedy only participates in the "demonic" insofar as it subjugates it. By overcoming these "chthonic powers," tragedy clears away the mythic in order to inaugurate the rule of a paternal, Hellenic culture.

Baeumler's work was protofascist from the beginning, not because it sought a return of myth but because it insisted on myth's suppression as a foundation for social order. Baeumler maintains this perspective throughout his career, from the 1926 Bachofen introduction all the way through his 1943 defense of Rosenberg's *Myth of the Twentieth Century*. The delegitimation of myth arises from his attempt to establish a "material" basis rather than an aesthetic (and, in Kant's sense, disinterested) foundation for its functioning. In making a fundamental distinction between myth and ritual in which ritual is allegedly more material than myth and the materiality of rituals is taken to be the source of the power of myth, Baeumler assumes that he does not have to explain the sacredness of rituals. But because the rituals are understood as pure materiality and are consequently left without a voice, philosophy is necessary to harness the power of ritual, establishing a de facto suppression of both myth and ritual as sources of aesthetically based patterns for human behavior and cultural identity in which individual judgment is central. The ideas of myth and ritual become instead tools for the implementation of a philosophical-political project. The goal of Baeumler's theories is not to affirm the aesthetic truth of myth and ritual, but to replace the mythic and ritual structures governing social life with philosophical ones.[42]

This goal links the fascist understanding of ritual and myth to an enlightenment one. The goal of both perspectives is to delegitimate myth as an organizer of social life based in a disinterested aesthetic attitude to the world and to replace it with concepts imposed by a philosophical leader with an instrumentalist approach. The difference between liberal and fascist methods is still of course supremely important, but it remains a disagreement about means, the former depending on arguments and the latter depending on political repression to bring about the establishment of a philosophical approach. To the extent, though, that liberal methods protecting free expression also allow for the continuing elaboration and reception of aesthetic forms, they also continue to support and even depend upon the kind of mythic processes that they often explicitly condemn.

The centrality of Baeumler's perspective for the Nazis can be seen in the passages from Rosenberg's *Myth of the Twentieth Century* that quote Baeumler's Bachofen introduction in order to defend the Nordic character of Apollo, the god of light, against the degeneracy of a Dionysian mysticism.[43] Though couched in mythic terms, the point of this suppression of the Dionysian is to legitimate, not a mythic dimension, but its suppression at the hands of an Apollonian domination through the concept. Such Nazi condemnations of popular traditions make it impossible to simply pose a fascist myth against an enlightenment antimyth in order to condemn the former in favor of the latter. Rather, a contemporary evaluation of myth must recognize a popular sphere of aesthetic experience, outside of philosophy, which functions, for good or for ill, as the source of values and social structure.

When contrasted with Einstein's aesthetic understanding of myth as an independent sphere of human experience, Baeumler's theory of myth turns out to be an antimythic affirmation of the authority of philosophy. But Baeumler does not merely turn away from myth in order to affirm the primacy of philosophy. Rather, philosophy must colonize the sphere of experience previously occupied by myth. The philosopher's view of the world must "take the place of the popular, mythic one."[44] This replacement is the basis of Nazi cultural politics, for it allows the Nazis to speak the language of myth while at the same time delegitimating active mythic traditions. Rather than ceding power to a popular dimension, the Nazis colonize this space with a conceptual and instrumental construction of values.

Once we understand the antimythic basis of Baeumler's theories, it becomes clear that his project accords surprisingly well with Bloch's attempt to functionalize myth for a left-wing political project. The main differences lie in the political tendency to which myth is to be subordinated and the use of repressive or benign means to bring about the elimination of mythic forms. In Bloch's analysis, myth consists of all aspects of a culture, such as tradition and ritual, which are somehow obsolete or out of place in the present. They are only significant insofar as their noncontemporaneity threatens the unity of a modern system, "the capitalist Now," and their ideal function is to aid in bringing about their own dissolution into a future built upon contemporaneity.[45] His theory seeks neither to suppress nor to completely unleash myth, but to allow these remnants of the past a controlled existence until they dissolve of their own accord into the future. Bloch does not advocate a return to myth but seeks to "release" it from fascist control in order that it might be subordinated to an emancipatory, that is, Marxist, goal.[46]

In spite of the fact that he has a historical rather than a biological understanding of the source of mythic experience, the structure of Bloch's argument is very similar to Baeumler's. Bloch discerns the objectivity of myth in its contradiction to a capitalist present and is only interested in how the power of such noncontemporaneity might be wrested away from support for fascism and sublated into a utopian Marxist future.[47] Baeumler meanwhile sees myth's objectivity in the silent symbol that always requires the intervention of the philosopher-politician to provide a meaningful interpretation of its significance. Neither Bloch nor Baeumler attributes to the popular dimension any legitimacy. Rather, they both attempt to mobilize the forces they see active in this dimension for political goals that are determined outside of it by a central authority.

While myth and ritual are only temporary historical contradictions for Bloch and popular symbols soon to be superseded by philosophical-political interpretations for Baeumler, Einstein treats them as part of a realm of human experience that is constantly relevant and continually changing. Einstein attempts to discern how myth might be valuable in its own right as a site of irrepressible psychic processes. This means that Einstein, in contrast to Bloch, detaches myth from a particular position in a universal history of mankind. But it is also true that Einstein does not locate myth in an inaccessible "foundation" of human existence, as Baeumler does, but investigates myth as part of those processes that evolve within a popular and aesthetic dimension of culture. In contrast to both Bloch and Baeumler, Einstein claims that myth presents an irreducible dimension of experience that, when left to unfold without philosophical or political intervention, can develop according to an independent aesthetic dynamic based in individual judgments.

Manfred Frank's New Mythology

Manfred Frank has pursued a project similar to Einstein's in his attempt to develop the idea of a new mythology. Extending Habermas's suggestion for how a mythic art might be rehabilitated as part of an architectonics, "which, as once with Schelling, should anchor the unity of theoretical and practical reason in the faculty of judgment,"[48] Frank describes how mythic art in the modern world, instead of competing with reason as a mediator of truth, might support reason by anchoring its legitimacy within aesthetic judgment. In describing the details of such a recovery of mythic art in his *Lectures on the New Mythology* (*Vorlesungen über die Neue Mythologie*), he also explicitly returns to Schelling's project of creating a new mythology based on art and linked to reason.

In contrast to Einstein, however, who champions myth and the sacred as a separate realm from reason, Frank seeks to "tame" myth and subordinate it to a rationalist project, thereby taking advantage of art's and myth's intimate connections to experience in order to legitimate the rule of communicative rationality. Frank never considers myth to be an independent sphere of human creativity and insight that could provide the basis for social structure. Instead, his conception of a new mythology pursues the same essential goals and uses the same fundamental arguments as those developed by Baeumler. Like Baeumler, Frank's main interest is not in the sacred but in legitimizing the rule of reason. He seeks to salvage "the universalist and late-enlightenment idea of a socialization that is 'mythically' legitimized by reason" from the turn to "particularism, nationalism, and anti-enlightenment" (*GE* 9). Though the two obviously differ—Baeumler uses myth to justify a society ruled by a philosopher-leader and based on racial segregation and Frank turns to myth in order to legitimate a society ruled by communicative interaction—they both ignore the possibility that myth might be the source of an aesthetic truth that is distinct from philosophical truth. As a consequence, philosophical concepts are the final authority and the only source of truth in both of their models for society. Myth and ritual are instrumentalized as legitimators of political projects whose final justification is based on rational arguments which are detached from the sphere of everyday experience.

Frank bases his theory of myth on Baeumler's distinction between myth and cult (*GE* 35–36), in which cult ritual functions as the moving force behind the myth. Because he recognizes that he shares this reading of myth and cult with Baeumler, Frank seeks to dilute the fascist legacy by constructing a linear history of this idea from the romantics through Bachofen to Nietzsche and then into modernism. On this point, Frank disagrees with Baeumler by arguing that Nietzsche took his idea of myth from Bachofen, Creuzer, and Schelling.

Baeumler himself recognizes the difference between his own interpretation of myth and Nietzsche's, and he ridicules Nietzsche's reading because of its aesthetic emphasis (B CCXLIX). Although he rejects it, Baeumler accurately describes Nietzsche's theory of myth as one in which the myth's symbolic character derives from its exemplary status, its ability to accurately relate by analogy to the experiences of the people to which it speaks. Consequently, the religious power of the myth derives from an aesthetic efficacy that is defined both in terms of inner form and reception. Through this aesthetic process, the symbolic meaning of the myth develops as a function of contemporary subjective experience.

As opposed to Nietzsche, who understands myth as a form of aesthetic experience, Baeumler considers art to be merely play and illusion. For him, the cult ritual is the basis of the significance and seriousness of myth. In defending the permanence and original meaning of the ritual against the ephemeral and changing character of the metaphor, Baeumler implicitly denies that aesthetic processes can have a defining impact on human experience. He consequently must criticize Nietzsche's aesthetic reading of the myth for isolating myth in an aesthetic realm where myth would no longer have any impact on life.

Whereas Baeumler recognizes Nietzsche's break with the romantic distinction between myth and cult, Frank skips over this part of Baeumler's argument in order to equate this distinction with Nietzsche's opposition of Apollo and Dionysus (*GE* 36–37), thereby placing his own work into a lineage beginning with Creuzer and running through Bachofen, Nietzsche, and Baeumler (*GE* 37). But by interpreting Apollo as myth and Dionysus as cult, Frank not only develops a false genealogy, he also obscures the crucial distinction that Nietzsche attempts to make between Apollonian art as illusion and Dionysian art as metaphysical expression.

Nietzsche emphasizes the aesthetic character of the Dionysian, arguing that there are two types of art—Dionysian, which mediates a metaphysical reality, and Apollonian, which is mere semblance. The Dionysian is not substance, but art as inner form and parable, while the Apollonian is art as representation and appearance (*BT* 19–20, 30–31). This opposition, which Adorno would later describe as one between semblance (*Schein*) and expression (*Ausdruck*) (*AT* 110–12), allows Nietzsche to develop an aesthetic theory of the sacred that still maintains a distinction between art that is sacred and thus an expression of reality (Dionysian) and art that is mere appearance and thus separate from reality (Apollonian). By distinguishing the two, Nietzsche can interpret myth and the sacred as part of a Dionysian aesthetic rather than an Apollonian one.

Ignoring the aesthetic reading of the Dionysian that Nietzsche offers, Frank claims that Nietzsche reads the Dionysian as a fundamental substance: "The drama is a mixed form consisting of magic-participative (or cultic) and narrative-mythic (Nietzsche says: epic) characteristics. In the tragedy the substantial character of the old cults breaks through the cover of the mythic distancing" (*GE* 51). Frank identifies the Dionysian with cult ritual and thus with the real while the Apollonian is tied to myth and representation. He thereby reduces all art to an Apollonian representational structure and denies the existence of the Dionysian, mimetic art that Nietzsche sets up as an alternative to reason for organizing social life. Though he suggests that he is following Nietzsche's interpretation, Frank actually recapitulates Baeumler's by equating cult with substantiality and opposing it to the distancing of myth.

Instead of locating the fascist element of Baeumler's theory of myth in the differentiation between myth and cult ritual, Frank accepts the validity of this distinction and attempts to separate Baeumler's earlier work on myth from the later fascist writings. Frank's critique of Baeumler's work limits itself to a criticism of Baeumler's relation of ritual to the "nonsacred" referent of blood. Here, Frank distinguishes between a blood religion, which is grounded in earthly concepts, and a "new religion," which would base itself upon the authority of a metaphysical world. According to Frank, it is only the latter that could provide a proper legitimation for a society, while the former can only be fascist. "The blood religion differentiates itself on one decisive point from every 'new religion' that we have come to know by this name: it does not have its source in the supernatural world but in nature itself. It is not a divine power that is mythologized, but the biological fiction of race and its accompanying 'racial soul' " (*GE* 130). Because Frank pursues the same project as Baeumler of searching for the "source" of the sacred, he bases his critique of Baeumler on the use of a natural rather than a supernatural source. Yet, this distinction is a relatively insignificant one; appeals both to race and to divinity can serve to legitimate a totalitarian system. The crucial move is the separation of myth from its legitimation in ritual.

Even though Frank condemns the fascist notion of a community of blood for placing values in biology (*GE* 129), he does not dispute the project of discovering such a nonaesthetic basis for myth. Like Baeumler, Frank subordinates the "merely" symbolic character of the myth to the more tangibly "real" character of the rite that participates directly in the sacred: "To narrate means: to incorporate into a symbolic order. The symbol is however only a representative of the thing, not the thing itself. By contrast the rite—for example omophagy (the consumption of a god manifested in wild animals or of the savior in the communion of the last supper)—allows the direct participation in the sacred, which one makes a part of oneself. It is a sacrament (as is the case for us with the rite of communion)" (*GE* 17–18). In distinguishing between mythic symbol and sacred rite, Frank, like Baeumler, denies that the aesthetic dimension in myth would be able to reenact human experience objectively. The myth can never itself be sacred because Frank defines the sacred as a material act rather than an aesthetic experience. Accordingly, Frank also discounts the aesthetic dimension of experience embedded in the sacrificial ritual in order to concentrate on the material practice as a "direct participation in the sacred" and thus as self-justifying. At this point, Frank's argumentation is virtually identical in structure with Baeumler's proposition that blood and race are the direct material manifestations of the sacred. In both cases, material reality is the final self-justifying reality from which all other values derive. Because they have discounted the aesthetic dimension in the construction of the sacred, they are both left with an opposition between a mute material reality, which is deemed sacred, and philosophical discourse, through which this reality gains concrete significance.

In this schema myth functions as an instrument of reason by giving voice to and justifying an otherwise mute material reality embedded in ritual. The propagandistic function of myth for Frank becomes evident in his example of how myth in ancient Greece functioned to justify Bacchic rites, in which women raced through the snow-covered mountains tearing apart animals and eating them raw: "This wild cult is justified by an accompanying narrative, that is, the myth that reports that the frenzied women are called by their god, whom they call Dionysus, in order to serve as midwives for his rebirth, which takes place every spring in the mountain peaks. The custom is consequently justified by the narratively constructed reference to something sacred, and the function of myth consists in nothing else but the carrying out of this justification" (*GE* 17). According to Frank a set of practices already exists and is primary. But the sacredness of the ritual must be communicated to the participants by means of an accompanying story. This myth exists only as a rationalization that is constructed to explain why it is that such a ritual would take place. Frank never explains what would cause these women to believe the myth and accept the sacred character of the rites. He suggests that the mere mention of a god will guarantee that the god will be considered divine and the rite will be justified as proper. Although Frank does not in the end evoke myth in order to justify the rule of a philosopher-leader but to justify a political system based on "universal norm-constructing communication" (*GE* 127), his use of myth as a legitimator of an existing practice is no less instrumental than Baeumler's. In both cases, any existing practice can be justified through myth because myth does not have any separate mechanism to guarantee its legitimacy. The arbitrariness of the designation of the sacred matches the arbitrariness hidden in Baeumler's fascist relation of myth to blood. Because blood does not speak, a leader is required who will arbitrarily determine the meaning of blood. For Frank, the experience of the sacred is based on the designation of something as sacred. Consequently, the sacred, since it is created through an arbitrary decision, only exists as a propagandistic legitimator. Frank does not allow for any independent process going on in the minds of the celebrants of a ritual or the receivers of a myth that would enable participants to pass judgment on either notion.

Because Frank senses the dangers of myth as he has constructed it, he rejects traditional myth in order to pursue a "new mythology" that he is at pains to distinguish from Baeumler's version of new myths. Yet, Frank's vision of myth still retains the same function as Baeumler's. As Frank expresses it, the new mythology serves "to save a legitimation-function for political rule prior to the belief in values."[49] Like Baeumler, Frank assumes that traditional religion and myth are no longer valid and that a new mythology is needed that would legitimate a particular political system in a "postreligious era" (*KG* 168). The primary difference lies in the character of the system for which the new myth is to be instrumentalized. As opposed to the establishment of racist policies, Frank seeks to use myth in order to legitimate communicative consensus-making in which Habermasian discursive interaction is the creator of norms and values (*KG* 165). Myth's role is simply to provide a sacred legitimation for such discourse. The primary difference between the traditional myth and the new myth is that, while the old mythology is a "naturally occurring product of history" (*KG* 185), the new mythology is an instrument "in the service of ideas" (*KG* 183). By trading in the former for the latter, Frank delegitimizes myth as the aesthetic mediator of human experience and a possible source of "naturally occurring" community structures and replaces it with myth as an ideological instrument for supporting the construction of discursive truth within expert cultures. His "new mythology" is a mythology of reason, "because the content of a fable referring to the sacred cannot establish the harmony of members of a society; rather the maintenance of the compact is based on the pure form of nonviolent intersubjectivity and communication" (*KG* 169). Reason can take the place of religion in Frank's conception because he does not consider the possibility that myth might be the mediator of a certain type of aesthetic truth that, unlike discursive reason, is intimately linked to experience.

The resulting relative insignificance of myth in his new mythology is most evident in Frank's examples of how modern art functions as its basis.

Though he attempts to develop his own aesthetic understanding of myth, his explanation for the aesthetic structure of myth does not connect myth with experience but alienates one from the other. He constructs mythic art along the lines of what Nietzsche calls an Apollonian aesthetics of semblance. In his reading of Rainer Maria Rilke's *Sonnets to Orpheus,* Frank refers to the relation between art and the experiences of suffering, love, and death, but he does so in such a way as to separate these experiences from everyday life. As a result, when Frank writes that "poetry itself and as such becomes the new mythology" (*GE* 206), this unity of art and myth does not expand the significance of myth as a source of aesthetic truth, but encloses and isolates myth within the confines of a work of art regarded as semblance rather than expression.

In his discussion of Rilke's first "Sonnet to Orpheus" as the model for the new mythology, he refers to the distinction between myth and ritual in order to justify the "purity" and thus the isolation of Rilke's "sacred speaking": "Now: a poem that—like Orpheus's song—constructs its temple in our ear—note well: that is its house of god, a space designated for worship!—such a poem has a similarity with cultic speech and is in this exact sense: symbolic: belonging to that *of* which it speaks. In other words (for its object is something that has, from out of the past into the timeless present of the myth, ascended beyond ['Oh pure ascension!'])—this speech is 'pure' or 'sacred speaking'" (*GE* 185). The aesthetic word in Rilke's poem can only become sacred to the extent that it is "pure" and only speaks about itself as being sacred. Art's position as a new mythology is one that is directed at itself and the idea of the sacred and consequently opposed to the world of experience.

The new mythology is to be differentiated from a traditional religious mythology based on this alienation from the world, and it turns out to be a version of Adorno's idea of the hermetic character of art in modern capitalist society.

> Here the movement into the unseen that the work of art describes is seen as an extension and surpassing of the movement that drives social reality itself into the unseen. With the difference that while social reality's sacred disappears away into a u-topos, a non-place, art can preserve the sacred in a utopia. Its unseen is not, like that of the capitalist-technological world, the negation of the concrete-sensual world, but rather the saving of this world destroyed by progress in the heart's inner space of the poem: in the poem as the sanctuary and asylum of mythical desires in a technical age. (*GE* 211)

Although Frank's vision of art as a place of asylum for mythic desires seems at first to be based on Adorno's notion of artworks as "plenipotentiaries of things that are no longer distorted by exchange, profit, and the false needs of a degraded humanity" (*AT* 227) there is a very important difference. Adorno sees works of art as plenipotentiaries for things in their nonidentical, nonreified state. As such, the artwork yearns for its own dissolution into a world where all things already exist in such a preconceptual state: "Through their difference from a bewitched reality, they embody negatively a position in which what is would find its rightful place, its own" (*AT* 227). Art does not present an alternative to reality so much as a vision of what reality is in its essence, before the intervention of the philosophical concept. By contrast, Frank's notion of art establishes a division between a technical reality where sensual experience has no place and an aesthetic reality that preserves mythic desires in an isolated "sanctuary." Unable to conceive of the sacred as a junction of aesthetic and social experience, he confines it to an Apollonian world of art understood as semblance. Whereas works of art for Adorno struggle to overcome their own autonomy and, with it, a social division of intellectual labor from sensual experience, for Frank their autonomy is essential for preserving the stability of this division.

Myth for Frank becomes an ideological weapon whose significance lies less in its cognitive value as a mediator of experience than in its instrumental value for defending philosophical truth. This instrumental use of myth is evident not only in Baeumler's attempt to defend ritual as a fundamental order, but also in Frank's attempt to use myth as a legitimator of communicative reason. For both, the true issue—race in the case of Baeumler and communicative reason in the case of Frank—has been predetermined. The assumed inability of myth to do anything but legitimate a set of practices that are understood as simply given denies myth its critical potential for altering practices and its legitimating potential for integrating human experience with social practice. These tasks are left to discursive rationality, which Frank, following Habermas, recognizes as separate from the sphere of everyday experience. Whereas myth would merge the creation and transmission of values with sensual experience, Frank maintains a strict division between the professional philosophers of truth and the rest of society, using myth merely to legitimate this split.

Frank consequently does not take myth seriously enough. By reducing myth to a legitimator of previously existing structures, he establishes these structures, whether a religious rite or a communicative practice, as stable and unchanging. But in assuming that religious rites have been superseded by rational communication and that this development is a foregone conclusion, only to be legitimated by myth, Frank has oversimplified his outlook on the modern world. By contrast, an attempt to grasp both the continuing importance of religious experience (whether in institutionalized religions or in new forms such as nationalism) and its unpredictable development will understand myth and ritual as both of the same order, participants in the same aesthetic process of reception and transformation based on the judgments of the audience.

Theories of myth that do not recognize its aesthetic character inevitably turn toward rationalist replacements for myth. This antagonism toward mythic processes is common to both fascist and liberal theories of myth. Such theories set the material or metaphysical reality of ritual against the ephemerality of art and presume a rigidity of the ritual that is then used either to justify a certain set of prejudices, using as grounds the constancy of the cultic ritual, or to try to eliminate modern forms of ritual. An opposition to the Nazi approach to myth therefore cannot consist of a rejection of myth but must begin with a renewed understanding of the aesthetic character of both ritual and myth. Such an understanding can lead, first, to insights into the reasons why sacrifice continues to persist as a crucial structure in the modern world and, second, to a set of conceptual tools for tracking the ways in which sacrifice develops to either enforce or overturn certain modes of thinking and interacting. If myth and sacrifice are not simply remnants of a barbarian past but essential components of human experience, then the next step must be to investigate the mechanisms that underlie their proliferation as well as the forces that constrain their development.

CHAPTER THREE

Theories of Sacrifice in the Modern World
Georges Bataille, René Girard, and Walter Burkert

The opening two chapters seek to demonstrate that sacrifice can be analyzed as part of an aesthetic process that defines the human relationship to nature. Adorno provides a strong argument for the validity of an aesthetic truth that might be opposed to a philosophical truth in providing insight about the world. Yet, because Adorno's vision of aesthetic truth creates a mimesis of history rather than a mimesis of nature that would accept the inevitability of violence, his aesthetics do not take account of the centrality of sacrifice for human culture. At the same time, this refusal to take violence as constitutive for culture also leads Adorno to the positing of a universal subject whose structure is deemed identical for all cultures, resulting in a Eurocentric vision of culture. The analysis of Adorno's aesthetic theory confirms his insight that aesthetic truth is possible as a kind of disinterested judgment about the world and that this aesthetic truth consists primarily of the mimesis of nature. As opposed to Adorno, however, chapter 1 argues, first, that the mimesis of nature is an experience of the particular way in which violence relates to human endeavor and so includes myth and ritual as well as works of art, and, second, that the mimesis of nature will necessarily contain a structure of sacrifice. Finally, this structure of sacrifice lies at the core of every culture where it determines that culture's particular structure of subjectivity by laying out the limits against which subjectivity is established.

Chapter 2 demonstrates that this acceptance of myth and sacrifice as aesthetic structures for determining subjectivity in a culture is to be differentiated from the use of myth and sacrifice as ideologies for justifying the use of violence. The acceptance of violence as an unavoidable limit of human endeavor does not need to translate into a supernatural or biological explanation of culture. On the contrary, such explanations undermine the aesthetic functioning of myth and sacrifice as cultural constructs that define social processes as being based on an aesthetic judgment about the relation between culture and nature. The substitution of supernatural or biological explanations eventually leads to philosophical determinations that are based on the ideological defense of particular interests.

By contrast, an aesthetic approach sees the proliferation of myths and rituals as part of a reception process within which the aesthetic truth of these structures can be confirmed by the everyday experience of individuals in the collective that is established on the basis of these structures. If myth and ritual are primarily aesthetic events and gain their legitimacy not from a supernatural or biological underpinning but from a collective reception that selectively chooses which myths and rituals to continue, then the significance of sacrifice would not lie in its materialist quality as naked violence, but in its symbolic structuring of the human relationship to violence. Together, the discussions of Adorno and Baeumler on myth and art provide an understanding of the possibilities and pitfalls in approaching sacrifice as an enduring category in modern society.

This chapter considers the idea that the aesthetic understanding of sacrifice is based on a malleability of the structure of the subject, in which a particular structure of sacrifice will imply a specific structure of subjectivity. A particular structure of sacrifice would not only be essential for the formation of a subject but would also be the basis of the particularity of a culture's identity. If the constitution of the subject through sacrifice is a generalized cultural process that adapts a culture to its situation, then this process can only successfully take place as an aesthetic mimesis of nature in which the sacrifice mediates to the subject the specific pattern of constraints within which a subject in that culture operates. Subject formation, mimesis of nature, and the establishment of a cultural identity all come together in the act of sacrifice, and the investigation of a specific economy of sacrifice will define the particularity of a culture and the impact of culture on subjectivity. This vision of sacrifice as an aesthetic process that carries out both a mimesis of nature and a determination of subjectivity places sacrifice at the center of a culture's attempt to define and maintain its own separate identity.

In making this argument, this chapter will counter objections to an aesthetic notion of sacrifice that are raised by alternative theories of sacrifice. These theories must assume a particular viewpoint on the source of violence in order to understand the structure of sacrifice, and the question of the source of violence may be used here as a way to initially categorize these different theories. In the first place, liberalism and socialism have sought since the eighteenth century to take advantage of rationalized social structures and human technology's mastery over nature to inaugurate a new period of freedom from violence in human affairs, and the development of Marxist theory by Georg Lukàcs, Walter Benjamin, Theodor Adorno, and Max Horkheimer was built upon the premise that sacrifice could be eliminated from human society. The violent upheavals of twentieth-century European culture might be interpreted as the culmination and final collapse of the idea that humankind can overcome sacrifice as a basic model for organizing social relations. Nevertheless, a progressive approach that assumes that violence is something that can be eliminated with the advance of civilization continues to shape current understandings in which sacrifice remains a sign of barbarism.

But in theories that accept the alternative premise that sacrifice and violence might be unavoidable in human society, there arises the question of the basic causes and functions of sacrifice in the ancient and in the modern world. Such questions have been taken up by writers such as Sigmund Freud, Georges Bataille, René Girard, and Walter Burkert, whose readings of society tend to emphasize continuities between past epochs and the modern world and who see violence as a perennial phenomenon rather than something that might be banned through human progress. While Marxists overestimate the possibilities for overcoming violence in the modern world, less optimistic thinkers can be divided into two groups depending on their view of the role of violence in the shaping of human culture.

Sigmund Freud describes these two possible alternatives in the two stages of his thinking on sacrifice. In *Totem and Taboo* (1913) Freud sees the origin of violence in nature, but rather than interpreting scientific progress as a way to move beyond sacrifice, he insists on the continuing power of nature to thwart human endeavor. Sacrifice then becomes a way of acknowledging this power and adjusting human actions according to a principle of renunciation. This approach underlies Carl Einstein's approach to sacrifice as an integration of necessity into culture and also provides a framework for Walter Burkert's investigation of ancient Greek sacrifice. However, Freud revises his theory after *Beyond the Pleasure Principle* (1920) to include a death drive that accompanies and in some cases replaces the reality principle as the source of violence in society. Thus, in *Civilization and Its Discontents* (1930) Freud pursues an even more pessimistic line of thought in which violence in society results from a death drive and an accompanying instinct for aggression that cannot be appeased and will only increase in intensity with the advance of civilization and its techniques for suppressing individual desires. This second approach paved the way for later theories, such as those by Georges Bataille and René Girard, which portray sacrifice as an expression of an unavoidable destructive force that underlies human life. But because this second perspective regards violence as an active force rather than a function of limitations on human endeavor, it sees the violence of sacrifice as a real violence rather than as part of an aesthetic reception. As a consequence, Bataille's and Girard's theories do not consider sacrifice to be a constitutive process. Instead, it is for them an outward manifestation of an underlying structure of violence that they see as repeating itself across all the various examples of sacrifice in different cultures. This reduction of sacrifice to a single structure of violence leads to difficulties in their ability to account for the variety of forms of sacrifice. The first approach, initially suggested by Carl Einstein and developed by Burkert, by contrast, provides a more effective tool for analyzing different examples of sacrifice because it considers sacrifice as both a recurring aesthetic structure in human culture and a phenomenon that is not unified but variable, demonstrating a particular structure in each of its different manifestations.

Georges Bataille on Sacrifice and Sovereignty

Bataille and Einstein worked together in Paris in the 1930s on the journal *Documents,* and their collaboration becomes apparent in their mutual interest in issues of myth and sacrifice. Yet, their theories took different directions. As we have seen, Einstein pursued an aesthetic understanding of myth that recalls the Kantian reading of the sublime by treating violence as the result of natural limits on human endeavor and sacrifice as an aesthetically based means of organizing the human relation to these limits. Bataille's theories are very different in that they use a "hydraulic" notion in which excess energy builds up in order to create violence, and sacrifice for him is an expression of this more general descent into unintelligible destruction and chaos. Central to this approach is his metaphysics of violence, in which sacrifice functions as part of what he calls a general economy of biological life, which includes human economy understood in the normal sense but then exceeds it by including a consideration of a level of life forces underlying human activity. From this general perspective human activity is a subcategory of a biological dynamic that is subject to rules of energy capture and release—"the play of *living material in general,* involved in the movement of light of which it is the result."[1] Within this play of living material, living things capture energy from the sun and use this energy to maintain themselves and to grow. Space is the basic limit of this capturing of energy (*AS1* 29). As a result, once biological matter expands to fill the space available, there is a buildup of an excess. At this point, nature has to come up with new ways to integrate this energy into biological substance or this energy has to be released. This release happens, for instance, when we reproduce and die (*AS1* 33–35). Bataille contends that this energy release, rather than any kind of accumulation, is the basic problem of biological and human existence.

Because Bataille begins with his vision of the way life energy underlies all human activity, his notion of sacrifice already presupposes a real-world vision of the metaphysical reality behind the world of appearances. Sacrifice is not a form of aesthetic insight, nor is it a means of shaping the human relation to the outside world. Instead, sacrifice is a manifestation of the inevitable violent intrusion of the general flow of life energy into the world of human utility. Bataille contends that sacrifice is simply an example of a way in which excess energy is released. Because nothing ever truly escapes the flux of life but in fact always belongs to it, the human reification of the world into things can only be temporary and will only last as long as it is in consonance with the deeper processes of energy buildup and release. In this sense, human activity does not really change this underlying flux but can only follow the deeper movement. At some point this deeper movement will always demand a release of energy.

Bataille uses the notion of excess rather than scarcity in order to understand forms of violence and sacrifice ranging from Aztec rituals to the Marshall Plan. Nature, as well as human society (understood here as subject to the same biological forces), always has the problem of finding a way to create death and destruction in order to release excess energy. So, for example, herbivores developed as a way of destroying plant matter, and carnivores developed as a way of destroying excess herbivores. Humans developed as both the best accumulators of energy and the best releasers of energy through the destruction of excess. Human societies produce so much material both in terms of human population and in terms of products that pressures build up to eventually destroy the excess. He refers to the world wars of the twentieth century as huge conflagrations that arose in order to destroy the excess built up over the nineteenth century (*AS1* 24–25). The release can be catastrophic, as in war, or it can be more agreeable to human ends. The key problem of human society for Bataille is to develop ways of destroying excess that do not result in unnecessary suffering. So rather than conducting wars in order to destroy people and goods, he suggests rituals that abolish the excess. These rituals include human and animal sacrifice, which destroy human and animal biological material directly, potlatch, in which gifts are given without recompense and are thus lost to future ends, the modern consumer society, in which excess is spent through luxurious living, or the American Marshall

Plan, in which goods are given without recompense. In this conception, consumerism becomes a virtue to the extent that goods and services are consumed rather than preserved for the future. For without this type of consumption, the excess human material would end up being destroyed through other more violent means such as war, starvation, or genocide. Bataille makes this argument because he considers the destruction of goods and services in consumerism and the death of humans in war to be equivalent processes from the point of view of a general economy of living matter. Only the human perspective creates a preference for consumerism over war (*AS1* 33–40). He also sees different forms of sacrifice in human society as different answers to the problem of how to destroy excess. For example, he writes about Aztec human sacrificial rites as ways of destroying excess production and energy (*AS1* 45–49).

Although human activity is on the one hand part of the biological life process in which solar energy is transformed into living matter, which is eventually destroyed in a release of that energy, Bataille recognizes that human activity must also be distinguished from the purely biological life process to the extent that humans make use of life energy for human goals. The key question then is whether human activity can be considered something that exceeds and alters this life activity in an essential way or whether human activity is in fact just an expression of biological life activity and has no independent existence of its own. Bataille contends that human activity can only experience a temporary congruence of human goals with life forces; these forces will follow their own development in spite of human wishes (*AS1* 20–21). Even though humans might pursue their own goals, these aspirations will always be subject to a more basic underlying life movement that is indifferent to human goals and will inevitably lead to a release of energy, which from the human point of view means death and destruction. While the human perspective sees such releases of energy as catastrophic, these life processes are simply part of the normal ebb and flow of energy and biological matter—two aspects of the same solar energy.

In addition to being simply a raw manifestation of this violent flux that exists beyond human ends, sacrifice is also a method by which individuals can affirm their own participation in this greater life flow. In this sense sacrifice is an embracing of the truth of this biological destruction. This human experience of the release of energy is determined by the character of human activity. For rather than being, like animals, an undifferentiated part of the biological world around them, humans live in a world of things that are subject to human utility and as such are for a certain time taken out of the flux of biological energy and subjected to human ends. This fundamental characteristic of human life creates both the human object world and the symbolic order within which humans conceive the world. But this domination of human utility is for Bataille a sign of degradation. "The first labor established the world of *things,* to which the profane world of the Ancients generally corresponds. Once the world of things is posited, man himself became one of the things of this world, at least for the time in which he labored. It is this degradation that man has always tried to escape. In his strange myths, in his cruel rites, man is *in search of a lost intimacy* from the first" (*AS1* 57). The integration of nature into a system of human purposes is degrading because human ends are for Bataille only a system of utility rather than a place of metaphysical values.

In sacrificing something, a sacrificer emancipates the object from the enslavement to utility that Bataille sees as the fundamental characteristic of human life. Sacrifice provides humans with an experience of the flux of the life world that is normally closed to them because of their embeddedness in a subject/object world based on human utility. In order to escape their subjugation to utility and reification, an object must be taken out of the network of human ends. This is best done by destroying it. "Sacrifice restores to the sacred world that which servile use has degraded, rendered profane" (*AS1* 55). The key is not the destruction or the killing itself but the removal of the object from a subjugation to human utility. The human or animal that is killed in a ritual sacrifice is emancipated from human ends in order to return to the freedom of an ever-changing flux beyond all goals.

In the case of a sacrifice in which the sacrificer is separate from that which is sacrificed, the sacrificed object is set "free" of utility, but not in the sovereign manner of the one who affirms the sacrifice. The sacrificer, as the one who carries out the sacrifice, is the one who is actively negating utility and affirming the underlying flux of the world. But the sacrificer participates in the "freedom" of the sacrificed object only to the extent that its sacrifice substitutes for her or his own death as something that would be a totally sovereign emancipation from human utility. Sacrifice that is not self-sacrifice is therefore always a substitution for the ultimate nonchalance in the face of death. Because sacrificial rituals inevitably carry out this substitution, they are always an impure form of this return to the flux of life. "This was a sacrifice of substitution. A softening of the ritual had occurred, shifting onto others the internal violence that is the moral principle of consumption" (*AS1* 55). The substitution always implies that something is held back, that there is a remnant of human concerns that is excluded from the general indifference to destruction that would be the consequence of a true release from utility and reification.

The pure form of sacrifice for Bataille is a form of self-sacrifice that he designates "sovereignty." This type of pure sacrifice occurs, for instance, when the king is sacrificed and thereby becomes the true sovereign, that is, a subject who rejects in the sacrifice the importance of death. "What the sovereign takes seriously is not the death of the *individual*, it is *others*: to the fact of surviving personally he prefers the prestige that will no longer add to his stature if he dies, and will continue to count only so long as others count."[2] The sovereign prefers prestige to life, Bataille here borrowing from Hegel the idea that self-consciousness "exists only in being acknowledged."[3] In this way, the sovereign places her- or himself above utility by rejecting death as something that has any hold over her or him. "The sovereign world is the world in which the limit of death is done away with. Death is present in it, its presence defines that world of violence, but while death is present it is always there only to be negated, never for anything but that. The sovereign is he who *is*, as if death were not."[4] Bataille takes Hegel's dialectic of lordship and bondage and foregrounds the staking of one's life as the moment in which it is "proved that for self-consciousness, its essential being is not [just] being, not the immediate form in which it appears, not its submergence in the expanse of life, but rather that there is nothing present in it which could not be regarded as a vanishing moment, that it is only pure *being-for-self*" (*PS* 114). In focusing on this moment of self-sufficiency of the subject as the one who defines sacrifice, Bataille commits himself both to an idea of freedom organized around the sovereignty of the subject and to sacrifice as a struggle between opposing subjects to demonstrate this freedom.

This understanding of sacrifice is similar to Kant's notion of the sublime to the extent that both Bataille (following Hegel) and Kant focus on the staking of one's life as the crucial moment that on the one hand recognizes the overwhelming violence of nature and on the other hand negates this violence by demonstrating a sovereign attitude toward it. The difference, however, lies in the fact that both Hegel and Bataille insist on the necessity of experiencing actual violence as opposed to an aesthetic presentation. For Kant, the overcoming of violence occurs only as an aesthetic experience in which the subject is not in actual fear and is thus able to make a disinterested judgment about both the character of the violence that threatens the subject and the ideal to which the subject appeals as that which transcends the materiality being sacrificed. For Hegel and Bataille, the encounter is a truly fearful one in which the subject engages in a "life-and-death struggle" with another subject (*PS* 114).

The actuality of fear and violence is necessary for both Hegel and Bataille because they see self-consciousness itself as the only ideal that is ultimately to be affirmed. While Kant sees sacrifice as always structured around the affirmation of an ideal that is expressed as the negative projection of the sacrifice, Bataille sees only an affirmation of the sovereign as "the one who *is*," or in Hegel's formulation, "pure being-for-self." Rather than subjugating her- or himself to an ideal, the sovereign affirms only the self in Hegel's and Bataille's accounts. Like Hegel's *Phenomenology of Spirit,* Bataille's explanation of general economy is focused on "the *self*-consciousness that man would finally achieve in the lucid vision of its linked historical forms" (*AS1* 41). This focus on the self rather than an outside ideal requires the actual encounter with fear and violence rather than the aesthetic experience of the sublime.

For Hegel, the person becomes an independent self-consciousness, not through the affirmation of an outside ideal, but through the encounter with real violence. "The individual who has not risked his life may well be recognized as a *person,* but he has not attained to the truth of this recognition as an independent self-consciousness" (*PS* 114). Because in Hegel's account the subject only affirms itself as an independent self-consciousness by experiencing actual violence, this violence begins to dominate the existence of the subject, who seeks not only to risk his own life but also to seek the death of others, so that "just as each stakes his own life, so each must seek the other's death, for it values the other no more than itself" (*PS* 114). This understanding of the subject as both self-sacrificer and killer depends upon the fearlessness in the face of death that Hegel describes as the experience that establishes a pure being-for-self. This necessity of real violence is linked in Hegel to the emphasis on individual sovereignty rather than on the establishing of principles that would transcend the individual. In taking over the focus on individual sovereignty, Bataille also commits himself to an insistence on real violence as the basis of sacrifice.

Bataille diverges from Hegel in rejecting the next part of his dialectic in which the bondsman gains mastery through a working up of material reality. It is in this labor that the subject in Hegel finally gains mastery over violence after having been seized by an absolute fear:

> If consciousness fashions the thing without that initial absolute fear, it is only an empty self-centered attitude; for its form or negativity is not negativity *per se,* and therefore its formative activity cannot give it a consciousness of itself as essential being. If it has not experienced absolute fear but only some lesser dread, the negative being has remained for it something external, its substance has not been infected by it through and through. Since the entire contents of its natural consciousness have not been jeopardized, determinate being still *in principle* attaches to it; hav-

ing a "mind of one's own" is self-will, a freedom which is still enmeshed in servitude. Just as little as the pure form can become essential being for it, just as little is that form, regarded as extended to the particular, a universal formative activity, an absolute Notion; rather it is a skill which is master over some things, but not over the universal power and the whole of objective being. (*PS* 119)

This mastery through labor is not just "a skill which is master over some things," but a labor that is a response to an "initial absolute fear." Here, Hegel seems to be indicating that the condition of labor that he imagines is the absolute subjugation through fear contained in slavery as practiced, for example, in the American colonies.[5] If so, Hegel's argument indicates that such slavery is a precondition for individual freedom by force of the fact that an escape from slavery is not just a simple development of a skill, but must violently transform the entire order. The kind of freedom that the slave's rebellion against the master establishes is consequently a mastery "over the universal power and the whole of objective being." Hegel sees slavery as the prelude to the ability of the human to finally gain mastery over nature. This means, however, that the reification that the slave experienced becomes the content of the former slave's mastery once he or she has attained freedom. The Hegelian subject is defined by reification, and the situation of Hegelian freedom consists in an outwardly projected reification: the physical subjugation of nature to human ends.

For Bataille, on the other hand, "the first labor established the world of *things*, to which the profane world of the Ancients generally corresponds" and "man himself became one of the things of this world, at least for the time in which he labored" (*AS1* 57). Because labor subjects nature to human ends, Bataille rejects labor for subjecting both the object and the subject to an enslavement to human utility. Both the master and the slave suffer from the degradation of slavery. "No one can make a *thing* of the second self that the slave is without at the same time estranging himself from his own intimate being, without giving himself the limits of a *thing*" (*AS1* 56). This rejection of labor and slavery as a way of overcoming subjection to the world of objects is a critique of the reification inherent to Hegel's idea of labor as a subjugation of nature and a rejection of the assumption that human power might be able to triumph over nature as a physical force. Instead, Bataille sides with Kant in affirming the overwhelming power of nature in comparison with human power in the physical world. Because he is focused on the flux of life that underlies and subordinates all human activity to a greater movement, Bataille does not see the independence of the subject as the goal of existence. Nor does he consider that a subordination of nature to human ends would constitute part of the freedom of the subject. However, because Bataille also refuses to accept any principles that would transcend the subject, he still retains the idea of the independence of a pure subject that affirms itself as pure being-for-self in the face of nature.

Because he rejects labor as a resubjugation of the subject to utility, Bataille argues that the truth of violence is the *only* thing that transcends the subject. Rather than continuing the dialectical development of the subject beyond the life-and-death struggle, Bataille sees the violent encounter as the culmination of the process of subject constitution. The attainment of self-consciousness only comes about to the extent that the subject faces destruction without fear. Violence becomes not only the opposite of the subject but also its essence. Bataille recognizes, however, that such an affirmation of violence in the sovereignty of the subject is also an affirmation of pure capriciousness.

This capriciousness constitutes the return of objects to their status before a subjugation to human utility, and Bataille's vision of a return to this intimacy recalls Adorno's critique of Hegel. Both criticize Hegel's idea of a successful physical subjugation of nature by the subject in labor as a form of reification, an objectification of nature that constrains nature to human ends. Bataille sees in labor the fundamental cause of reification because it implies a living for the future and a subjugation of oneself to outside ends rather than a living for the moment that defines the sovereign. The key in both Bataille and Adorno is to find an escape from the reified world of things into a nature that is prior to the subject/object split and to individuation. Just as Adorno sets the reified world of instrumental reason against a possible freedom of nature in a state of non-identity, Bataille criticizes objects and reason as linked into a system in which the object is identical with itself. As with Adorno, who seeks a situation in which "nature, no longer oppressed by spirit, frees itself from the miserable nexus of rank second nature and subjective sovereignty" and for whom "such emancipation would be the return of nature" (*AT* 197), Bataille sees reason and the object world as parts of a system that denies the independence of nature.

Bataille, like Adorno, seeks to uncover an "intimate world" opposed to the rational one. But, crucially, Bataille is willing to recognize the violence that Adorno seeks to banish from nature. The linking of work to a subjugation to things requires both of them to reject the entire symbolic order as part of this subjugation as well. The freeing of objects from a structure of domination must consequently be impossible without a destruction of the entire symbolic order. In Adorno, this antagonism toward the symbolic order is developed in his idea of reification as a historical phenomenon and his resulting utopianism that rejects sacrifice as a necessary part of human life. For Bataille, however, the antagonism toward the symbolic order is more radical and leads to the idea that any type of human order and harmony is a form of reification. The key difference from Adorno's conception lies in Bataille's understanding of what a laying bare of an obscured nature would imply. While Adorno conceives of a return of nature to itself as part of a reconciliation with the human world and consequently for him "the sublime speaks against domination" (*AT* 197), Bataille recognizes the escape from utility as possible only through insanity, violence, death, and dissolution. "The world of intimacy is as antithetical to the *real* world as immoderation is to moderation, madness to reason, drunkenness to lucidity. There is moderation only in the object, reason only in the identity of the object with itself, lucidity only in the distinct knowledge of objects" (*AS1* 58). The liberation of objects from utility does not occur within a utopian end of violence but is possible only through the sovereign acceptance of death in sacrifice and the consequent embracing of the truth of violence.

Bataille criticizes reification and seeks to emancipate objects not in order to attain a utopian harmony of man and nature but in order to uncover the truth of chaos and destruction. He affirms the importance of sacrifice as the path toward a realization of this truth. "Sacrifice destroys an object's real ties of subordination; it draws the victim out of the world of utility and restores it to that of unintelligible caprice."[6] The end result of sacrifice is an unleashing of this caprice and an insight into the basic violence and chaos of the vital life behind the object world.

Yet, because he considers violent caprice to be the basis of true sacrifice, Bataille's readings of ritual sacrifice inevitably fail to coincide with his theory. The examples of Aztec human sacrifice, potlatch, Islam, Tibetan Buddhism, and the American Marshall Plan that he provides in *The Accursed Share* all ultimately follow the schema of the Kantian sublime to the extent that there is always a subordination of the sacrifice to another goal, thereby ruining the chaos and caprice of the sacrifice. Aztec sacrifice, for instance, functions in Bataille's account within the context of their beliefs, not as gratuitous violence, but within a set of carefully prescribed rituals and myths that both limit sacrifice to prisoners of war—that is, people from outside the community—and at the same time involve the "adoption" of the sacrificed captive by the sacrificer, "who regarded his victim as a son, as a second self" (*AS1* 53–54). As a consequence, the sacrifices were meant to emulate a kind of self-sacrifice in which one sacrifices oneself in order to guarantee the continuing power of the sun (*AS1* 53). But in spite of his description of the social order that the sacrifices serve to confirm, Bataille describes the Aztec rituals as following "the moral principle of consumption" (*AS1* 55), an idea that does not arise from his sources and that he must therefore insert into his account. In doing so, he must look past the specific relationships and principles that the sacrifices establish for the Aztec social order, effacing them in favor of his overarching principle of consumption.

The examples that Bataille successfully adduces to illustrate his understanding of sacrifice as a form of sovereignty include both the gratuitous and capricious violence in his literary texts, such as *The Story of the Eye*, and the descriptions of inhumanly cruel individuals that he culls from history, such as the child murderer Gilles de Rais.[7] These examples exhibit the domination of an individual's search for pleasure at all costs and the consequent subordination of everything to that pleasure. Although these examples exert a kind of voyeuristic fascination over the reader, they do not result in a feeling of the sublime. On the contrary, their effect, as Bataille intends, is generally to destroy any sense of the possibility of ideals that would transcend the independence of a particular subject and its individual caprice and pleasure. Consequently, as they would simply imply a total destruction of life and society, these examples are in no way reproducible on a larger social scale, nor are they meant as an interpretation of the way in which sacrifice in human society generally proceeds. Rather, their meaning lies only in their exemplification of the catastrophic results of a setting of the individual above the collective in a system of sacrifice. Without any outside ideal to which the individual is to be subordinated, the affirmation of individual sovereignty and pleasure is an affirmation of capricious violence as the final meaning of the world. Although this is Bataille's intention, there is no independent justification for it other than his decision to nihilistically reject all symbolic order and with it, all ideals.

In an alternative to both Adorno's and Bataille's conception of reification, Einstein subscribes neither to Adorno's equation of sacrifice with reification (i.e., with market exchange) nor to Bataille's understanding of sacrifice as a pure destruction of objects. Rather than simply affirming or destroying the symbolic order, sacrifice for Einstein transforms it into something that links materiality to spirituality, transcending the material by linking it to spiritual ideals and concretizing these ideals by projecting them out of the forms of materiality. "It is important that belief presupposes despair—in this way it becomes an immediate force, a dramatic force, not opinion. Belief without action, without sacrifice, is almost like a theory and is in any case just a pretentious assertion."[8] Here, the sacrifice establishes the materiality of the belief. For Einstein, sacrifice does not lead, as with Bataille, to a suspension of the symbolic order and a fleeting glimpse of a world of flux but rather to an affirmation of a spiritual ideal that founds a symbolic order through the materiality of sacrifice.

This form of sacrifice grounds a particular symbolic order rather than destroys it. For Bataille, the insight that results from sacrifice is always the same one—an insight into a basic uselessness and chaos. Although Adorno shares aspects of Bataille's critique of reification, Adorno opposes sacrifice as part of the ideology of reification by pointing to the unnecessary character of violence and the promise of utopian reconciliation. For Einstein, the result of the sacrifice is a materialist affirmation of an ideal with a particular content that then affirms the details of the symbolic order that is implied in this ideal. Referring to the work of Paul Claudel, Einstein writes: "Claudel is not concerned with things, but with their principles, which are embodied in humans, yet, not entirely—principles exceed the human. In order to be king, the king must sacrifice himself, and in the same way the saint gives himself over to the miracle."[9] Every sacrifice for Einstein is a particular one that lays out the founding principle of a system of culture. Rather than suspending the symbolic order, the sacrifice designates materiality as something that is linked to the symbolic order. Materiality, the world of things, is intertwined with the symbolic order that enables the conception of the world as a set of things. Sacrifice establishes a symbolic order, not as an abstract set of ideals, but as a particular projection from the sacrifice as a confrontation with violence and materiality. This confrontation does not subjugate nature physically, as Hegel would have it, nor does it unleash nature as total chaos, as Bataille envisions, nor does it imagine nature as reconciliation, as Adorno does. Rather, each instance of sacrifice reconfigures the relation to nature anew. The performance of the sacrifice follows an aesthetic reception of the patterns of violence in nature that leads to a linking of material reality to sacred ideals on the one hand and a physical manifestation of these ideals on the other.

Bataille would call this linking of materiality to the sacred a continuing subjugation of the world to reification and utility because it means that each thing is considered only in terms of its usefulness for some outside ideal. But if sacrifice establishes the final goal of all human purposes rather than simply negating these purposes in favor of an underlying biological energy flux, then all material things and this energy flux would be subordinated by extension to this final, metaphysical goal as well, rather than to a self-interested human purpose.

René Girard on Sacrifice and Scapegoat

As with Bataille's conception, René Girard's theories are distinguished by their focus on violence rather than human ideals as the primary issue in sacrifice. His approach is in some ways similar to Freud's in *Civilization and Its Discontents* to the extent that both see human aggression as the basic problem of sacrifice and thus understand sacrifice as something that is independent of a situation of scarcity or necessity that threatens a culture's ideals. Yet, the turn away from necessity as the source of violence and toward human aggression as a self-perpetuating process of increasing violence has the consequence that violence becomes both too important for Girard's theory and yet not important enough. Violence becomes too important because the hidden content of every sacrifice according to Girard is always the same insight into the collective violence of a human group that focuses on a single innocent victim. Yet, violence is not important enough because Girard ultimately argues, like Adorno, that violence, as an irrational result of an imitation of others' desires, can be eradicated from human culture through a proper type of consciousness that identifies with individual victims rather than with the murderous group. Violence is a correctable human malady and not a consequence of objective necessities and conflicts. Therefore, sacrifice is both a unified phenomenon in Girard's account and a sign of barbarism that can be overcome through adherence to a proper consciousness that is given by Christian culture.

Like Bataille, Girard argues both that a single structure of violence underlies all examples of sacrifice and that the function of the sacrifice is to express this violence directly. For Girard, humans have a natural tendency toward aggression and violence, and this inherent tendency must always be given an outlet: "If left unappeased, violence will accumulate until it overflows its confines and floods the surrounding area."[10] Girard derives this pressure toward continual accumulation of violence from the fact that an act of violence will always engender other acts of violence because of the desire to imitate. He sees this mimesis of violence as the basis for all of culture because culture always arises out of a prior state of disorder dominated by violent rivalries.

Girard divides the imitation of acts of violence into two categories: acquisitive mimesis and conflictual mimesis. Although he bases culture on acquisitive mimesis, which "divides by leading two or more individuals to converge on one and the same object with a view to appropriating it,"[11] this form of mimetic violence is no different than the idea that resources are limited and people will struggle to obtain them. In order to move beyond scarcity (and thus natural limits) as the basis of culture, Girard must emphasize the proliferation of a type of violence whose object is not the acquisition of a particular limited resource but the mere continuation of aggression against a rival (*VS* 31). This "conflictual mimesis" is central to Girard's theory because it determines the way in which sacrifice is structured as a reaction to violence.

Although Girard argues that acquisitive mimesis leads into conflictual mimesis, in fact the two are theoretically separate. Whereas acquisitive violence can be explained by an economic theory in which scarcity creates a situation of competition for limited resources and thus an imaginary (but unattainable) state of abundance could theoretically do away with violence, mimetic violence has no situational explanation but rather is caused by a human tendency toward violence independent of its goals. With conflictual mimesis, the point of violence is no longer to acquire a particular object. In fact this type of violence only begins when the goal disappears. "Once the object has disappeared and the mimetic frenzy has reached a high degree of intensity, one can expect conflictual mimesis to take over and snowball in its effects" (*TH* 26). For Girard, violence becomes an end in itself. Such violence without an object cannot stop of its own accord but must be constantly confronted (*VS* 10).

Given such a predicament, the only way to maintain culture is through the continual creation of victims—scapegoats killed to limit aggression to particular times and places. Girard imagines a primal scene in which an act of aggression leads to acts of vengeance and a general violence of all against all. The only way for a culture to escape this general violence is to direct all aggression at one surrogate victim, who is picked arbitrarily to be the focus of all violence. "Since the power of mimetic attraction multiplies with the number of those polarized, it is inevitable that at one moment the entire community will find itself unified against a single individual. Conflictual mimesis therefore creates a *de facto* allegiance against a common enemy, such that the conclusion of the crisis is nothing other than the reconciliation of the community" (*TH* 26). The initial death of an innocent victim is the founding act of a culture because it limits violence to a single act rather than letting it run rampant. Not the symbolic significance but the physical act of ritual sacrifice, channeling aggression toward a single victim, becomes the basis of culture. Without such sacrificial violence, human society would destroy itself in a process whereby natural aggression would repeat itself in continuing acts of vengeance and feuding. Within this framework, where the primary violence that humans face is their own aggression, the role of sacrifice is to channel this human violence into limited expressions that do not destroy the society as a whole.

Once the killing of the scapegoat diffuses the "sacrificial crisis" and grounds the society, all later sacrifices refer back to this primal scene by substituting a ritual victim for the initial surrogate victim. "Ritual sacrifice is founded on a double substitution. The first, which passes unperceived, is the substitution of one member of the community for all, brought about through operation of the surrogate victim. The second, the only truly 'ritualist' substitution, is superimposed on the first. It is the substitution of a victim belonging to a predetermined sacrificial category for the original victim" (*VS* 102). Girard argues that the original surrogate victim that founds a culture must be innocent, but contends that non-Christian religion must hide this innocence in order to continue. For this reason, while "the surrogate victim comes from inside the community" and is the real scapegoat on which the community blames the outbreak of violence, "the ritual victim must come from outside; otherwise the community might find it difficult to unite against it" (*VS* 102). Thus, Girard separates the initial scapegoat whose death founds a culture from the victim of a ritual sacrifice. He does this in order to affirm the innocence of the victim in sacrifice while emphasizing that this innocence must be hidden in a sacrificial culture. Whereas the scapegoat is arbitrarily chosen and innocent of any real offense, the victim of a ritual sacrifice is seen by the perpetrators of the sacrifice to be guilty.

Girard's mixing of innocence and guilt in the victim is an attempt to explain the identity of the sacrifice with the scapegoat. Because he sees mutual aggression as the single most important form of violence that is constantly threatening human society, Girard understands the scapegoat mechanism as the hidden meaning of *every* sacrifice. But because different examples of sacrifice do not always demonstrate a clear scapegoat logic, he uses the double character of sacrifice to explain variations in how and when sacrifice is carried out.

Girard grounds the necessity of sacrifice in the threat that human culture will lose the distinction between pure and impure violence that maintains the stability of the social order. "The *sacrificial crisis,* that is, the disappearance of the sacrificial rites, coincides with the disappearance of the difference between impure violence and purifying violence. When this difference has been effaced, purification is no longer possible and impure, contagious, reciprocal violence spreads throughout the community" (*VS* 49). Once the violence spreads, the entire community descends into a chaos of violence that keeps on breeding more violence. This violence can only be stopped when the community chooses an innocent victim upon whom to project all guilt and then sacrifices this victim. Girard concludes that the maintenance of ritual sacrifice is crucial for the stability of a social order.

> The sacrificial distinction, the distinction between the pure and the impure, cannot be obliterated without obliterating all other differences as well. One and the same process of violent reciprocity engulfs the whole. The sacrificial crisis can be defined, therefore, as a crisis of distinctions—that is, a crisis affecting the cultural order. This cultural order is nothing more than a regulated system of distinctions in which the differences among individuals are used to establish their "identity" and their mutual relationships. . . . The hidden violence of the sacrificial crisis eventually succeeds in destroying distinctions, and this destruction in turn fuels the renewed violence. In short, it seems that anything that adversely affects the institution of sacrifice will ultimately pose a threat to the very basis of the community, to the principles on which its social harmony and equilibrium depend. (*VS* 49)

Girard suggests that sacrificial rites create the distinctions that underlie any cultural order by heaping guilt on an innocent sacrificial victim and drawing a boundary between the victim and the rest of the community. Because the function of the sacrifice is always to create this distinction between guilty victim and innocent community, Girard also asserts that every rite has the same structure. The universal structure of sacrifice means that the distinctions that sacrifice creates will always be the same distinction between sanctioned violence and unsanctioned violence. This will be the primary distinction that grounds every cultural order for Girard, and he interprets every sacrifice as telling the same story. This story then overwrites all other interpretations of the world: "In my opinion, the sole possible model remains the sacrificial crisis and its resolution" (*VS* 96).

This unified character of sacrifice has two consequences for Girard's method. First, as he points out, the verification of his thesis requires him to take examples from all different cultures and contexts. Second, because not all rites fit precisely within his model, he must posit a constant delusion about the real meaning of the sacrifice. This delusion stems from the unwillingness to admit that the surrogate victim is an arbitrary scapegoat.

> No single rite will reproduce, point for point, the operations my hypothesis proposes as the origin of all rites. A delusion concerning its own factual basis—*not* the absence of that basis—is characteristic of religion.

And the source of this delusion is none other than the surrogate victim; or rather, the fact, which remains unperceived, that the surrogate victim is arbitrarily chosen. The ritualistic mind strives to reproduce the operation of violent unanimity without understanding its mimetic nature. If my hypothesis is correct, no single religious form will suffice to illuminate the whole picture, but a multiplicity of examples will cast light on its various aspects until everything gradually becomes clear and certainty prevails.

In order to verify my hypothesis, then, it must be applied to many different forms of ritual and myth, as far apart in content, history, and geography as possible. If it is correct, the complex rites will provide the most striking confirmation. (*VS* 104)

In offering his scapegoat theory, Girard uses a semiotic structure of analysis that affirms a basic arbitrariness in the meaning of sacrifice because the victim is arbitrary and the distinctions on which the victimization is based are also arbitrary. Girard even explicitly links the arbitrariness of the victim to the arbitrariness of the sign in a semiotic system of distinctions. This arbitrariness is coupled, however, to a total lack of variation when Girard links every sacrifice to the same scapegoat mechanism as the underlying but sometimes obscured final truth of sacrifice.

Within this framework, the only possible variation in the structure of sacrifice is a variation in the level of delusion about the underlying reality of the scapegoat mechanism. Girard differentiates in *Violence and the Sacred* between societies that use sacrifice in order to quell violence and modern societies that have overcome sacrifice by using a justice system to put all violence in the hands of the state. Later, in *Things Hidden Since the Foundation of the World*, Girard revises this dichotomy in order to distinguish between sacrificial societies that do not understand the fact that the victim is a scapegoat and nonsacrificial societies, Christianity being the primary example, in which the scapegoat mechanism has been uncovered for what it is and thus overcome. In both cases, Girard tries to account for variations in sacrificial rituals by insisting on variations in the level of delusion about the final truth of internal violence as the defining form of violence for human society.

Having demonstrated the necessity of sacrifice, Girard changes tack in order to argue that this ritual sacrifice is irrational because the victim is innocent. He distinguishes between Christianity, which recognizes the innocence of sacrificial victims, and sacrificial religions, which emphasize the victim's guilt and justify violent sacrifice. Because it emphasizes Christ's innocence, Christianity is the only religion that unmasks the injustice of the scapegoat mechanism and of ritual sacrifice. In preaching love of enemies and attempting to discourage violence toward rivals and victims, Christianity presents the only chance to escape a culture based on sacrifice. On the one hand, sacrifice is necessary for the founding and maintenance of a culture but, on the other hand, it becomes unnecessary once Christianity reveals that sacrificial victims are innocent. While Christianity identifies with the victims, all other religions, relegated to the status of "myth," only know violence against their victims. These mythic religions demonstrate a uniformly unreflective character. By contrast, Christianity arrives at the truth of sacrifice—that is, the victim is innocent and the sacrifice is in fact arbitrary and unnecessary.

Girard's opposition of mythic with Christian culture in the end denies the importance of violence for the structure of human culture. If the Christian insight is that the victim is innocent and chosen arbitrarily and thus not at all guilty, then the sacrifice is in fact not necessary but merely part of an irrational structure of mimetic violence. Once the delusion has been overcome, mimetic violence, as a purely human violence, seems to be overcome along with it. In the end, Girard disputes the necessity of sacrifice and defends the individual victim against the society that would seek to create scapegoats. This account discounts the structuring influence of the ritual experience in the construction of the sacrifice. If every instance of sacrifice is a retelling of the same scapegoat story, then the ritual is not itself constitutive of the relationship to violence. Rather, the basic storyline is predetermined, and the specific sacrifice is simply an ideological construct that hides the underlying truth that the sacrificial victim is an arbitrarily chosen scapegoat.

The only variations Girard's theory recognizes are in the degree of consciousness in the sacrificer about the truth of the underlying mechanism. Consequently, Girard must reduce every instance of sacrifice to the scapegoat mechanism. As opposed to Girard's approach, this study investigates whether each individual instance of sacrifice might have a constitutive effect on social structure. If so, acts of sacrifice would be events that have a shaping influence on the human relation to violence. Sacrifice would on the one hand respond to the constant problem of death and violence. On the other hand, each specific sacrifice would outline a culturally specific solution. Instances of both mythic and modern sacrifice would not be differentiated by the opposition between a sacrificial and a nonsacrificial society, as Girard argues, but by each sacrifice's unique mode of structuring the human relation to violence.

In order to establish this alternate method, consider the distinction between sacrifice and scapegoat that Girard denies. For him, every sacrifice is in fact a reenactment of the scapegoat mechanism, and any attempt to distinguish the two is part of the ideology of the victimizers, who are unwilling to recognize the injustice of the sacrifice. Significantly, Girard, in developing this argument, avoids consideration of the description of the distinction between sacrifice and scapegoat in the Jewish Bible, in which a strict separation between the two indicates that sacrifice might not be a unified phenomenon.

> And Aaron shall cast lots upon the two goats; one lot for the Lord, and the other lot for the scapegoat. And Aaron shall bring the goat upon which the Lord's lot fell, and offer him for a sin offering. But the goat, on which the lot fell to be the scapegoat, shall be presented alive before the Lord, to make an atonement with him, and to let him go for a scapegoat in the wilderness. (Leviticus 16:8–10, King James version)

The sacrificial goat is an innocent victim. The scapegoat, however, "shall bear upon him all their iniquities unto a land not inhabited" (Lev. 16:22). The scapegoat, which bears guilt, is not killed but sent out into the wilderness. Here, we find the two types of sacrificial victim that Girard describes: the innocent sacrifice and the guilty scapegoat. But while Girard asserts that the first is the hidden meaning of the second, in Leviticus the two are not presented as two versions of the same sacrifice. Rather sacrifice and scapegoat are clearly differentiated and serve two separate functions.

The sacrifice is a pure offering to God, in which the sacrificer makes an offering of something valuable and untainted. Those who refuse to make sacrifices become themselves tainted because they are not willing to follow the rituals by which the society consecrates and limits killing. The proper punishment for such people is the same as for the scapegoat—banishment from the community.

> What man soever there be of the house of Israel, that killeth an ox, or lamb, or goat, in the camp, or that killeth it out of the camp, and bringeth it not unto the door of the tabernacle of the congregation, to offer an offering unto the Lord before the tabernacle of the Lord; blood shall be imputed unto that man; he hath shed blood; and that man shall be cut off from among his people. (Leviticus 17:3–4)

The key distinction is between those who make sacrifices and those who do not. Whereas Girard sees sacrifice as a controlled outlet for violence, this passage, in differentiating a killing that is not a sacrifice from a killing that is, demonstrates an alternative logic of sacrifice in which its significance is not in the release of violence. Instead, Leviticus emphasizes the need to offer the sacrifice to God according to the laws of the community rather than keep the sacrificed animal for oneself. The man who does not offer the killed animal as a sacrifice becomes guilty of a transgression against the community's rules and is banished like the scapegoat. He is considered guilty of murder because killing must be a sanctioned community decision rather than an individual one.

This distinction between sacrificial and nonsacrificial killing lies at the heart of Walter Burkert's theory of sacrifice, in which he bases his notion of sacrifice on the situation of the hunter and sees killing as necessary for life because of the hunter's need to kill for survival. As Burkert points out, "man became man through the hunt, through the act of killing,"[12] and sacrifice is the acknowledgement of the need for violence in the development of human life. The focus on the hunt illuminates the function of specific instances of animal sacrifice that are performed, not as an arbitrary victimization, but as a consecration of a killing that is committed in any case for food. Relying on the work of Karl Meuli, Burkert demonstrates that animal sacrifice was simply a way to ritualize the feasting process after a kill. If, as Burkert suggests, "all orders and forms of authority in human society are founded on institutionalized violence" (*HN* 1), the opposite of sacrifice cannot be a nonviolent structure, but an unbounded kind of killing that is not limited by social rules.

Consequently, the distinction between sacrifice and scapegoat is a distinction between two types of socially sanctioned killing. The sacrifice is a recognition of the necessity of violence for the continuation of society and is carried out as a kind of self-sacrifice that is to be honored and emulated. It grounds the social order by establishing the ideals for the sake of which a sacrifice should be carried out. The scapegoat, by contrast, is the opposite of the sacrifice in that it describes a situation in which sacrifice, and thus the social order dependent upon it, is refused. The violent reaction to those who refuse to sacrifice is banishment or death as punishment. The scapegoat is thus equivalent to the *homo sacer* of the Roman tradition, described by Giorgio Agamben as someone who is both unfit for sacrifice yet also available to be killed without any consequence for the killer. Both the scapegoat and the *homo sacer* represent a specific category of individuals who are considered to have been expelled from the community and open to punishment because of either a failure to sacrifice or an unsuitability for sacrifice. Neither, however, should be considered to be the basis of the other process of sacrifice. While sacrifice builds up the ideals of a society, the scapegoat is punished for the denial of sacrifice and a consequent transgression against these ideals. The sacrifice and the scapegoat are opposite but linked phenomena, and this relationship is what accounts for the double character of sacrifice that Girard attributes to the scapegoat mechanism's choice of an innocent victim and the simultaneous guilt attributed to the victim.

Although there is a clear distinction between the sacrifice and the scapegoat, the two are also intimately connected. Sacrifice and scapegoat are different because their importance lies not in ritual violence, as Girard argues, but in the relationship to death and violence that they symbolize. The function of the sacrificial goat and of the scapegoat is not to provide a vent for built-up aggression but to remind individuals continually of their obligations to the community. The sacrifice is an enactment of a self-sacrifice in which one gives up something valuable in order to affirm a spiritual relationship. The sacrificial victim must in this case indeed be innocent and pure—a recognized part of the group whose sacrifice dramatizes an instance of individual self-denial for the sake of community rules and ideals. The sacrifice thus represents a voluntary limitation that is necessary to establish social rules and a social identity. The scapegoat by contrast is an object of punishment and is guilty of a particular transgression against the rules established by the sacrifice. Those unwilling to agree to sacrifice thereby exclude themselves from the community and are banished as scapegoats.

Walter Burkert on Sacrifice and Social Order

If we are dealing here with two separate categories, it will be necessary to rethink the logic of sacrifice in order to understand the reasons why both sacrifices and scapegoats continue as cultural phenomena into the present day. Girard himself affirms that sacrifice lies at the basis of a community and guarantees its stability. In basing sacrifice on mimetic violence and rivalry, however, Girard denies the possibility that the basis of religious sacrifice might be in principles that the community seeks to uphold. But if sacrifice is necessary for the origin of culture, it might also be necessary for its continued survival, and if a culture is indeed founded on a spiritual basis, an alienation from this basis would threaten the entire culture.

To the extent that a culture must come to terms with conflicts that necessitate choices between competing values, a particular vision of sacrifice will be needed in order to structure these choices. Sacrifice presents a human response to the violence that opposes a culture's goals, and its justification lies in the desire to defend these goals. Sacrifice implies a submission to a specific set of ideals, but only if sacrifice is conceived not as an arbitrary and irrational act of violence but as the disinterested recognition of forces that oppose a culture's aspirations.

Burkert describes this sense of sacrifice as the key component of human culture that separates humans from other animals and allows human survival in spite of inherent physical vulnerabilities.

> If man nonetheless survived and with unprecedented success even enlarged his sphere of influence, it was because in place of his natural instincts he developed the rules of cultural tradition, thus artificially forming and differentiating his basic inborn behavior. Biological selection rather than conscious planning determined the educational processes that helped form man, so that he could best adapt himself to his role. A man had to be courageous to take part in the hunt; therefore, courage is always included in the conception of an ideal man. A man had to be reliable, able to wait, to resist a momentary impulse for the sake of a long-range goal. He had to have endurance and keep to his word. In these matters men developed behavior patterns that were lacking in anthropoid apes and were more closely analogous to the behavior of beasts of prey. Above all, the use of weapons was controlled by the strictest—if also artificial—rules: what was allowed and necessary in one realm was absolutely forbidden in the other. A brilliant accomplishment in one was murder in the other. The decisive point is the very possibility that man may submit to laws curbing his individual intelligence and adaptability for the sake of societal predictability. The educative power of tradition attempts to bind him in an irreversible process analogous to biological "imprinting." (*HN* 18–19)

To be part of a community means to give up part of one's individual freedom—to make sacrifices in one's own life for the sake of the community. Sacrifice in myth or in ritual refers to this everyday need in the life of each member of a community. Because the power of myths and rituals, and the corresponding strength of the community, lies in the internalization of a sense of individual sacrifice in the life of each member, "not just the religious cult, but the order of society itself takes shape in sacrifice" (*HN* 84). Myths and rituals do not create but only reinforce this sense of sacrifice by reminding the community of a prior exemplary sacrifice on the part of one of its members. It is in this way that sacrifice forms the basis of culture.

Burkert's analysis demonstrates the functional importance of sacrifice for a community. In this conception, sacrifice is not just a form of ideology that is constructed to hide an underlying truth, as Girard asserts. It is not a form of exchange, as in Horkheimer and Adorno's analysis. Nor does sacrifice destroy the symbolic order as Bataille contends. It establishes and perpetuates the fundamental value distinctions of a symbolic order and plays a central role in maintaining the stability and coherence of that order. Burkert's conception explains the importance of sacrifice for cultural stability.

Yet, within his attempt to legitimate sacrifice, Burkert offers conflicting explanations for its truth value. In parts of his argument, he emphasizes the ritual character of sacrifice and the need for real bloodshed to ground the truth of the sacrifice. "However, the bloodshed and the refined methods of torture are very real and guarantee the seriousness of the ritual. The gruesome 'evil' at work in the ritual fulfills a function, i.e., to preserve a social structure over the course of generations. Once again, life rises up from the peril of death" (*HN* 45–46). Because Burkert sees the necessity of sacrifice in the aggressive instinct of humans that must constantly express itself in violence, he argues that the sacrifice can only be effective to the extent that it involves real bloodshed. The bloodshed and torture guarantee the truth of sacrifice by demonstrating that the ritual is not just a game or a show but has consequences for reality as well. According to Burkert, this bloodshed also performs the social function of diverting aggression to the outside world. But with the advance of civilization, the diversion of aggression becomes an ever more violent affair. Thus, he points to the death penalty and war as modern forms of sacrifice only to the extent that they involve real violence and not just a form of aesthetic spectacle: "to some extent, this too was still a game, a show. With the progressive growth of consciousness, civilization came to demand absolute seriousness—one could no longer *pretend* to kill men. For this reason the death penalty became the strongest expression of governmental power, and, as has often been shown, the criminal's execution at a public festival corresponded to a sacrificial ritual. . . . There is another, far more serious, way to divert aggression toward the outside world: by integrating large groups of men in a common fighting spirit, i.e., war" (*HN* 46–47). Real violence is that which grounds the truth value of a sacrifice, and Burkert suggests that such violence is essential to culture.

Here, Burkert's definition of sacrifice consists of two parts, bloodshed and theatricality, that work together to perpetuate sacrificial ritual. He rejects the notion that a ritual is based on an "an antecedent 'idea'" and argues that, "thanks to its theatrical, mimetic character and the deep impression that its sacred solemnity can impart, ritual is self-perpetuating" (*HN* 27, 29). Ritual perpetuates itself based on both a theatrical tendency to imitate and a real violence that lends seriousness to the otherwise inconsequential spectacle. Although in the first case he argues that ritual "dramatizes the existing order" and creates an imitation of it (*HN* 25), he does not explain why the existing order is as it is or why the ritual should not take a different form. The intimation is that ritual is the way it is because of the violence that it dramatizes. But violence exists in other situations besides ritual, and it is not clear from Burkert's explanation why ritual violence would be repeated rather than any other kind of violence. He notes earlier that ritual separates outer violence from inner prohibition against violence. The separation is carried out through the fear and guilt that the ritual enactment of violence evokes. Yet, the ritual in fact is supposed to quell the fear and the guilt of killing during the hunt, and in that case its sacred solemnity does not come from the violence itself and how "some danger is evoked arousing anxiety" (*HN* 26). Instead, this solemnity seems to be a result of the way in which the ritual is able to quell anxiety.

The difficulties of Burkert's two-part definition of sacrifice result from the separation of the imitative aspect in the narrative structure from the serious aspect in the real violence. Although the truth of the narrative structure of sacrifice is only guaranteed by the bloodshed and the bloodshed only attains meaning through the simultaneous drama, Burkert can only link the two aspects arbitrarily. For the two aspects of imitation and seriousness to function together to create the sacrifice, they would have to be linked in a more determinate way.

Sacrifice as Aesthetic Event

At the same time that he uses violence as the measure of the "seriousness" of a culture, Burkert also develops a symbolic understanding of sacrifice. In this approach, though the real death of a member of the community may be the event to which a narrative of sacrifice refers, this death is not the act that actually establishes the ritual of sacrifice. The creation of the ritual depends on a symbolic relationship. In a demonstration of this symbolic significance of the sacrifice, Burkert offers the example of an animal sacrifice performed by the Plataeans to commemorate their victory in battle over the Persians.

> Both battle and burial were reenacted in the bloody ritual. Death and victory alike were present in the act of killing. The Plataeans evidently had already experienced their victory as a sacrifice in the year of the battle: the votive offering they presented at Delphi after 479 [B.C.E.] was a bull. The ritual celebrating the defeat of the Persians is therefore not a creation

of the historical event but, rather, a traditional form assimilating that event. A unique occurrence was thereby given universal significance and transformed into an enduring obligation that lasted through centuries. Of course, this could not prevent the destruction of Plataea in 427, but the victors built a sanctuary of their own for observance of the cult. The actors are interchangeable, the ritual remains. (*HN* 57–58)

As Burkert points out, the sacrificial ritual assimilates the event of victory in war into the cultural tradition as an "enduring obligation." The historical event provides the authority for a set of rituals whose function is to link the ritual sacrifice to the original sacrifice carried out by the warriors in battle. This link is not a material one, nor is it an objective one. It consists of an obligation that forms the basis of an ethic of sacrifice in battle for the sake of the larger community. The symbolism of this tradition survives as a cultural construct, even after the physical destruction of the people within which the tradition originates. If the ritual can survive the death of the original actors and perform the same social function within a new community, then the sacrifice must have a symbolic value that grounds its truth beyond any historical truth value.

The symbolic importance of myth and ritual lies in the fact that those who die for the community do not have to appear directly in order to create such commitment. Instead, the symbolic process links three distinct aspects of sacrifice—the narrative, the ritual, and the actual event—into a system of commitments and promises that serve to maintain the cohesion of the group. For the Plataeans, the story of sacrifice in battle establishes the principles and parameters of cultural identity and institutions. The ritual serves as a recommitment of the people to this story of sacrifice and the identity that it implies. In this sense, the ritual functions as a promise that, in the event of a future threat to the community, the people will make a similar sacrifice.[13] Finally, the real sacrifice in war, which was at the root of the initial story, is also the point at which the promise made in the ritual is fulfilled both in the past and in a possible future situation of crisis. All three elements—myth, ritual, and actual event—function as mutually supporting elements essential to the structure of sacrifice. Without the actual sacrifice in a future time of need, the promise made in the ritual remains an empty one. Without the initial story, there is no specific cultural structure that would make up the content of the promise. Without the promise acted out in ritual, the actual sacrifice would never come about as its fulfillment. As the "portability" of the ritual from one people to another indicates, the narrative of sacrifice, rather than the real event, is what endures, producing the template for potential action in the future.

Although the event of death forms the basis of the story, the significance of the ritual is not based on violence itself, but on the construction of the mechanisms that commemorate the violence in terms of a specific vision of sacrifice. The story of sacrifice establishes the cultural form that is to be affirmed when carrying out the religious rituals. The violent death itself only has a shock value that cannot go beyond the single moment. In order for the death to form the basis of a ritual that enacts a promise to repeat the sacrifice, it must acquire a symbolic significance.

This symbolic process of sacrifice is based on a dramatic structure, which Burkert describes as a recapitulation of the experience of the hunt. "Ritual must constantly reestablish the deadly outdoor realm of the hunting era within the circle of civilization, both to call that civilization into question and to renew it. Both are divine, and perhaps both aspects of sacrifice, the dread of death and the certainty of life, are subject to the same god" (*HN* 134). Here Burkert describes the truth of the ritual, not in terms of its raw violence but in its ability to recapitulate a social development. While Burkert makes a good case for a basic structure of ritual that enacts a commitment to a particular order, the idea that this structure is a recapitulation of the historical progress from hunting society to agricultural society is not clearly established by his examples. Instead of pointing to a common historical referent for diverse rituals, his examples indicate that the common function of all rituals is to create a commitment to a particular structure of sacrifice.

Burkert's analysis suggests that sacrifice generally follows a particular narrative schema. The unifying factor is not a particular historical referent, such as a primal scene of scapegoating or of killing during the hunt. Rather, we can consider every example of sacrifice as generally moving through three parts of a narrative sequence:

> Here the three parts of the sacrificial action—preparation, "act," restitution—are expanded into three related festivals that can be characterized as: (1) a symbolic sacrifice of a girl; (2) an "unspeakable sacrifice"; and (3) a sacrifice of renewal. The rhythm of anticipatory renunciation, followed by the savage "act" and, finally, pleasurable gratification, reflects the age-old situation of the hunter. In the city-culture, however, it is symbolically transformed into a New Year's festival following a period of dissolution, that is, a breakdown of the normal order. The same structure appears in Dionysiac orgies, almost as an atavistic regression. And, further on, we encounter the customs of fishermen who, although situated somewhere between hunting and city cultures, adapted themselves to the

same tradition. Through changing economic and social conditions, the fundamental structure of ritual remains. (*HN* 135)

The fundamental structure of the sacrificial action is not tied to a particular historical event or cultural form, but consists only of a narrative structure that recapitulates the three aspects of sacrifice (ritual, act, and story) in the three stages of (1) promise of renunciation, (2) fateful decision, and (3) restoration of order. This structure can be occupied in different ways in separate cultures, and each particular manifestation of this structure indicates the parameters of a unique culture.

The specific structure of sacrifice to be affirmed will vary, however, from group to group, depending on its particular circumstances and its understanding of its values. In providing a unified theory of sacrifice based on the situation of the hunt, Burkert uses many examples to demonstrate the transformative power of sacrifice. Although the variety of examples shows the ubiquity of sacrifice and its importance, their very variety begins to undermine the idea that there could be a unified model of sacrifice. Instead of being a single act with a variety of manifestations, sacrifice seems to function differently in each separate context. Consequently, the focus of study shifts away from what is common to all sacrifice and toward the character of each individual example and how it functions within a particular culture.

The variations in different models of sacrifice will depend upon the extent to which a group's values might diverge from those of another group. The implied link between sacrifice and ethics is based on the idea that ethical behavior will depend on how a particular system of values can establish itself on a representational level. If values cannot become binding for a group without the existence of supporting representations, then there would be a fundamental link between sacrifice and a community's values. These values may even originate through the mechanisms of sacrifice.

This approach requires an aesthetics of sacrifice that links the theatrical aspect to the actuality of sacrifice. Charles Peirce offers part of such a theory in his distinction between signs used as indices and signs used as symbols.[14] As Terence Deacon has pointed out in his interpretation of Peirce, signs used as symbols are to be distinguished from signs used as indices based on the fact that while an index indicates a physical link between the sign and the referent, such as in the example of a weathercock indicating the direction of the wind, a sign used as a symbol only points to other signs in order to establish its meaning.

An indexical relation governs the animal rituals, such as the triumph ceremony of the graylag geese that Burkert cites from Konrad Lorenz (*HN* 23). This ceremony, performed by geese in a pair-bonded relationship in order to demonstrate their solidarity, consists of a series of movements that resemble attacks, but rather than really attacking, the participants deviate in the last instant in order to avoid harm.[15] Because the ceremony of the animals is not prompted by a real enemy, Burkert argues that it "is meant to demonstrate and draw attention to the couple's solidarity and is confirmed by corresponding behavior in the partner, who understands the ritual communication because of its predetermined stereotypy" (*HN* 23). The referent of the ritual is the solidarity of the couple. But because this solidarity is physically enacted in the ritual by the difference between a real attack and a ceremonial one, there is no sense in which the ritual could possibly be a deception. The ritual is a real index of the reality of solidarity that it signals, and in this sense the ritual is a performative establishment of this solidarity.

Although this indexical character is shared by all animal rituals, human rituals exist within a context of signs in which they can be either indices or symbols. The specific character of the human ritual as opposed to the animal one is that the former is conducted in a situation in which the ritual does not function as an index of an underlying reality but as a symbol that links the elements of the ritual to other signs in the culture such as speeches, myths, images, other ritual practices, or even another culture's myths and rituals. The fact that the human ritual must be understood as a sign existing within a network of signs, and thus in a tradition, radically separates human from animal ritual.

Deacon describes this distinction by referring to the peacemaking rituals of the Yanomamö Indians of the Amazon rainforest.[16] Like the triumph ceremony of the graylag geese, their peacemaking "feasts" involve a process in which the opportunity for aggression is provided, but the aggression is not carried out. But this similarity only foregrounds the profound differences between the animal and the human ritual. In the case of the geese, the triumph ceremony is continually carried out, even and especially in situations where there is a potential conflict with other hostile geese outside the family. The necessity of the repetition stems from the fact that the ceremony does not consist of any kind of promise for future behavior in a way that would require a symbolic understanding of the ceremony. Instead, the ceremony is contextually bound, not just to the immediate situation but also to the specific paired couple and its offspring. Because it is purely indexical and performative in its establishment of solidarity, there is no way for the ceremony to function as a "sign" of peace that could be extended to a new context. For instance, once a gosling reaches a certain age, there is no way for it to be integrated with another nest by use of the ceremony as a gesture of peace. The adopted family would simply identify the gosling as an enemy and attack it.[17]

By contrast, the Yanomamö feast involves two potentially hostile villages that are trying to make peace in a situation of mutual distrust. In order to establish peace, they depend upon the same kind of indexical demonstration that the geese use. All the members of one village lie defenselessly in their hammocks as guests while the members of the opposing village have the opportunity to attack them. If the ritual goes as planned, they do not really attack, but instead provide food to those in the hammocks. By establishing a situation of peace, the hammock ritual is indexical and performative like the ritual of the geese. But there are also cases in which the ritual situation leads to an attack on the guests. This possibility indicates that the ritual is much more complicated than a performative gesture. It actually consists of the three parts of a sacrificial action: the initial invitation to the feast that is the promise of renunciation, the hammock ritual, in which the promise is fulfilled or broken, and the ensuing feast to celebrate the new order. In those cases in which the hosts attack the guests, the promise of renunciation is broken, and the alliance, for which the feast would have served as the fulfillment, is dissolved.

If all goes well, the feast paves the way for a new ritual in the future in which the two villages switch places, and the previous guests invite the previous hosts to a new feast, and those who had played the potential attackers in the first feast now lie in the hammocks and allow the previous potential victims the opportunity to attack. If the potential attackers provide food and peace is still maintained, then the two villages can begin to deepen their relations. The food that the first village provided to the second village is now reciprocated by the second village at the new feast. The giving of food at the feast is thus not just a performative act of peace. It also inaugurates a whole process of feasting, whose character of constant reciprocation establishes a history and thus a public sphere within which every action is invested with a symbolic meaning. Every enactment of the ritual is more than a single performative gesture, but consists of the three-part process of promise, real sacrifice, and order. The entirety of the three-part sacrificial action inaugurates and anchors the other activities of exchanging food and dancing that establish and regulate relations between the two villages. The two villages establish thereby a foundation for the symbolic relations that define a shared public space.

The real possibility of a breakdown into aggression makes the feast process into a visible index of the opposing parties' peaceful intentions.

In that sense, the ritual is similar to that of the geese. The difference lies in the fact that the ritual is not just a performative act, but must initiate a set of ensuing symbolic relations, creating friends out of enemies based on a promise about future actions, something that would be impossible for the geese. Because it consists of promises that ground an accompanying set of future relations, the ritual can establish the peace that ushers in a whole set of subsequent relationships contingent upon this peace: sharing food, bartering, and possibly marriage can become possible over time between the two villages. The ritual does not function as a single indexical moment; rather it embeds the indexical ground into an entire set of symbolic relationships that all relate back to the ritual as the initial promise that founds the symbolic order.

As long as this symbolic order continues to function smoothly, the ritual can serve as the promise that reaffirms the entire order. But the symbolic character of the ritual means that, within human ritual, deception is also possible, and the believability of the ritual can be put into question. Consequently, Burkert notes: "In groups shaped by aggression, especially in the younger generation, forces that question the acceptance of tradition become active. Willfulness stands in the way of the impulse to imitate. Thus, along with its theatricality, human ritual must always have a strong underlying component of seriousness, and this means that time and again there is a regression from symbolism to reality" (*HN* 42). This possibility of an empty ritual performance dictates for Burkert the necessity of the sacrifice as that which guarantees the connection of the symbol to the reality, and indeed that may be one of the key functions of sacrifice. That is, the sacrifice is the one point in an entire cultural system in which the symbolic relations are finally put to the test of reality in order to guarantee the legitimacy of the entire symbolic structure that comprises the culture's traditions and self-understandings. While the structures of myth and the promises of ritual refer to each other in a set of symbolic relationships that are self-reinforcing, the whole system will stand or fall in those moments of crisis in which these promises of sacrifice must be fulfilled. At these crisis points, the real sacrifices that must be made are not just *indexical* in the sense of affirmations of the symbolic order but are *performative* as establishments of this order. Such a performance does not have to be provided for each individual sign, but must only be demonstrated at those moments of crisis in order to establish and maintain the legitimacy of the symbolic structure as a whole. While the real sacrifice may indeed function primarily as the act that performs the binding quality of the symbolic system, it is also important that the sacrifice itself functions within the symbolic system as the stabilizing point around which the other elements of the system are defined. Thus, the real sacrifice functions uniquely within a cultural system as the moment at which the symbolic and indexical functions of the sign are linked together in the performative act. In this way, the act of sacrifice is the fulfillment of the promise embedded in ritual sacrifice and the establishment of the system of order that is displayed in the accompanying narrative of sacrifice.

As we have seen from some of Burkert's examples, stories of sacrifice serve as symbolic representations of previous acts of violence, such as a victory in war. If this is the case, then the symbolic force of sacrifice would not be based on ever-new acts of violence but rather on the ability of the dramatic structure to establish a kind of aesthetic truth that is convincing enough to the audience to motivate future acts of sacrifice should the need arise. Here, we return to aesthetic structures such as the sublime, in which an experience of violence is attained even though no actual violence is carried out. Sacrifice begins as a three-part structure in which the specific terms of its promise, fateful decision, and restoration of symbolic order must become convincing for an audience. The audience must take a specific manifestation of sacrifice to be an accurate portrayal of its understanding of how its values are to be weighed against opposing forces.

While the stories and myths of sacrifice set up the parameters for symbolic order through an aesthetic process, these stories remain only stories until they establish a set of promises for future behavior. The key is the extent to which the invocation of violence creates a link to communal values through the experience of the sublime as an overcoming of violence for the sake of an overarching purpose. Although violence is the context for the situation of sacrifice, it is not the brute facticity of real violence that grounds the ritual, but the way in which this violence requires an act of sacrifice that would reaffirm the values embedded in the stories of sacrifice. The sublimity of the experience is a measure of the extent to which the presentation of sacrifice is able to evoke a commitment to the persons, creatures, objects, or ideals for whose sake the sacrifices are being performed.

CHAPTER FOUR

The Genealogy of Nazi Morality

Walter Burkert contends that the origins of Greek tragedy lie in sacrifice and that the tragedy is consequently in its essence a structuring of our human relationship to the fact of death.[1] This argument suggests that the key issue of sacrifice is not willful execution but the humanizing of death, and the opposite of sacrifice is not life, but mechanical death without ritual. Ritual animal sacrifice for instance seems to have been carried out in ancient Greece as part of the process of slaughtering animals for food. The sacrificed animal was eaten by the celebrants, and only a small portion of the flesh was burned as an offering to the gods.[2] As opposed to killing the animal mechanically and without remorse, the sacrificial ritual creates a human relationship to death that, according to Karl Meuli, is based on a "respect for life." Whatever one's understanding of the significance of the ritual (a totem ritual to the animal spirit to deal with the guilt of killing, a way to gain favor with the gods, or a commitment to the community), the choice of sacrifice or nonsacrifice does not lie in whether death will or will not take place, but in whether death is to be granted the significance of a ritual process or is to be regarded as a mere mechanical function, part of a process of consumption and symbolically insignificant. Nonsacrifice is not the avoidance of death, but routinized death, death that is carried out as a matter of course. There is something natural about death without sacrifice in the nonhuman realm—the death of an animal in the grip of a predator, for instance. But death without sacrifice in a human context becomes something very different, something which cannot be called animal because nonsacrificial death is the only possibility in the animal world. In the human world nonsacrificial death can only be understood in the opposition to death as sacrifice.

The Nazi use of sacrifice defined their relationship to death to the extent that one of their primary goals was to grant meaning to the otherwise senseless deaths of German soldiers during World War I. This process was not limited to a recovery of the past, but extended itself into a shaping of the future. At the Nazi tenth party congress in 1938, Rudolf Hess opened the ceremonies with a ritual commemorating those Nazis who died serving the nation, after which he added, "We have commemorated those who have sacrificed their lives for their political beliefs, beliefs which also animate us. Their sacrifice should be for us and for all who come after us a commitment to hold unwaveringly to the political beliefs for which they died."[3] In the course of this ritual the earlier deaths become a sacrifice that the Nazis mobilize as a "commitment" to support their political goals. The sacrifice is consequently neither a psychological scapegoating process nor an attempt to influence deities. Rather it functions as a symbolic act that links past death to a subsequent promise that both determines the status of the dead and the spiritual self-understanding of those who come after them. The Nazi understanding of sacrifice links the world of the living to the world of dead heroes by using their example as the model for future sacrifices to be made for the sake of the nation and the Nazi movement.[4] Their sacrificial rituals helped to forge a national community in support of their ongoing political project.

The understanding of sacrifice developed in these *Reichsparteitag* rituals has been linked to the killings carried out in concentration camps.[5] But although Hitler's rhetoric concerning the Jews emphasizes how their elimination would be a necessary and productive step in creating a new utopian social order,[6] the extermination of the Jews and others deemed non-German must be considered to be of a different order than the sacrifice of German soldiers. Contrary to the attempts to classify the extermination of the Jews as continuous with the rituals developed in the *Reichsparteitage* and an example of a "religious sacrifice,"[7] this designation must be reserved for the Nazi efforts to heroize fallen German soldiers.

Giorgio Agamben argues that the situation of those considered "non-Aryan" in Nazi society falls into a different category, that of the *homo sacer*, the sacred man, a concept from archaic Roman law that designates one who, having committed a certain crime, is unavailable for sacrifice and may be killed without any consequences for the killer. To the extent that he is able to explain the Nazi treatment of "non-Aryans" as a form of *homo sacer*, Agamben distinguishes sacrifice from nonsacrifice (*homo sacer*) in the Nazi cultural system. While sacrifice designates those German soldiers who died for the nation and became a model for future sacrifices for this same nation, *homo sacer* designates all those who are not available for such sacrifice.

In Agamben's interpretation, the category of sacredness arises out of the establishment of sovereignty, and the condition for the extermination of the Jews in Germany was not a cultural one but a political one having to do with the structure of the nation-state in the modern world. "If our hypothesis is correct, sacredness is instead the originary form of the inclusion of bare life in the juridical order, and the syntagm *homo sacer* names something like the originary 'political' relation, which is to say, bare life insofar as it operates in an inclusive exclusion as the referent of the sovereign decision."[8] In defining the *homo sacer* as primarily the result of a political relation, Agamben deemphasizes the cultural component in constructing Jews as *homines sacri* in Nazi society. Instead, Agamben borrows from Carl Schmitt's theory of sovereignty in order to argue that the designation of Jews as *homines sacri* was intimately connected to the state of exception that Schmitt's *Political Theology* sees as the core of sovereignty.[9] *"The sovereign sphere is the sphere in which it is permitted to kill without committing homicide and without celebrating a sacrifice, and sacred life—that is, life that may be killed but not sacrificed—is the life that has been captured in this sphere"* (HS 83). In explaining the status of the Jews in Nazi Germany as a consequence of the structure of sovereignty in the state of exception, Agamben defines the treatment of the Jews as a political problem rather than a cultural and ideological one.

Although Agamben provides an excellent critique of this politics of the body, he remains trapped within it to the extent that he sees it as a structural component of any form of sovereignty and political life in the modern world. The separation of cultural from political explanations leads Agamben to take the concentration camp to be a phenomenon associated not solely with the Nazis. Discounting the differences that culture makes for the political organization of a society, he argues that "today it is not the city but rather the camp that is the fundamental biopolitical paradigm of the West" (HS 181). In conflating totalitarian and liberal democratic systems, this approach obscures the cultural particularity of Nazi ideology and denies the possibility of defining the specific characteristics of a totalitarian system that is by no means inevitable or pervasive in the modern world. This failure to recognize any alternative to the totalitarian reduction of humanity to bare life stems from the lack of a cultural theory of the human, a failing that becomes evident in the inability to admit the legitimacy of any situation in which one person might have the power of life and death over another. For this absolute subjugation of the individual cannot itself be criticized, as this subjugation is what creates the parameters within which individual identity might develop—for example, as the result of an interaction between parents and children within an education process. Although this process represents on the one hand integration into a particular culture and its possibilities, it will also take the form of a subjugation of individuals in which sacrifice and education are the crucial defining structures. An alternative to Agamben's biopolitical perspective must approach sacrifice as part of a cultural marking of the human that takes human existence out of the biological realm and turns it into something that is in its essence culturally mediated.[10]

Whereas Yvonne Karow and Michael Ley subsume the extermination of the Jews under the category of sacrifice, Agamben's refusal to consider cultural explanations leads him to deny that the idea of *homo sacer* has any significant relationship to sacrifice. "In modernity, the principle of the sacredness of life is thus completely emancipated from sacrificial ideology, and in our culture the meaning of the term 'sacred' continues the semantic history of *homo sacer* and not that of sacrifice (and this is why the demystifications of sacrificial ideology so common today remain insufficient, even though they are correct)" (*HS* 113–14). In one sense, this separation of *homo sacer* from sacrifice makes sense when considering the Nazi model of sacrifice. The sacrifice of Germans for the nation on the one hand and the victimization of those considered non-German and thus deleterious to the nation on the other hand were carefully distinguished within Nazi culture. This differentiation made possible a type of "Nazi conscience" that Claudia Koonz describes as "a secular ethos that extended reciprocity only to members of the Aryan community, as defined by what racial scientists believed to be the most advanced biological knowledge of the day."[11] While the deaths of Germans serving the nation were endowed with deep meaning by the Nazis, as seen in Rudolf Hess's remarks at the 1938 party congress, Agamben argues that the second category of non-Germans were not sacrifices for the Nazis at all, but were treated like the *homo sacer*, incapable of being sacrificed but available to be killed without any consequences for the killer. While the first category of death comprised instances of sacrifice celebrated by the Nazis that defined the entire symbolic economy with which the Nazis mobilized the German people, for Agamben the second category of death was not meant to leave any type of symbolic trace.

Yet, this account, in which the elimination of the Jews was to be carried out as a matter of "hygiene" and in such a way that it was to have as little cultural and aesthetic significance as possible, does not explain the importance in Nazi rhetoric of *both* sacrifice for the nation and anti-Semitism. As crucial as it is to draw the distinction between sacrificial and nonsacrificial death when considering the significance of sacrifice for the Nazis, these two opposed forms of death are nevertheless linked. But because Agamben does not treat this distinction as a cultural one but rather as a "biopolitical" one in which the "Jewish body and German body" are distinguished from each other "as life unworthy of being lived

The Genealogy of Nazi Morality

and as full life" (*HS* 173), Agamben's discussion falls short of providing a full explanation of the aspects of the Nazi worldview that led to the Holocaust. The key distinction is not between unworthy life and full life, as the Nazis did not place the full life of the individual at the center of culture. Rather the opposition must be thought of as one between sacrifice and scapegoat, in which the former designates the individual who can be sacrificed and the latter designates the individual who refuses sacrifice or, in the case of Jews, was considered by the Nazis to be biologically incapable of sacrifice. It is only from this standpoint of sacrifice that the *homo sacer* makes sense in Nazi ideology, not as part of an overall biopolitical paradigm, but within a cultural construction of German identity. Even as the official Nazi rituals concentrate on the sacrifice of German soldiers as the paradigmatic model for a German subjectivity consecrated to the national community, this integration of the individual into the nation is linked to a designation of Jews as nonhuman based on their supposed unsuitability for sacrifice. The Nazis linked their demand that all Germans participate in the total mobilization for the nation to the status of all those individuals who cannot be successfully integrated into the national community and pose a potential threat to this community.

Such individuals who could not participate in sacrifice fell into two groups. First, there were political enemies such as Communists, who were seen to adhere to an alternative set of ideals and would therefore presumably refuse to participate in any sacrifices for the nation. These political enemies were persecuted and imprisoned for the same reasons, though in a much more brutal way, as alleged political enemies in other countries, such as in the U.S. treatment of Japanese-Americans during World War II and of Communists after the war. The basis for the persecution in all these cases was a perception of unacceptable difference in cultural or political identity and in values that would lead to an unwillingness to make the kinds of sacrifices that would demonstrate a commitment to the nation.

What made the Nazis different was their designation of a second group of people who were not just culturally or ideologically prevented from sacrificing for the German nation but were biologically incapable of any sacrifice at all. Although the Nazis drew on a longer tradition of anti-Jewish sentiment, the specific Nazi form of anti-Semitism emphasized the biological incapacity of Jews to participate in German national identity. Sacrifice and anti-Semitism are linked in Nazi ideology, not through the idea that Jews must be sacrificed, but in the conviction that Jews are incapable of sacrifice.

In a 1933 speech outlining the Nazi approach to art, Hitler moves from a typical affirmation of sacrifice to anti-Semitism by a series of steps that leads to the idea of a Jewish incapacity for sacrifice. He begins with a standard idealist approach: "If the National Socialist mission is to attain its inner justification, then it must lift the German out of the depths of an exclusively materialist view of life and into the heights of a dignified representation of that which we understand to be the concept of the 'human.'"[12] Hitler's description of sacrifice draws on views that are common to virtually all German affirmations of the importance of sacrifice, from Kant and Hegel to Nietzsche and Heidegger, in which materialism is rejected in favor of an orientation toward ideals. Indeed, the appeal to Germans to rise beyond a focus on materialist interests and toward a more dignified idealism cannot be distinguished from similar statements by politicians that would include, for instance, John F. Kennedy's entreaty in his 1961 inaugural address: "Ask not what your country can do for you—ask what you can do for your country." The basic attitude that condemns materialism in order to argue for a sacrifice of material goods for the sake of ideological or spiritual goals is common to virtually all political ideologies and religions, and Hitler's use of this rhetoric builds upon both Christian and nationalist discourses. In emphasizing self-sacrifice and self-denial, all these discourses appeal to people to forgo self-interested motivations in order to affirm some set of ideals. Because such praise of self-denial cannot be criticized in itself and is in fact praiseworthy, Hitler can use his call for self-denial to establish the ethical force of his argument.

The key move in Hitler's speech that distinguishes the Nazi approach to sacrifice is the rejection of the idea that materialism and idealism are two impulses that exist within every human. Here, he begins by pushing his ideological point in a biological direction by linking it to a distinction between humans and animals. "For if the human is really to be categorized as a higher form of life, then the human must separate himself from the animal. If the human were to remain in his strivings within the limits of his primitive needs, then he would never have lifted himself beyond the sphere of the merely animal" (AH 66). In linking a certain stance with "the sphere of the merely animal," Hitler introduces the biological terminology that then establishes his racist discourse. Once he establishes the distinction between human and animal, he goes on to assert that certain individuals or even groups will always remain within a materialist attitude, while others are chosen by providence to uphold idealist goals:

> The human must also obey here the commandment that providence has laid upon him. For the fact that a part of humankind does actually ful-

fill their life tasks through the satisfaction of the lower biological needs is just as natural for these peoples as it would be unnatural for those races that have been chosen by providence for something higher to, then, against the admonishing voice of their conscience and the burning compulsion of their essence, regress to this most primitive view of life or even, what would amount to the same thing, to allow themselves to be defiled to such a state. (AH 66)

This division of human races into materialist and idealist groups sets up the basis for an imperialism that sees its mission as a world-historical one of spreading an idealist attitude to the rest of the world.

Additionally, however, Hitler affirms that this division between materialists and idealists exists within Germany as well. "Since nature in such a case now establishes a living contradiction, this antagonism has entered into those peoples in which two essentially divergent racial components sought to exist side by side" (AH 66). This discrimination between the materialist and idealist racial groups within a people then leads to the question of the relationship between the two groups, and the answer to this question no longer involves the limitation of individual aspirations that is found in the traditional notion of sacrifice. Instead, Hitler's splitting of the people into the noble and the base segments of the population leads to a bifurcation in the structure of sacrifice. "In the same way, however, that the perpetuation of every human society requires that certain principles be represented without regard for whether all individuals declare themselves to be in agreement with them, the cultural image of a people must also be formed *in accordance with its finest elements* and, thanks to their breeding, the sole natural-born carriers of the culture" (AH 66). On the one hand, he still insists on the subordination of the individual to certain principles. On the other hand, his distinction between two racial groups means that only one group has the capacity to participate in the sacrifice of the individual for the group. The other group, which is made up of those who do not just refuse to sacrifice but are existentially incapable of making such sacrifices, is condemned to an inferior status akin to an animal existence. So while Hitler establishes a traditional notion of sacrifice understood as the idealistic subordination of individual, material interests to spiritual and ideological goals, he also, through his racist distinctions, divides humanity into one group of noble, idealist beings whose lives are built around sacrifice for higher ideals and another group of animal-like, materialist beings who are incapable of sacrifice and whose materialism poses an implicit threat to the nation's idealist attitude.

Hitler's separation of German society into Germans and Jews involved both the construction of a notion of sacrifice in which Germans were expected to subordinate individual, material concerns to nationalist ideals and the designation of Jews as those who are biologically unable to participate in these sacrifices. This linking of the Nazi notion of sacrifice to this division within German society indicates that Nazi anti-Semitism was not a purely political dynamic, nor a product of the construction of sovereignty itself, but was the result of a particular cultural construction of both German sacrifice and a Jewish incapacity to participate in this sacrifice.

This distinction corresponds to the separation between sacrifice and scapegoat noted in the previous chapter, in which the former becomes the basis for the establishment of cultural ideals and the latter designates those who are unwilling or unable to make such sacrifices. But while the typical punishment for the scapegoat is banishment, the Nazis rejected this punishment because they saw the Jews as, on the one hand, biologically incapable of sacrifice and, on the other hand, so indistinguishable from "sacrificeable" Germans that the threat they posed as enemies would be a constant, hidden danger.

State versus Family Households as Competing Contexts for Sacrifice

Hitler's understanding of the relationship between sacrifice and enemy was not an anomaly in his time and place, but was in fact part of a broader understanding of sacrifice that had become established in German culture. On the one hand, sacrifice was treated as a necessary measure for defending the integrity and survival of the German nation. Even upon Germany's invasion of Poland, some commentators attempted to treat the war and its sacrifices as part of a defensive measure, for example in the opening to the editorial of a southern German newspaper: "For the last week the law of self-defense has dominated our national life. The private sphere of every German has been integrated into its inexorability. And it is the deep, calming felicity of our national hour of trial that the German people has merged into a voluntary community of readiness, which, in solemn, resolute greatness, makes the sacrifices that the fate of its fatherland demands of it."[13] The call to sacrifice for the nation both places national identity before "personal" ties and justifies sacrifices based on the need to defend the national community against outside enemies. Although the insistence on the defensive character of the war was disingenuous, the need to paint the war as a defensive one is also an implicit acknowledgement of the limits of this understanding of sacrifice. Sacrifice for the nation that is posed as the subordination of the individual to national identity does not immediately create a justification for imperialist aggression. One way to justify the war was to emphasize its defensive character. But Hitler's construction of the enemy also contains the legitimation for aggression to the extent that the Germans understand their expansion as part of a broader, universalist project.

Here, the Nazis were not alone in seeing a link between sacrifice for the nation and an imperialist project. In a meditation on sacrifice written in support of the Nazis, the Protestant writer and journalist Tim Klein describes his understanding of sacrifice by describing examples such as parents sacrificing for their children, workers sacrificing for their colleagues, and soldiers sacrificing for the nation. He then goes on to describe the connection between those who are willing to make such sacrifices and those who are not:

> It fills us with a confidence in the unquenchable springs that will always continue to break forth from the depths of the people into the light that such an unwavering belief and such selflessly performed sacrifices were possible. That is it. For it is always there where the limits of the human and of the people are extended that both are revealed in their true greatness. There are those half-hearted ones who remain content with their own bare being and existence. They do not want the limits of the human, they do not want to cast their stone toward the farthest possible goal, they lie buried in their own egos and imagine that they live, they scoff at those that desire and reach beyond themselves, they allow themselves without shame to be outdone by animals. In this way they separate themselves from the people, from humanity.[14]

This reflection on the importance of sacrifice and the simultaneous condemnation of those who refuse to sacrifice provides an example of the link between the German soldier and the Jew as the two complementary poles constructed during the Nazi period. Klein points out the selfishness of all those who are not willing to be integrated into a system of sacrifice and declares that this unwillingness to sacrifice excludes them from both the nation and humanity itself. This understanding of the relation between sacrifice and nonsacrifice was not limited to the Nazis, but was a current idea that the Nazis adopted as their own. Yet, Klein himself was forbidden by the Nazis from publishing on account of his outspoken Protestant stance,[15] indicating that the specific Nazi appropriation of the notion of sacrifice excluded alternative institutional contexts for sacrifice.

Not only Klein's text, but also the Nazi opposition to it based on its Protestant perspective, provides us with the basis for a cultural understanding of Nazi sacrifice that distinguishes it from other models of sacrifice. The original issue out of which the category of *homo sacer* arises is not a purely political dynamic concerning sovereignty, as Agamben suggests, but a cultural one that defines the parameters of sacrifice. The decision to define the enemy as outside culture and humanity is not part of a particular political dynamic but a cultural one. On the one hand, rationalist culture rejects tradition as a basis of authority and seeks seemingly more objective and universal legitimations, such as biological and racial distinctions, for their principles. On the other hand, such a culture sees only its own tradition as a humanizing one and regards other traditions as barbaric or even nonhuman. The key issue is the status within the political order of alternative traditions with their own models of sacrifice. Once the nation sees itself as the sole definer of culture that replaces all other traditions, it can consider all local traditions within it as well as all external traditions outside of it as backward or inhuman. The specifically Nazi move was not the affirmation of sacrifice, but the argument that some peoples exist entirely outside a conception of sacrifice, that is, that such a thing as a bare life of the human could even exist.

In order to understand the importance of such suppressions of alternative traditions, it will be useful to emphasize a distinction that Agamben fails to make between a household subjugation and a state subjugation of the individual. In describing the origins of the idea of bare life as a power of life and death, Agamben describes the Roman law granting the father the power to kill his son. "This power is absolute and is understood to be neither the sanction of a crime nor the expression of the more general power that lies within the competence of the *pater* insofar as he is the head of the *domus:* this power follows immediately and solely from the father-son relation (in the instant in which the father recognizes the son in raising him from the ground, he acquires the power of life and death over him)" (*HS* 87–88). Agamben argues that this power of the father over the son is parallel to the power of the sovereign over the people, and in making this parallel he designates all sovereignty as implicated in the reduction of human life to bare biological existence. "And when we read in a late source that in having his sons put to death, Brutus 'had adopted the Roman people in their place,' it is the same power of death that is now transferred, through the image of adoption, to the entire people. The hagiographic epithet 'father of the people,' which is reserved in every age to the leaders invested with sovereign authority, thus once again acquires its originary, sinister meaning" (*HS* 88–89). In arguing here that the essence of sovereignty is the power of death over the subjects in the same way as the father has the power of death over the son, Agamben neglects the particular character of the ideal that is supposed to be affirmed through the sacrifice, both in the father's sacrifice of the son and in the sovereign's sacrifice of the subject.

The fact that this power of life and death originates in the father-son relationship before it is transferred later to the sovereign means that this power is not originally a power over life as such but a recognition that there is no bare life as such. Human life only exists as a specific culturally formed life into which a son is raised and educated by the father. This raising of the son is not the creation of a bare life but always the forming of a person in a specific cultural tradition that comes from the parents. As a consequence, there is no son without the father, not just in a biological sense, but in a subject-constituting sense. The power of life and death is originally not a political power but a culturally mediated relationship.

To the extent that the sovereign might have the same consciousness-constituting power over her or his subjects that the father has over the son, the parallel between household sovereignty and state sovereignty indicates a cultural aspect of sovereignty that goes beyond pure violence. Once the power over life and death (*vitae necisque potestas*) is transferred to the sovereign, there arises the question of what happens to this cultural aspect. It may be argued that this state power is not an expression of the responsibility of the father for the formed life of the son but only of the violence of the sovereign and that there can be no parallel between the father and the sovereign because of this difference. Agamben provides an example of how strongly the difference was felt in ancient Rome when citing the case of the son who "demands that his father," rather than an executioner, "be the one to put him to death" (*HS* 89–90). Such a demand can only make sense if the condemned son sees the father rather than the state to be the legitimate executioner. But this preference for the father indicates the son's embracing of the authority of the father and, by extension, the acceptance of the father's forming influence. Because Agamben denies the reality of this cultural forming and focuses only on the power over the body that both paternal and state violence suggest, he precludes a discussion of the cultural constitution of the subject and forecloses all possibility of finding anything to oppose the violence of the state. "Like the concepts of sex and sexuality, the concept of the 'body' too is always already caught in a deployment of power. The 'body' is always already a biopolitical body and bare life, and nothing in it or the economy of its pleasure seems to allow us to find solid ground on which to oppose the demands of sovereign power" (*HS* 187). If, contrary to Agamben, the body is from its origin not bare life but always a cultured life, the reduction to bare life can only be accomplished once the individual is liberated from the original cultural subjugation that brought the individual into being as a human. Yet, this stripping away of a preexisting tradition cannot create a bare life either; rather it can only function to reconfigure the person within a new organization. A critique of bare life can only begin once it is recognized that any understanding of the human beyond bare existence must begin with the subjugation of the individual to a particular cultural tradition through the education process. It is the character of this tradition that then becomes the point of contention.

Education as Preparation for Sacrifice

The difficult truth here is that the German Enlightenment tradition of thinking about education provided the Nazis with the basic attitudes that allowed them to consider certain segments of humanity to be less valuable than others, even to the point of declaring them "inhuman." This idea of a link between the German idea of *Bildung* (education or cultural formation) and Nazi education policies runs against the basic thesis of Hannah Arendt's *The Origins of Totalitarianism*: "Totalitarian movements are mass organizations of atomized, isolated individuals. Compared with all other parties and movements, their most conspicuous external characteristic is their demand for total, unrestricted, unconditional, and unalterable loyalty of the individual member. . . . Such loyalty can be expected only from the completely isolated human being who, without any other social ties to family, friends, comrades, or even mere acquaintances, derives his sense of having a place in the world only from his belonging to a movement, his membership in the party."[16] Identifying as the key characteristic of totalitarianism a psychological structure that links the individual directly to the party, Arendt seeks to explain the historical development that led up to this isolation of individuals. In her account, the nation-state was the pinnacle of a European development toward a social system based on equality of rights and a world order based on a peacefully coexisting "family of nations." While the nation-state allowed both the self-determination of peoples and a natural limitation on the growth of a polity, its decline created the conditions for the rise of totalitarianism (*OT* 161). She traces the downfall of the nation-state to the growth of both an antinationalist imperialism and a "tribal" form of nationalism that together broke down the structures of the nation-state through their expansionist tendencies and their racist ideologies. "The tribalism of the pan-movements with its concept of the 'divine origin' of one people owed part of its great appeal to its contempt for liberal individualism, the ideal of mankind and the dignity of man" (*OT* 235). Arendt tries to set up an opposition between tribal nationalism and a nation-state system in which liberal individualism, the ideal of mankind, and the dignity of man become those ideologies that control and temper nationalism, and make it a civilizing force in contrast to tribal nationalism.

One of the main difficulties of this approach is that, as Ernest Gellner has argued, the development of the idea of the sovereign individual was also one of the key prerequisites for the rise of nationalism itself.[17] Arendt points this out herself in recognizing that "man had hardly appeared as a completely emancipated, completely isolated being who carried his dignity within himself without reference to some larger encompassing order, when he disappeared again into a member of a people. . . . The whole question of human rights, therefore, was quickly and inextricably blended with the question of national emancipation; only the emancipated sovereignty of the people, of one's own people, seemed to be able to insure them" (*OT* 291).

The rise of nationalism and the defense of individual rights are not only inseparable but are two faces of a single development. As such, individual rights only make sense within a nation that guarantees these rights as stemming from a particular heritage. Citing Edmund Burke, Arendt concedes that the Rights of Man (*les droits de l'homme*) do not make sense as a concept and must be replaced with something like the Rights of an Englishman (*OT* 299). Similarly, a discussion of the particular structure of the individual within Nazism cannot make any appeal to a concept of universal human rights or a liberal individual but must consider the particular development of the individual and its structure within the German tradition. Unlike the French tradition, in which the declaration of the Rights of Man was central to the understanding of the role of the individual in society, or the U.S. tradition, in which nationalism is inextricably linked with the Declaration of Independence and the U.S. Constitution, in Germany the key to both individual and nation has been the concept of culture: *Bildung*.

What are the links between *Bildung* and totalitarianism? First, as Georg Bollenbeck has shown, Nazi cultural policies succeeded by exploiting prejudices of the *Bildungsbürgertum* about the moral imperative of culture embedded in the idea of *Bildung* in order to condemn avant-garde culture as a degenerate "cultural bolshevism."[18] There was an implicit agreement between the Nazis and the *Bildungsbürgertum* in their evaluations of the cultural tradition, and this basic agreement was founded on a notion of culture that links individual development with national unity. Working within this framework, the *Bildungsbürgertum* did not have the means to resist the rise of the Nazis based on any type of cultural argument.[19] Further, the moral aspect of *Bildung* in turn assisted in the Nazi reorganization of subjectivity that takes it out of the orbit of family and religious bonds in order to integrate subjects into National Socialist structures of sacrifice. The consecration of the subject to the nation in death has its corollary in another consecration to the nation in life, in the field of education.

Sacrifice and education are linked together by the fact that they both consecrate the individual to certain external goals. While sacrifice accomplishes this in death, education does this in life, and a certain structure of sacrifice will imply a corresponding form of education that supports it. Because the consecration of the subject in sacrifice presumes a particular disciplining of the subject that forms it into the particular cultural path leading to the sacrifice, Nazi education policy demonstrates the same structures as the Nazi rhetoric of sacrifice. Just as the Nazi vision of sacrifice bifurcates into the two paths of sacrifice of the individual and the elimination of those who cannot be sacrificed, Hitler's vision of education has two complementary tasks. As Karl Christoph Lingelbach describes, "The political-pedagogical reflections are based on the determination of 'the first task of the state, to increase precisely the racially most valuable core of the people and its fertility.' Hitler seeks to achieve this in two ways. While the 'racial hygiene' measures are designed to exclude from the body of the people all 'foreign races' and 'all those who are visibly sick and genetically impaired,' education has the positive task of a strengthened state-sponsored 'care' for the children of healthy parents."[20]

While Hitler's hygienic goal defines an enemy to be eradicated, the positive form of education is a preparation for sacrifice, a preparation of youth for their future consecration "in the service of the general good."[21] In order to create the possibility of sacrifice for the sake of the nation, "the entire forming and educating task of the peoples' state must find its fulfillment in the fact that it burns both instinctively and rationally a race consciousness and a race feeling into the heart and mind of the youth that is entrusted to it."[22] Hitler's goal is to establish a cultural forming of the people in the direction of a notion of national sacrifice that defines the nation racially and therefore includes a specific racial designation of the enemy.

This separation of humanity into superior and inferior segments was not a Nazi innovation. It was already a part of the discourse of development and education in Germany from the early nineteenth century. This continuity becomes apparent when we consider again the writings of

Alfred Baeumler, who, as an extension of his work on sacrifice and ritual, became one of the primary leaders of the effort to build a Nazi pedagogical practice, publishing extensively about pedagogical issues during the Nazi period all the way through 1943. He was one of the key functionaries in effecting the transformation of German education into a specifically National Socialist institution.[23]

Baeumler's cultural policies developed as a system for reconfiguring the subject in terms of the Nazi movement. As he understood it, in order to fulfill the primary task of instilling a race consciousness into the hearts and minds of German youth, the education system must not just create a sacrificial consciousness but replace previously existing notions of sacrifice with the Nazi one. His main concern during this period was to develop a form of education that would dissolve the community and family notions of sacrifice and replace them with race- and nation-based understandings.[24] As a consequence, though much of his work suggests that he supports myth and community as the foundations of society, his specific recommendations, included in essays published in the 1930s and 1940s, tended to increase the power of the Nazis to intervene in and manage community life. The primary effect of Nazi education policy was not to support myth and tradition as such but to replace the community development of culture with a Nazi-imposed version.

Baeumler's pedagogical project was linked to the humanistic attempt in nineteenth and early twentieth-century German culture, summed up in the concept of *Bildung*, to develop the individual as the basis and fundamental unit of cultural life. Baeumler's embracing of the idea of *Bildung* was not an example of a Nazi distortion. Rather, his use of the term built upon the key defining features of the idea in a way that demonstrates the extent to which the Nazi view of culture, at least in Baeumler's understanding, was an outgrowth rather than a repudiation of the idea of *Bildung*. Embedded in both the ideal of *Bildung* and Baeumler's mobilization of it was the project of detaching the individual from a family and community context in order to then fit that individual into a national project. In this sense, Baeumler's work parallels the attempt to transfer the idea of *vitae necisque potestas* from a household into a state context in a convincing way. The tie between the eighteenth- and nineteenth-century conception of *Bildung* and Baeumler's is significant because it is summed up in the trajectory of Baeumler's work from the individualist position in his 1923 Kant book to the nationalist views of his work of the 1930s and 1940s.

The ease with which Baeumler was able to appropriate the term *Bildung* and give it a Nazi interpretation stems from the fact that from the beginning of its modern usage, the concept of *Bildung* was linked to the interests of the nation. The concept developed in the eighteenth century as a term that accompanied enlightenment and was regarded by some as virtually synonymous with it: "Education [Bildung] breaks down into culture and enlightenment" ("Bildung zerfällt in Kultur und Aufklärung").[25] In the course of its use, however, *Bildung* began to be distinguished from the alternative word for education, *Erziehung,* based on three primary characteristics. First, in contrast to *Erziehung,* which referred to the acquisition of a fixed set of practices, *Bildung* emphasized the free development of the individual. Second, the self-development of the individual, once detached from the specific rituals and practices of a specific group, becomes a process that is linked to the development of humanity and the human race as a whole, Moses Mendelssohn writing for instance of *Menschenaufklärung* (human enlightenment) as opposed to *Bürgeraufklärung* (citizen enlightenment).[26] Finally, though differences remained concerning the precise role of society in education, the focus on individual development on the one hand and the development of humanity on the other led to the concept of *Bildung* becoming integrated into a form of national education.[27]

While Mendelssohn understands *Bildung* primarily as "the education of a nation,"[28] it was Johann Gottlieb Fichte who developed the idea of *Bildung* into the form that was most easily applied by the Nazis. The linking of *Bildung* with *Nationalerziehung* (national education) lies at the core of Fichte's conception of education: "By means of the new education we want to mold the Germans into a corporate body, which shall be stimulated and animated in all its individual members by a common interest."[29] Education is crucial for the project of national unity because such unity must be embraced enthusiastically and thus can only be properly established with a form of education that, instead of consisting of rote learning, seeks to "to stimulate directly the spontaneous activity of the pupil" (JF 21). This spontaneous activity will, according to Fichte, naturally develop according to a fixed set of laws and within a new national community. "Under the new system of education the pupils, although separated from the adult community, will nevertheless undoubtedly live together among themselves, and so form a separate and self-contained community with its organization precisely defined, based on the nature of things and demanded throughout by reason" (JF 28).

Although he emphasizes the free activity of the individual as crucial for a strong affective link between individual and nation, he maintains, first, that this education must detach the individual from prior social distinctions in order to form a new national community and, second, that the free activity will inevitably lead to a uniform set of rules. "This creative mental activity which is to be developed in the pupil is undoubtedly an activity according to rules, which become known to the active pupil until he sees from his own direct experience that they alone are possible—that is, this activity produces knowledge, and that, too, of general and infallible laws" (JF 21). The contradiction between free activity and a single set of rules is resolved in Fichte's conception by the idea that these rules are the manifestation of general and infallible laws toward which all spontaneous activity must naturally develop, and this underlying belief forms the link between *Bildung* and nationalism that Baeumler would later develop.

Finally, though Fichte does not engage in the type of racial stereotypes used by the Nazis, his grounding of culture in language nevertheless maintains a distinction between the German language and the Romance languages in which he holds that only German maintains the proper relationship between concrete meanings and abstract concepts that allows for proper reflection and understanding.

> Within the range of German speech such a wrapping-up in incomprehensibility and darkness arises either from clumsiness or evil design; it is to be avoided and the means always ready to hand is to translate into right and true German. But in the neo-Latin languages this incomprehensibility is of their very nature and origin, and there is no means of avoiding it, for they do not possess any living language by which they might examine the dead one; indeed, when one looks at the matter closely, they are entirely without a mother tongue. (JF 58)

In claiming an objective advantage of German over other languages for enhancing abstract thinking, Fichte links his own German nationalism with an interest in the progress of humanity in general that would then later become important for the Nazi self-understanding as representatives of a world-historical mission.

Baeumler had a keen sense for Fichte's linking of universalist notions with the development of German national consciousness. Although Hans Sluga has argued that Baeumler was opposed to the idealist tradition, and particularly Fichte's version of it,[30] an address Baeumler published in 1942 demonstrates that he feels a particular affinity to Fichte's linking of a universalist philosophical project with German nationalism. Baeumler writes approvingly of German intellectual history as a movement in which "theology has been displaced by philosophy," with Fichte playing the role of a philosophical "preacher of the German nation."[31] The key to this rise of the nation as the basis for what Koonz describes as a "secular ethnic faith" is, however, the idea of the free individual.[32] As Baeumler emphasizes throughout his Fichte address, "The German thinker cannot speak of law and order without speaking of the free personality" (*BG* 193). This insistence on individual freedom of personality becomes the basis for Baeumler of both a religiously held nationalism and a genius aesthetic that forms the basis of his theory of values. "The idealistic doctrine of freedom is inseparably linked to the doctrine of the primacy of the will before cognition, that is, with voluntarism. We are not here in order to piously honor a mysteriously revealed 'word,' but rather in order to launch ourselves actively and formatively into the world" (*BG* 189).

Baeumler's use of Fichte is not an aberration, but fits well into Fichte's schema of an individualism that is detached from traditional bonds. Although Baeumler's invocation of voluntarism seems to imply a total detachment of the individual from all outside limitations, this isolation of the individual is, in fact, just the first step, allowing the individual's subsequent integration into a unified humanity of such individuals and a concomitant practical recruitment for a national project. The connection between humanity and nationalism was obviously determined by the German political situation of 1808, when Fichte was writing in the midst of the Napoleonic Wars, but nevertheless remains a theme in Baeumler's work when he writes of the *"unity of race and personality"* (*BG* 188; emphasis in original). In the Nazi biological perspective, race superiority becomes the new version of the idea of humanity because both indicate a hierarchy of humans in which the human is to be distinguished from the inhuman. At the same time, Baeumler links race with personality in order to emphasize that the superiority of the German race is linked to the free development of the individual into a German national collective. For both Fichte and Baeumler, then, the idea of universal humanity is inseparable from a universalizing nationalism.

Fichte's linking of individual freedom to national identity very clearly fits with Baeumler's views on the subject, suggesting deep continuities between the latter's variation of National Socialist cultural policy and a longer German tradition of *Bildung*. A similar connection between Baeumler's and Wilhelm von Humboldt's ideas on education may seem to be somewhat counterintuitive because Humboldt adamantly defended the freedom of individual inquiry against intervention by the state.[33] Yet Fichte's linking of individual development to national education is actually not far removed from Humboldt's defense of individual development against an immediate instrumentalization by the state. Because of his insistence on the freedom of the individual, Humboldt's conception also depends on the detachment of the individual from traditional hierarchies and its integration within the nation, even though he emphasizes the limits of the state. He writes, for instance, "that this connection of the individual with his nation lies right at the centre from whence the total mental power determines all thinking, feeling and willing."[34] The individual and the nation are thus inextricably linked in Humboldt's notion of cultural formation.

Yet, this resemblance does not necessarily demonstrate a real link between *Bildung* and totalitarianism because Arendt may be correct in arguing that the Nazis took a basically healthy nationalism and perverted it into a race-oriented tribal nationalism. She distinguishes the two by locating the roots of tribal nationalism in a romantic concept of the individual that emphasizes the individual personality. "For this peculiar behavior, romanticism provided the most excellent pretext in its unlimited idolization of the 'personality' of the individual, whose very arbitrariness became the proof of genius. Whatever served the so-called productivity of the individual, namely, the entirely arbitrary game of his 'ideas,' could be made the center of a whole outlook on life and world" (*OT* 168). Arendt criticizes the focus on the productivity of the individual as a romantic notion that became complicit in the rise of race thinking because innate personality became the new mode of differentiation that would replace the rights and qualities of birth that characterized the aristocracy (*OT* 168). But whereas she claims that this idea is confined to romantics such as Clemens Brentano, it is actually also common to Humboldt's more liberal notion of the idiosyncratic development of the individual through education. Although Humboldt is credited for developing some of the basic tenets of a liberal notion of the limits of the state and a corresponding understanding of *Bildung* that emphasizes the freedom of the individual, it is in fact precisely these ideas that link him to the romantic notion. Humboldt's perspective is linked to the romantic view by a common focus on the individual as a free entity, loosened from traditional bonds and free to respond to inner affinities and embark on an individual development.

In his programmatic elaboration of the idea of *Bildung* in *The Limits of State Action,* Humboldt writes: "The true end of Man, or that which is prescribed by the eternal and immutable dictates of reason, and not suggested by vague and transient desires, is the highest and most harmonious development of his powers to a complete and consistent whole. Freedom is the first and indispensable condition which the possibility of such a development presupposes; there is besides another essential—intimately connected with freedom, it is true—a variety of situations."[35] Humboldt considers the true purpose of man, dictated by eternally unchanging reason, to be the forming (*Bildung*) of his powers into a unified whole. This vision of *Bildung* emphasizes individual development in which freedom and diversity are both essential.

While Arendt makes a distinction between a romantic idea of the individual in which "the 'innate personality' was given by birth" and an alternative notion, followed by Humboldt, in which language is the basis of particularity,[36] this is in fact not the crucial distinction in determining a tie to a "tribal nationalism" (*OT* 169). The key idea that creates the parameters for race-thinking is not that nationality is established by birth but that the free development of the individual, released from a specific role and place in society in order to be able to experience a variety of situations, should be the goal of mankind. This idea first detaches the individual from other social institutions such as family or church in order to emphasize the link between individual and nation. For the key characteristic of the idea of nation is its basis in natural affinities and not on any traditional bonds or fixed roles. The affinities between individual and nation are the content of *Bildung* that creates the specificity of the individual and the corresponding link to the particularity of the nation:

> To penetrate fruitfully and powerfully, therefore, into the general course of cultivation, the issue for a nation is not merely one of success in particular scientific endeavours, but primarily of the total exertion in that which constitutes the centre of man's nature, which finds its clearest and completest expression in philosophy, poetry and art, and which streams out from thence over the entire mode of thought and disposition of the people. In virtue of the connection here in view, between the individual and the mass surrounding him, every significant activity of the former belongs, albeit mediately only, and in some degree, to the latter as well. But the existence of languages proves that there are also mental creations which in no way whatever pass out from a single individual to the remainder, but can only emanate from the simultaneous self-activity of all. In languages, therefore, since they always have a national form, *nations*, as such, are truly and immediately creative.[37]

Language becomes the primary example of a natural affinity between the "simultaneous self-activity" of all individuals and the unity of the entire nation. Instead of gaining particularity from a specific position and role assigned within a feudal order, the individual for Humboldt attains the specific status as individual through free development, and the nation attains both unity and a particular character through the collective activity of the individuals within it.

The Genealogy of Nazi Morality

This conception is linked to a tribal nationalism in two ways. First, because the measure of the specificity of a nation does not lie in a fixed set of social relationships but rather in the creative growth of cultural achievements, the corresponding social order is inherently unstable and built to expand. Rather than remaining within the bounds of the nation-state, Humboldt's nation sets up what Arendt describes as the tribal nationalist pan-German project by seeking the freedom to develop as it pleases and to unite individuals through their language. Second, the specificity of the nation as created through language, although not racist in character, fulfills the same function as the racial understanding of nation, namely to create sharp demarcations between nations in such a way that, as Arendt puts it, "peoples are transformed into animal species so that a Russian appears as different from a German as a wolf is from a fox" (*OT* 234). Just as Fichte assumes that differences between languages lead to varied capacities for conceptual thinking, Humboldt not only demonstrates a separation of human nations from each other in his comparison of separate languages but also presupposes a hierarchy of languages and a progress from one language to another. The key characteristic of Humboldt's notion of progress in language is that, in contrast to Rousseau's idea of progress—in which each culture is placed on a single path of progress and the differences of cultures are merely reflections of their different positions on the same ladder of development—Humboldt affirms both the idea of progress and the notion of creative genius that dictates the incompatibility of one language with another:

> We cannot, unless the facts imperatively demand it, presuppose a *gradual progress*, since every significant enhancement appertains, rather, to a peculiar creative force. An example may be drawn from the structure of the Chinese and Sanscrit languages. One might certainly suppose here a gradual progression from the one to the other. But if we truly feel the nature of language as such, and of these two in particular, if we reach the point of fusion between thought and sound in both, we discover there the outgoing creative principle of their differing organization. At that stage, abandoning the possibility of a gradual development of one from the other, we shall accord to each its own basis in the spirit of the race, and only within the general trend of linguistic evolution, and thus ideally only, will regard them as stages in a successful construction of language. By neglecting the careful separation here proposed of the calculable stepwise progress and the unpredictable, immediately creative advance of human mental power, we banish outright from world-history the effect of *genius*, which is no less displayed at particular moments in peoples than it is in individuals.[38]

While he maintains that languages stand in a hierarchy in which, for example, Chinese is at an earlier stage than Sanskrit, he rejects the idea of a gradual progress from one to the other because each language has "its own basis in the spirit of the race." The different languages still describe a "general trend of linguistic evolution," but do so only ideally. There is no bridge from one language to another, and each existing language is in fact stuck in its place in the hierarchy. Movement toward the more advanced stages can only be accomplished by abandoning one language for another one in a superior position in the hierarchy, meaning that the Chinese, for instance, will always remain on an inferior level. Finally, the role of the creative genius in both the individual and the nation suggests that there is indeed some kind of inner quality that motivates the hierarchy of both individuals and nations.

With this understanding of language and nation, Humboldt arrives at a theory of cultural difference that fits well with the most extreme forms of tribal nationalism that Arendt describes. Not only do the nations present different species of humanity based on linguistic diversity, these differences between nations also reflect a hierarchy of nations in a movement toward perfection. Moreover, any possibility of cultural advance for a more backward nation cannot occur as a result of its own progress but can only come about through the replacement of its culture by a more advanced one.

Arendt draws a distinction between a healthy nationalism of the nation-state with defined borders and respect for other peoples on the one hand and a tribal nationalism that is both race-oriented and expansionist on the other hand. She uses the distinction, first, in order to paint the German development of nationalism as an anomalous one that was conditioned by its specific circumstance of lacking a nation-state and, second, to argue that totalitarianism, by embracing a tribal nationalism, which for Arendt is a perversion of true nationalism, contained a rejection rather than a continuation of nationalism. But in fact the German development was not an exception to the rule of healthy nation-states but rather a specific and independent case of the rise of nationalism, and the National Socialist understanding of nation fit within the parameters of this trajectory.

The primary distinguishing point in the Nazi form of nationalism was the linking of the process of *Bildung* to the idea of a universal humanity as the justifier of German aggression against others. This idea was one that developed in the course of the establishment of a German idealist culture that saw itself as a successor to traditional culture. With Humboldt, for instance, the belief in equality of peoples does not hold, even though he maintains the goal of a universal humanity. He constructs a hierarchy of nations in which all stand in a closer or more distant relation to the pinnacle of human development. Paradoxically, this pinnacle occurs when a particular nation has developed the ideas of freedom and universal humanity: "The operative principle here, of universal *humanity*, is an advance to which only our own age has truly ascended; and all the great discoveries of recent centuries are working together to bring it to reality."[39] The concept of universal humanity is precisely that which distinguishes one nation from all others in its development and sets it ahead of these other nations, but as a result the universality it proclaims is already undermined by the civilizational trajectory that the concept presumes. The specific character of the Humboldtian notion of *Bildung* that made it a precursor to the Nazi vision was that it combined a universalist ideal and trajectory with a strong sense of national particularity. This combination allowed the Nazis to claim the superiority of the German nation based on universal principles.

The similarities with a Nazi conception are even present in Humboldt's understanding of the state, a topic that would seem to provide a basis for demonstrating that Humboldtian *Bildung* and Nazi totalitarianism are entirely incompatible. Humboldt indeed argues for strong limitations on the power of the state, but does so in order to emphasize the importance of individual *Bildung* for the greatness of the nation. Because "the very variety arising from the union of numbers of individuals is the highest good which social life can confer, and this variety is undoubtedly lost in proportion to the degree of State interference," Humboldt seeks to limit the state's power to interfere in the "free play of individual energies" and the situation of "individual members of a nation living united in the bonds of a civil compact."[40] The individual's development is hampered by the state to the extent that the state imposes limitations on individual development, but the development is helped by a relation of the individual to the nation, in which the nation represents an association of affinity rather than of force. Consequently, Humboldt's limitation of the state serves to support the freedom of individuals to associate as the nation.

The key idea that creates the parameters for Baeumler's conception of *Bildung* is not that nationality is established by birth but the idea, introduced by Humboldt, that the free development of the individual, released from a specific role and place in society in order to be able to experience a variety of situations, naturally fits into a nationalist development that supports a universal history of mankind. This idea detaches the individual from other social institutions—such as family or church—in order to emphasize the link between the individual and the nation. For the key characteristic of the idea of nation is based on natural affinities and not on any traditional bonds or fixed roles. The affinities between individual and nation are the content of *Bildung* that creates the specificity of the individual and the corresponding link to the particularity of the nation. Although Humboldt emphasizes the freedom of the individual, the true goal is the greatness of the nation:

> If we may think it possible for a language to arise in a nation precisely as a word evolves most meaningfully and evidently from the world-view, reflects it most purely, and itself takes form so as to enter most readily and concretely into every vicissitude of thought, then this language, if it does but retain its life principle, must evoke the same power, in the same direction, with equal success in every individual. The entry of such a language, or even one that approaches it, into *world-history*, must therefore establish an important epoch in man's course of development, and this in its highest and most wonderful products. Certain paths of the spirit, and a certain impulse carrying it on to them, are not thinkable until such languages have arisen. They therefore constitute a true turning-point in the inner history of mankind; if we are to see them as the summit of language-making, they are also the starting-points for a more mentally abundant and imaginative cultivation, and it is to that extent quite correct to maintain that the work of nations must precede that of individuals; although the very observations here made are indisputable evidence of how in these creations the activity of each is simultaneously swallowed up in that of the other.[41]

Humboldt looks to the "self-activity of all" as the basis for *Bildung* and a community of individuals because it is grounded in free individual activity as opposed to static traditional frameworks. But the freedom of individual development is not the key concern. This development is conceived as always developing along national lines, in which "the work of nations must precede that of individuals" and only the development of certain languages can "constitute a true turning-point in the inner history of mankind." Not only does Humboldt's conception of *Bildung* tend to be a homogenizing one that replaces traditional structures with a new national culture, it also treats specific nations as inherently superior to others in terms of a universal history and evolution of mankind. Although he bases this inherent superiority of certain nations on language rather than on blood, his critique of state structures still provides the framework for a similar Nazi shift in emphasis from the state, with its conservative structures, to the "movement," with its proximity to a community of freely developing individuals.

From Education to Soldierly Sacrifice

At the 1934 Nuremberg Party Congress, Hitler emphasized that National Socialism was not to be founded upon state power: "*It is not the state that commands us, but we who command the state. It is not the state that has created us, but we who create our state.*"[42] Rather than depending on state orders, Hitler declared that the power behind the Nazis arose from its supporters having come together through "*the command of their hearts.*"[43] That heartfelt power derives, not from the state, but from the spirit of sacrifice that drives the movement: "It would be blasphemous if we were ever to allow that to sink which had to be fought for and achieved with so much work, so much effort, so much sacrifice, and so much privation. *No! The movement lives, and it stands solidly grounded, and as long as even one of us can breathe, he will lend this movement his energies and defend it, just as in the years that lie behind us.*"[44] The affirmation of the Nazi movement as a voluntary association based on the commitment and sacrifice of its members as opposed to the state as a static structure is the essential move that creates the conditions for the rise of National Socialism. Not only does it deemphasize the role of forced associations including not only the state but also the household, but the emphasis on the movement as the core of the nation also creates an interest in inner disposition that is not part of state authority but is central to totalitarian forms as Arendt describes them. As a result, this limiting of the state for the benefit of the nation is also one of the primary characteristics of the Nazi organization of power. As Arendt points out, the institutionalization of Nazism did not mean that the state gained power but that the Nazi *movement,* defined as a voluntary association that was not only separate from the state but also outside its structure, set up its own offices and structures that made the state apparatus irrelevant (*OT* 395–96). The point of this duplication according to Arendt was to make sure that the movement stayed active and did not stabilize into a set of fixed structures embodied in the state, and it is this aspect of constant activity and development that is perhaps the key to understanding the tie between *Bildung* and totalitarianism. The Nazis were not satisfied with taking over a state structure and setting up a military dictatorship with fixed hierarchies. Instead, they emphasized movement and development before stasis and institutionalization.

In this preference, the Nazis are simply articulating the same antagonism toward the state that motivates Humboldt's own defense of individual and nation:

> Like causes produce like effects; and hence, in proportion as State interference increases, the agents to which it is applied come to resemble each other, as do all the results of their activity. And this is the very design which States have in view. They desire comfort, ease, tranquility; and these are most readily secured to the extent that there is no clash of individualities. But what man does and must have in view is something quite different—it is variety and activity. Only these develop the many-sided and vigorous character; and, there can be no one, surely, so far degraded, as to prefer, for himself personally, comfort and enjoyment to greatness; and he who draws conclusions for such a preference in the case of others, may justly be suspected of misunderstanding human nature, and of wishing to make men into machines.[45]

Whereas states promote comfort, ease, and tranquility, Humboldt sets up variety and activity as the ultimate ends of human activity, and the rejection of this continual striving for "greatness" becomes for Humboldt the sign of an ultimate degradation of the human, to the point where he describes the rejection of this ideal as a wish to "make men into machines." He thereby inaugurates a point of view that sees an alternative cultural construction of human goals as something that is not just a sign of cultural difference but the basis for a distinction between healthy individuality and "degradation." Humboldt's remarks, though they cannot be read as directly influencing Nazi perceptions, certainly establish the type of intolerance for alternative perspectives that feeds into Nazi structures. At the same time, by setting up a desire for "comfort and enjoyment" as the enemy of a striving for "greatness," Humboldt demonstrates that he is also working with a notion of sacrifice in which the individual must give up personal comfort in order to harness energy for the sake of the development of a cultural "greatness."

As a consequence, this particular vision of sacrifice was not foreign to German sensibilities formed within the tradition of *Bildung*, and when Hitler spoke to the Hitler Youth during the 1934 Nuremberg Party Congress, his words affirmed the primacy of sacrifice for the sake of development and the idea that individual development and national development were one:

> Then the proud happiness seizes us all to be able to see in you *the completion of our work* and with it the consciousness that the millions of the

Great War, the numerous comrades among us, did not make their sacrifice for Germany in vain, that there is rising up for us in the end *a united, free, proud, honor-loving people*.

And I know, it cannot be any other way; for you are flesh of our flesh and blood of our blood, and in your minds there burns the same spirit that dominates us. You cannot be anything else but bound with us, and when the great columns of our movement march victoriously through Germany today, then I know you will join the columns, and we all know: *Before us lies Germany, within us marches Germany, and behind us comes Germany!*[46]

Even though the specific reference to flesh and blood are absent from Humboldt, this absence is less important than the overall structure of sacrifice for the sake of development and the equation of individual with nation that both Humboldt and Hitler share. The consequent call for the unity and development of the nation becomes the basis for an idealist notion of sacrifice for this national development.

When the National Socialist Party confronted the German people for the first time, it consciously refused to accept any commitment to the interests of any specific confessionally or economically limited group. Its appeal was from the first moment one that was directed at heroic instincts. The party raised hopes, not for those people who are only interested in advantages for their own businesses or for groups related to themselves, but rather for those, idealists often derided by others as fantasizers, who, without regard for their own interests, are committed with faithful hearts to their people and their country and are ready, if necessary, to sacrifice their very existence for the eternal life of both.[47]

Hitler emphasizes here the rejection of any prior local commitments that would disturb the unity of the nation and thus is speaking to the Germans as freely developing individuals. He then links this elimination of prior loyalties to an embracing of the notion of sacrifice as the rejection of material interests in a way that allows the individual to affirm her- or himself while at the same time understanding this affirmation to be a sacrifice to the nation, understood here as the collected group of free, German individuals. For Hitler the loss of self in the nation allows a recovery of individuality on a higher level.

It is within this framework established by Hitler that Baeumler constructs his pedagogical theory as a linking of individual to nation in the concept of *Bildung*. This concept is not a traditionalist but a modernizing one. For Baeumler, the nation can only become the organizer of social life when it links the education of individuals to a unified political goal and provides a nationalist structure of sacrifice that is based on a dissolution of local and family bonds. His pedagogical program is designed as a means of destroying preexisting traditions and replacing them with the rituals of a national community. This double movement is embedded in his particular interpretation of *Bildung,* which emphasizes individual development as something that detaches the individual from a family context in order to then integrate the individual into a national community. Although he initially opposes the idea of liberal individualism embedded in the history of the concept of *Bildung* (BG 111), he ultimately defends *Bildung* as a form of education that emphasizes individual development. Such development is an essential part of Nazi education for Baeumler because it is one of two necessary steps in the construction of a national community that he designates as *Bildung* and *Erziehung.*

In describing these two notions, Baeumler describes *Bildung* as a specific form of the more general idea of *Erziehung:*

> Education [*Erziehung*] is everything: inner and outer event, event that is brought about and experienced, process in the individual and at the same time life of the community. Formation [*Bildung*] by contrast is something that only can occur in the individual. Those who develop capacities and powers, form themselves. But this concentration of the process of formation in the *subject* in no way justifies the reproach of individualism against the formation process as a whole. The individual *must* develop his own powers if he is to totally become what he can be. *Formation does not express anything else but that this development occurs according to a specific law.* (BG 112–13)

Baeumler is careful here to criticize the liberal idea of *Bildung* as detached from any specific law of development in order to be able to retain *Bildung* as a development of individual capabilities. In affirming both individual development and the rule of a specific law, Baeumler undertakes to establish the trajectory that moves the individual from a traditional community into a national one.

In describing this trajectory, however, he conflates the two communities in a way that obscures the antitraditionalist element of his argument. First, the traditional (family, religious) community must be dissolved in order to create the free individual. Second, the individual can be integrated into the national community once the earlier community has been superseded. This two-step process is the process of *Bildung* and *Erzie-*

hung in Baeumler's conception. But he refers to the two steps not as a series, but as one contained within the other in order to be able to move the individual from the household community into the national one as if they were united rather than in opposition: "Family, home, country [*Familie, Haus, Heimat*] expand themselves in the course of life to people and fatherland without ever allowing the smaller circle to dissolve into the larger one." Yet, when he continues in the next sentence to describe the path from the "small community" into the "large one," it becomes clear that the transformation is based on a suppression of family bonds in favor of nationalist ones: "The path, however, from the small community to the large one, which is the path destined for every human, can only be traversed by the individual with all his power if the individual has attained the capacity, through the formation [*Bildung*] of all of his powers, to place *everything he is capable of* in the service of the community" (*BG* 113–14).

In order to be integrated into the larger community of the nation, the individual's powers are developed in such a way that the individual focuses on him- or herself and his or her own development rather than subordinating this development to the needs and practices of the small community. This focus on the individual's *Bildung* then becomes the basis for the integration of the individual into the larger national community through a process of national *Erziehung*: "*insofar* as the school forms [*bildet*] the powers of the individual, it also *educates* [*erzieht*] him for the community" (*BG* 115). This sentence completes the conflation of the small community with the large community by using the single word "community" (*Gemeinschaft*) in such a way that both meanings are connoted at once even though the real goal of the process is the dissolution of the former for the sake of the latter. For this form of *Erziehung* is not the same as the eighteenth-century form, in which *Erziehung* preceded *Bildung* and was primarily concerned with fitting the individual into the specific practices of a household community. Instead, Baeumler's process of *Erziehung* takes as its starting point the enlightenment process of *Bildung* and makes it into the "primal process of community life": "Insofar as the growing person learns to produce and reproduce mental constructions, 'he forms himself,' and this formation is a primal process of *community life*, even though it occurs in the subject and is nothing other than the ordered development of the powers of the individual" (*BG* 113). The community life Baeumler refers to is actually the national community to the exclusion of the household community, and the development of the individual as an individual becomes the prerequisite for the subordination of individual identity within national identity.

The antagonism to family and household in Baeumler's conception of *Erziehung* becomes immediately clear in his construction of the interpersonal basis of the national community as a *Männerbund* [men's association]. "A state originates, neither through mere thoughts nor through mere opinions, it is a product of forces, and the force that actually constitutes it is the one that appears in an association of free men [*Bunde freier Männer*]" (MW 32). The concept of the *Männerbund* is essential for Baeumler's idea of the nation because it fits the process of education into a community-building project whose goal is the detachment of the individual from a prior household and integration into the "association of free men." Recalling Fichte's notion of a "separate and self-contained community" of pupils (JF 28), this *Bund* forms the structure of the new national community, which, as Baeumler realizes, needs an affective basis and a structure of sacrifice to orient individual action.

The overriding concern that constitutes the *Bund* is no longer the life of the community nor the advancement of a metaphysical idea, but the pursuit of political goals: "It is only in relation to the state that the association [*Bund*] exists; the association is nothing without a political idea" (MW 32). Here, Baeumler's construction of the national state as a collection of men's associations oriented around the political goals of the state shifts the structure of sacrifice away from the immediate household and toward the national community. Instead of going to war to protect one's family or to defend a religious or moral ideal, German men are to sacrifice themselves for the reality of the fatherland. "Their death and that reality for which they fell is one and the same: for insofar as they fell, they testified to the reality of the Germany that they envisioned" (MW 19–20).

Contrary to Agamben's argument, in which sacrifice is no longer a significant concept for the Nazis, the Nazis cultivated the idea of sacrifice and mobilized it as part of a National Socialist constitution of the subject. This idea of sacrifice is not at all what Agamben means when he describes *homo sacer* as the condition of those enemies that are excluded from the protection of the state and become unfit for sacrifice but may be killed without any consequence for the killer (HS 81–86). Rather than promoting the creation of a *homo sacer*, a kind of bare life, Baeumler in fact rejects such a reduction to materiality: "This word [human material] is inappropriate for soldierly education [*Erziehung*]. For this education only takes place where there is a community and an idea that fulfills and animates this community. Such a community is, however, no longer 'material' (MW 158). Rather than treating the soldiers as bare life, a kind of human material, Baeumler seeks the consecration of fallen German soldiers to the German national community, this consecration then becoming the basic sacrificial structure that Baeumler uses to understand the relation between education and community. "The soldierly system of education must take hold of every German, regardless of who he is, regardless of where he works" (*MW* 164). The key to education into this national community is integration into a present political reality. "Next to the soldier of the armed forces and of tradition there stands today the traditionless soldier of the revolution, the storm trooper" (*MW* 164). This storm trooper becomes Baeumler's model for Nazi subjectivity because he represents the subjugation of the individual to the reality of a nationalist political agenda rather than to what Baeumler considers a static and meaningless cultural tradition. The anticultural and antitraditional stance is important to the structure of teaching to the extent that Baeumler seeks to orient the teaching of culture around present political concerns rather than around what he sees as timeless and thus irrelevant cultural artifacts (*BG* 25).

Both the Germans to be sacrificed for the nation and the German Jews declared to be unfit for such sacrifice had to undergo the same process of being pulled free of traditional bonds. While Baeumler uses the education process to effect this change on Germans, Agamben describes how "Jews could be sent to the extermination camps only after they had been fully denationalized (stripped even of the residual citizenship left to them after the Nuremberg laws)" (*HS* 132). In the case of both the German and the Jewish subjects, the Nazis sought to strip them of culturally specific aspects of their subjectivity. The result of this process was a new subject of sacrifice in the case of the German, a political enemy in the case of Communists, and a dehumanized enemy in the case of the German Jew. The specifically Nazi element of this process undoubtedly consisted of the Nazi ideology of racial superiority, which created the unbridgeable distinction between German and Jew and motivated the Nazi drive to eliminate alternative traditions, both through the homogenization of German subjectivity as well as through the brutal eradication of all those people whom they considered to be impossible to assimilate. The structures of this Nazi ideology can be traced back to the tradition of *Bildung* first developed in the work of Fichte and Humboldt and then continued by Baeumler. As opposed to a nationalism that recognizes an equal value of all nations and traditions, their idea of an evolution of cultures toward a European and German superiority established the kind of distinction between peoples that could legitimate the Nazi distinction between Germans and Jews.

Sacrifice as Resistance

Resistance to this process on the part of both non-Jewish and Jewish Germans consisted of a reaffirmation of the alternative traditions threatened by the Nazi process of individuation. In the case of non-Jewish Germans, Agamben describes the transformation of the Euthanasia Program for the Incurably Ill "from a theoretically humanitarian program into a work of mass extermination" but also points out that "Hitler ended it in August 1941 because of growing protest on the part of bishops and relatives" (*HS* 140). Such protest from families and the church demonstrates that the possible opposition to the Nazi vision of sacrifice could only come from institutions that maintained alternative models of sacrifice. Just as the German resistance to euthanasia depended upon the maintenance of alternative traditions with their own notions of sacrifice, the Jewish resistance to mass extermination depended on the ability of the Jews to maintain the strength of alternative ways of constituting subjectivity through their own models of sacrifice. This idea challenges the notion that the primary danger of Nazi ideology was its affirmation of sacrifice and the accompanying dissolution of subjectivity.[48] Rather than basing itself in the idea of individual subjectivity as the highest value, resistance to the Nazi cultural project came from a subordination of the individual to an alternative set of cultural goals.

Arnold Schoenberg's cantata, *A Survivor from Warsaw*, illustrates how resistance to the Nazis could only develop to the extent that individuals could be subordinated in such a way that the nonsacrificial death of the camps could be reinterpreted as sacrifice. The narrator recounts to us a story in which precisely the point of contention within the camp is whether the prisoners can be thought of as possessing only bare existence or whether they in fact are still culturally marked in such a way that their lives, even in death, transcend the confines of Nazi power. This latter possibility can only be grasped to the extent that the inmates can escape being defined in terms of their bare life. In order to do this, they must inscribe their existence within a sacrificial trope, consecrating their existence to something beyond the individual through the reactivation of "the forgotten creed."

The first part of the cantata consists of the narrator's account of what he remembers of a Nazi extermination camp, and this description of the dehumanizing violence of the Nazi sergeant seems to confirm Agamben's argument that the modern state has developed a system of power that reduces individuals to their bare life, their existence as such, and has thus denuded them of any particular quality that could oppose the proliferation of state power. This part ends with a scene in which the Nazi sergeant begins to round up the prisoners in order to bring them to the gas chamber:

> Narrator:
>   There I lay aside half conscious. It had become very still—fear and pain—Then I heard the sergeant shouting: "*Abzählen!*" ["Count off!"]
>   They started slowly, and irregularly: One, two, three, four, "*Achtung.*" The sergeant shouted again: "*Rascher! Nochmals von vorn anfangen! In einer Minute will ich wissen wieviele ich zur Gaskammer abliefere! Abzählen!*" ["Faster! Once more, start from the beginning! In one minute I want to know how many I am going to send off to the gas chamber! Count off!"]
>   They began again, first slowly: one, two, three, four, became faster and faster, so fast that it finally sounded like a stampede of wild horses, and all of a sudden, in the middle of it, they began singing the Shema Yisroel.
> Chorus:
>   Sh^{e}ma Yisroel Adōnoy elōhenoo Adōnoy ehod   V^{e}ohavto es Adōnoy elōheḫo b^{e}ḫol l^{e}vov^{e}ḫo oov^{e}hol nafsh^{e}ḫo oov^{e}ḫol m^{e}ōdeḫo   V^{e}hoyoo hadd^{e}voreem hoelleh asher onōḫee m^{e}tsavv^{e}ḫo hayyōm al l^{e}voveḫo   V^{e}shinnantom l^{e}voneḫo v^{e}dibbarto bom b^{e}shivt^{e}ḫo b^{e}veteḫo oov^{e}leḫt^{e}ḫo baddereḫ oov^{e}shoḫb^{e}ḫo oov^{e}koomeḫo.[49]

As many commentators have pointed out, the music that accompanies the narrator before the singing is atonal, the brief motives and lack of thematic continuity reminiscent of the depiction of the dissolution of subjectivity in Schoenberg's 1909 opera, *Erwartung*.[50] But once the chorus begins singing the text of the Shema Yisroel, a Jewish prayer of praise for God, the character of the music changes dramatically. The chorus takes up some of the thematic fragments from part 1, such as the military fanfare motifs, and organizes them into a twelve-tone row with a thematic continuity.

The opposition between the narrator's speech and the chorus's singing is not the opposition between a German order and a Jewish order,[51] but an opposition between the dissolution of order that the Nazis tried to create in the camp (as described by the soloist) and the creation of order enacted by the prayer (as sung by the choir). The depiction of the camp emphasizes the irrationality and chaos in which no rules seem to hold. The narrator points out at one point: "The sergeant and his subordinates hit everyone: young or old, strong or sick, guilty or innocent—it was painful to hear the groaning and moaning." In the midst of this arbitrary violence, a shift occurs when the sergeant decides to have the prisoners count off before being taken to the gas chamber. In having the prisoners count off, the Nazis unwittingly allow the reestablishment of order that leads to the beginning of the prayer.

Once the order is reestablished, the rest of the narrator's story is retroactively integrated into the order of the prayer. The thematic fragments of the music accompanying the narrator can now be recognized as broken pieces from the chorus's twelve-tone row, and the scattered memories and the descent into trauma of the narrator are redeemed and given meaning by the memory of the prayer. As the narrator points out at the beginning of his account, the dissolution of his consciousness and memory are only halted by the grandiose moment of prayer that creates the possibility of memory: "I cannot remember ev'rything, I must have been unconscious most of the time; I remember only the grandiose moment when they all started to sing, as if prearranged, the old prayer they had neglected for so many years—the forgotten creed!" The prayer becomes the defining moment for the narrator, and the chaos of the camp can only be remembered to the extent that these experiences are subordinated to the experience of the prayer. Without this experience, the narrator would have nothing to tell. It is only the ordering force of the prayer on the narrator's consciousness that provides the structure that imparts meaning to the rest.

The text of the prayer emphasizes this consciousness-constituting character of the religious tradition by demanding that the entire life of the community be permeated by the prayer and its praise of God in such a way that the children are educated into it. The English translation of the Hebrew prayer reads:

> Hear, O Israel: the Lord our God is one Lord: And thou shalt love the Lord thy God with all thine heart, and with all thy soul, and with all thy might. And these words, which I command thee this day, shall be in thine heart: And thou shalt teach them diligently unto thy children, and shalt talk of them when thou sittest in thine house, and when thou walkest by the way, and when thou liest down, and when thou risest up. (Deuteronomy 6:4–7, King James Version)

Rather than an affirmation of individual sovereignty or even of an individual right to survival, the prayer subordinates the individual to the Jewish God in both an inner spiritual consciousness and in the process of education, and the resistance to the dehumanization of the Nazi camp does not lie in an affirmation of the body but in an alternative subordination of the body to a cultural ideal. The key to the grandiosity of the prayer lies not in its liberation of the individual but in its particular form of subordination.

Both the success and the specific horror of the Nazi state lies in its proximity to the ritual subjugation of the individual in the prayer. Both the Nazi state and Jewish culture depend upon an education that subjects the individual to a greater force. But whereas the Jewish prayer depends upon the freedom of individual subjects to aesthetically receive and affirm the rules of a particular tradition and subject themselves voluntarily to that tradition's idiosyncratic construction of the sacred, the Nazi construction of sacrifice, though also dependent on representational processes, explicitly rejects aesthetic processes as a source of legitimation. Instead of allowing for a free aesthetic development of structures of sacrifice that could lead to the affirmation of alternative traditions, the Nazis, convinced of the objective validity of their ideology, utilized aesthetic representations as a means of manipulation within a framework of terror.

The new ethic of self-development begins by valorizing the individual as the basic and sovereign unit of society in order to destroy the previous rituals that grounded the individual's existence within a previous structure of sacrifice. Once individuals stand alone as the basic manipulable units of human existence, they become open to influence from all sorts of competing conceptions of culture, each with its own rituals and myths of sacrifice. In such a situation, the Nazis, in order to maintain their preeminent role within German society, had to forcibly deny all alternative traditions any status as sources of their own independent meaning.

Consequently, the opposition to the Nazi national completion of the individual was neither an affirmation of the sovereignty of the individual nor a rejection of ritual violence. Rather than an appeal to a universal humanity, the only adequate response to the Nazis in the camp—as shown in Schoenberg's cantata—is a willful embracing of a specific ritual, a commitment to "the forgotten creed." This affirmation of the validity of a particular tradition becomes essential to undermining the Nazis' own claim to be the representatives of a universal progress of humanity. With this shift in focus from universality to particularity, the key question is no longer whether sacrifice and ritual are valid concepts for the modern world, but rather how to distinguish and evaluate different ways of structuring sacrifice.

Conclusion

This book has argued that sacrifice structures the human relationship to violence. Key to this argument is the premise that human values cannot be established within a particular community without a set of supporting representations organized around a vision of sacrifice. To the extent that ethical values must translate into action in human society, sacrifice will play a key role in establishing the fundamental principles of a cultural order. The performative character of sacrifice in the establishment of values suggests that sacrifice is not a thoughtless or dogmatic action. As a defining moment for the structure of a society, sacrifice does not create a link to a metaphysical truth (biologically or supernaturally based) behind "normal" life. Rather, its performance enacts the value system of a society through an act of will. The act of sacrifice is a performative affirmation of ultimate values that establishes the structure of the society that ensues from the sacrifice. Although a performative sacrifice may occur only rarely, as with instances of martyrdom in Christianity, such acts of self-sacrifice then suffice to ground an entire cultural system and the stories of sacrifice that it entails, though the continuity of this system still requires the ongoing expression of commitment embedded in shared rituals.

For those who adhere to the dream of a rational ethics, in which universally binding values can be established for human action on the basis of rational insight and agreement without any consideration of representational structures, this understanding of sacrifice, and the premises upon which it is based, may appear to be backward and regressive. Without the vision of a universal ethics based on reason, there would seem to be no hope for an escape from a relativism that would have to affirm any existing social system whose representations enjoy popular support, even Nazism, because there are no objective criteria that could be used to draw distinctions.

The first response to these objections is to point out that an opposing vision of sacrifice is essential to any serious attempts to resist and turn

149

back social and political forms such as Nazism. While the Nazis obviously established a specific notion of sacrifice, those who fought against the Nazis could only develop the resolve and commitment to do so by embracing their own alternative visions of sacrifice. This was as true of the allied armies as of the scattered resistance to the Nazis within Germany. An appeal to reason would not have sufficed to destroy Nazism, if only because for most individual allied soldiers it was irrational, from the point of view of individual interests, to enter into combat. The decision to fight would have had to have been motivated by a sense of the collective goals that would be affirmed if one were to sacrifice one's own life. This need for a notion of sacrifice in combating an enemy means that the simple employment of sacrificial myths cannot be the basis upon which to criticize a culture.

It becomes all the more important then to consider the goals rather than the fact of sacrifice as the key issue. If the critique of Nazi myth cannot consist of a condemnation of the Nazis' appeal to sacrifice itself, it must move on to look at the particular ends of sacrifice that they advocated and the ways in which sacrifice is distributed and structured within their society. But such a look at the particular structure of sacrifice is in fact the same consideration that lies at the heart of every individual aesthetic judgment that leads, collectively, to the affirmation and legitimation of a particular cultural system. The key to values and ethics, then, is the way in which individual judgments about the proper structure of sacrifice lead to the establishment and stability of a particular collective vision. To the extent that aesthetic truth exists as something that is situationally valid, it restricts the relativist implications of an approach to ethics grounded in the consideration of sacrifice.

The consequence of linking sacrifice and ethics is, however, that ethics becomes inseparable from politics. This point becomes especially clear when we consider how anti-Nazi examples of sacrifice have become established as contemporary models. Claus von Stauffenberg undoubtedly demonstrated moral courage in risking and then losing his life in leading the failed July 20, 1944, assassination attempt against Hitler. But because he understood his actions as an attempt to defend German national culture against Nazism, the evaluation of his moral commitment cannot be separated from the kind of political vision that accompanied it. Similarly, the executions of Hans Scholl and Sophie Scholl cannot be separated from the liberal, Christian ideas upon which the flyers of their White Rose resistance group were based, and the resistance group around Herbert Baum was motivated by Jewish-Communist ideas. In all these cases, resistance to the Nazis was inseparable from the adherence to an alternative set of values that could justify the sacrifices made.

Today, it is primarily the Scholls who have been lionized in German culture, presumably because their liberal ideals best match those of Germans today. Karl Heinz Bohrer has criticized the failure to properly appreciate Stauffenberg's similar sacrifice because its German nationalist goals are no longer popular, emphasizing that Stauffenberg demonstrated the same level of moral commitment as others such as the Scholls.[1] But even many Nazis saw themselves as morally committed in the defense of their values, and the level of commitment alone cannot serve as a basis for our judgments about an individual's actions. The particular values motivating this commitment and the accompanying structure and distribution of sacrifice all become relevant for our judgments about examples of sacrifice from the past and our expectations and commitments for the future. Sacrifices become necessary if we want to make good on our promises in a world of uncertainty. But while our willingness to make such sacrifices provides a measure of our strength of character, the specific content of our promises will ultimately define this character as well as the contours of the social world we inhabit.

NOTES

Introduction

The epigraph to this introduction comes from Plato, *Protagoras,* trans. Stanley Lombardo and Karen Bell (Indianapolis: Hackett, 1992), 17–18.

1. See, e.g., Henri Hubert and Marcel Mauss, *Sacrifice: Its Nature and Function,* trans. W. D. Halls (Chicago: University of Chicago Press, 1964); James George Frazer, *The Magic Art and the Evolution of Kings,* vol. 1, pt. 1, of *The Golden Bough* (New York: Macmillan, 1935); and Edward B. Tylor, *Primitive Culture: Researches into the Development of Mythology, Philosophy, Religion, Art, and Custom,* 2 vols. (London: John Murray, 1871).

2. Sigmund Freud, *Civilization and Its Discontents,* trans. James Strachey (New York: Norton, 1961), 111–12.

3. Georges Bataille, *The Accursed Share: An Essay on General Economy* (New York: Zone Books, 1988).

4. Max Horkheimer and Theodor W. Adorno, *Dialectic of Enlightenment,* trans. John Cumming (New York: Continuum, 1972), 48–62.

5. René Girard, *Things Hidden Since the Foundation of the World,* trans. Stephen Bann and Michael Metteer (London: Athlone Press, 1987). See also Wolfgang Palaver, *René Girards mimetische Theorie im Kontext kulturtheoretischer und gesellschaftspolitischer Fragen* (Hamburg: LIT Verlag, 2003), 299–301.

6. Giorgio Agamben, *Homo Sacer: Sovereign Power and Bare Life,* trans. Daniel Heller-Roazen (Stanford, Calif.: Stanford University Press, 1998).

7. J. P. Stern, *The Dear Purchase: A Theme in German Modernism* (Cambridge: Cambridge University Press, 1995), 63–71.

8. Ibid., 83.

9. Hubert and Mauss, *Sacrifice,* 13.

10. Claudia Koonz, *The Nazi Conscience* (Cambridge, Mass.: Belknap Press, 2003).

Chapter 1

1. Max Horkheimer and Theodor W. Adorno, *Dialectic of Enlightenment,* trans. John Cumming (New York: Continuum, 1972), 11–14. Cited hereafter as *DE.* For an account of the ethical implications of Adorno's philosophy that defends his privileging of the "complex" concept, see Jay Bernstein, *Adorno: Disenchantment and Ethics* (Cambridge: Cambridge University Press, 2001).

2. Jürgen Habermas, *The Philosophical Discourse of Modernity,* trans. Frederick Lawrence (Cambridge, Mass.: MIT Press, 1987), 125. Cited hereafter as *PD.*

3. Peter Uwe Hohendahl, *Prismatic Thought: Theodor W. Adorno* (Lincoln: University of Nebraska Press, 1995), 205–9, 241–42.

4. For another description of this distinction between a rational and an aesthetic totality, see Carl Einstein, "Totalität," in *1907–1918*, vol. 1 of *Werke*, ed. Rolf-Peter Baacke with Jens Kwasny (Berlin: Medusa, 1980), 226–29.

5. Theodor W. Adorno, *Aesthetic Theory*, ed. Gretel Adorno and Rolf Tiedemann, trans. Robert Hullot-Kentor (Minneapolis: University of Minnesota Press, 1997), 100–118. Cited hereafter as *AT*. For an analysis of Adorno's distinction between semblance and expression, see Robert Hullot-Kentor, "The Impossibility of Music: Adorno, Popular and Other Music," *Telos* 87 (Spring 1991): 97–117. Compare Walter Benjamin's idea of mimesis as a recognition of "ingenuous similarity." Walter Benjamin, "On the Mimetic Faculty," in *Reflections: Essays, Aphorisms, Autobiographical Writings*, ed. Peter Demetz, trans. Edmund Jephcott (New York: Schocken, 1986), 334. For a discussion of the relation between Benjamin's and Adorno's concepts of mimesis, see Shierry Weber Nicholsen, *Exact Imagination, Late Work: On Adorno's Aesthetics* (Cambridge, Mass.: MIT Press, 1997), 137–80.

6. Friedrich Nietzsche, *The Birth of Tragedy and Other Writings*, ed. Raymond Geuss and Ronald Speirs, trans. Ronald Speirs (Cambridge: Cambridge University Press, 1999), 38. Cited hereafter as *BT*.

7. On this distinction, see Hohendahl, *Prismatic Thought*, 241–42, and Nicholsen, *Exact Imagination*, 66–73.

8. W. Tatarkiewicz, "Mimesis," in *Dictionary of the History of Ideas: Studies of Selected Pivotal Ideas*, ed. Philip W. Wiener (New York: Scribner's Sons, 1973), 3:226. In noting the origin of this term, Martin Jay fails to draw any consequences for Adorno's notion of mimesis. Martin Jay, "Mimesis in Adorno and Lacoue-Labarthe," in *The Semblance of Subjectivity*, ed. Tom Huhn and Lambert Zuidervaart (Cambridge, Mass.: MIT Press, 1997).

9. Norbert Bolz also notes this difference between Nietzsche's and Adorno's theories of art, but then goes on to criticize Nietzsche for a lack of "historico-philosophical" understanding. The key issue, however, is how Adorno uses the idea of history in order to escape the contradictions posed by nature. See Norbert W. Bolz, "Nietzsches Spur in der Ästhetischen Theorie," in *Materialien zur ästhetischen Theorie: Theodor W. Adornos Konstruktion der Moderne*, ed. Burkhardt Lindner and W. Martin Lüdke (Frankfurt am Main: Suhrkamp, 1980), 390.

10. Frederic Jameson, *Late Marxism: Adorno, or, The Persistence of the Dialectic* (London: Verso, 1990), 239.

11. Ibid., 225.

12. Nicholsen follows Adorno in making the assumption that violence can originate only from the subject and not from nature. See Nicholsen, *Exact Imagination*, 75.

13. Immanuel Kant, *Critique of Judgment*, trans. Werner S. Pluhar (Indianapolis: Hackett, 1987), 98–99. Cited hereafter as *CJ*.

14. Lambert Zuidervaart, *Adorno's Aesthetic Theory: The Redemption of Illusion* (Cambridge, Mass.: MIT Press, 1991), 165–66. See also Heinz Paetzold, "Adorno's Notion of Natural Beauty: A Reconsideration," in *Semblance*, ed. Huhn and Zuidervaart, 220.

15. Tom Huhn, "Kant, Adorno, and the Social Opacity of the Aesthetic," in *Semblance,* ed. Huhn and Zuidervaart, 245.

16. Albrecht Wellmer, "Adorno, Modernity, and the Sublime," in *The Actuality of Adorno: Critical Essays on Adorno and the Postmodern,* ed. Max Pensky (Albany: State University of New York Press, 1997), 125.

17. Jean-François Lyotard, *Lessons on the Analytic of the Sublime,* trans. Elizabeth Rottenberg (Stanford, Calif.: Stanford University Press, 1994), 189.

18. Ibid., 189–90.

19. Wellmer, "Adorno," 130.

20. Ibid., 131.

21. Ibid.

22. For an account of the symbolic relations involved in this process, see David Pan, "J. G. Herder, the Origin of Language, and the Possibility of Transcultural Narrative," *Language and Intercultural Communication* 4, nos. 1–2 (2004): 1–10.

23. Nicholsen, *Exact Imagination,* 24–31.

24. Ibid., 49.

25. Zuidervaart, *Adorno's Aesthetic Theory,* 146, and Hohendahl, *Prismatic Thought,* 191, 211.

26. Hohendahl, *Prismatic Thought,* 239.

27. Ibid., 233–35.

28. Ibid., 235, 251.

29. Nicholsen, *Exact Imagination,* 113–24.

30. Ibid., 123.

31. Rüdiger Bubner, "Concerning the Central Idea of Adorno's Philosophy," in *Semblance,* ed. Huhn and Zuidervaart, 172.

32. Ibid., 167.

33. Although this reading is admittedly a significant departure from Kant's analysis, I adhere very strictly to Kant's specific analysis of the sublime and its mechanisms in order to arrive at my conclusions. Unfortunately, Kant was too committed to retaining reason as a basis for morality to recognize the necessity of the aesthetic moment of myth for establishing a moral sense in a community. Kant designates religious enthusiasm as a kind of "madness" (*CJ* 136), and, as Lyotard notes, this "enthusiasm is an *Affekt,* a strong affection, and as such it is blind and cannot, therefore, according to Kant, 'deserve the approval of reason.' " Jean-François Lyotard, *The Differend: Phrases in Dispute,* trans. Georges Van Den Abbeele (Minneapolis: University of Minnesota Press, 1988), 166.

Chapter 2

1. Philippe Lacoue-Labarthe and Jean-Luc Nancy, *Le Mythe Nazi* (Paris: Editions de l'Aube, 1991), 8, 10; here and elsewhere, non-English language texts quoted in this book are my translations unless noted otherwise.

2. Ibid., 22.

3. Ibid., 53, 67.

4. Lawrence Birken, *Hitler as Philosophe: Remnants of the Enlightenment in National Socialism* (Westport, Conn.: Praeger, 1995), 12–20.
5. J. P. Stern, *The Dear Purchase: A Theme in German Modernism* (Cambridge: Cambridge University Press, 1995), 70.
6. Ibid., 71.
7. Hermann Kurzke, *Thomas Mann: Life As a Work of Art*, trans. Leslie Willson (Princeton, N.J.: Princeton University Press, 2002), 248–66, 320–40, 364–87, 416–18, 494–513.
8. Hans Sluga, *Heidegger's Crisis: Philosophy and Politics in Nazi Germany* (Cambridge, Mass.: Harvard University Press, 1993), 127. For a description of Baeumler's career and his role within National Socialist administration of culture and education, see Sluga, *Heidegger's Crisis*, 126–31, 223–30, and Monika Leske, *Philosophen im "Dritten Reich": Studie zu Hochschul- und Philosophiebetrieb im faschistischen Deutschland* (Berlin: Dietz, 1990), 203–37.
9. Alfred Baeumler, *Kants Kritik der Urteilskraft: Ihre Geschichte und Systematik*, vol. 1, *Das Irrationalitätsproblem in der Ästhetik und Logik des 18. Jahrhunderts bis zur Kritik der Urteilskraft* (Halle: Niemeyer, 1923).
10. Alfred Rosenberg, *Der Mythus des 20. Jahrhunderts* (1930; Munich: Hoheneichen, 1934), 43.
11. For more details about Baeumler's role in the Nazi hierarchy, see Sluga, *Heidegger's Crisis*, 224, and George Leaman, "Deutsche Philosophen und das Amt Rosenberg," in *"Die besten Geister der Nation": Philosophie und Nationalsozialismus*, ed. Ilse Korotin (Vienna: Picus, 1994), 51–56.
12. On the centrality of Baeumler's pedagogical ideas for Nazi policies, see Karl Christoph Lingelbach, *Erziehung und Erziehungstheorien im nationalsozialistischen Deutschland* (Frankfurt am Main: dipa-Verlag, 1987), 80–94, 188–202, and Winfried Joch, *Theorie einer politischen Pädagogik: Alfred Baeumlers Beitrag zur Pädagogik im Nationalsozialismus* (Bern: Herbert Lang, 1971), 20–38.
13. Thomas Mann, *Pariser Rechenschaft* (Berlin: Fischer, 1926), 61–62.
14. Helmut Koopmann, "Vaterrecht und Mutterrecht: Thomas Manns Auseinandersetzungen mit Bachofen und Baeumler als Wegbereitern des Faschismus," *Text und Kritik* 8, no. 2 (1980): 281.
15. Hubert Brunträger, *Der Ironiker und der Ideologe: Die Beziehungen zwischen Thomas Mann und Alfred Baeumler* (Würzburg: Königshausen und Neumann, 1993), 125–26, 143.
16. As Marianne Baeumler, Hubert Brunträger, and Hermann Kurzke point out, Mann's attack "seems at this point in time to have been objectively unjustified since Baeumler, as mentioned, celebrates the victory of paternal law and reason described in Bachofen's work." M. Baeumler et al. *Thomas Mann und Alfred Baeumler: Eine Dokumentation* (Würzburg: Königshausen und Neumann, 1989), 154.
17. Alfred Baeumler, "Einleitung: Bachofen, der Mythologe der Romantik," in Johann Jakob Bachofen, *Der Mythus von Orient und Okzident* (1926; Munich: Beck, 1956), XXIX. Cited hereafter as B.
18. Brunträger, *Der Ironiker*, 130.

19. Manfred Frank, *Gott im Exil: Vorlesungen über die Neue Mythologie, II. Teil* (Frankfurt am Main: Suhrkamp, 1988), 33–37, 108–9. Cited hereafter as *GE*.

20. Concerning the Enlightenment aspects of the *völkisch* and racist currents of Nazi ideology see Birken, *Hitler as Philosophe,* 23–32, and Zygmunt Bauman, *Modernity and the Holocaust* (Ithaca, N.Y.: Cornell University Press, 1989), 61–82.

21. Georg Lukács, *The Destruction of Reason,* trans. Peter Palmer (Atlantic Highlands, N.J.: Humanities Press, 1981), 536–39.

22. Walter Benjamin, *Illuminations,* trans. Harry Zohn (New York: Schocken, 1968), 241.

23. Walter Benjamin, *Reflections,* trans. Edmund Jephcott (New York: Schocken, 1986), 179; Benjamin, *Illuminations,* 188.

24. On Bloch's life, see Vincent Geoghegan, *Ernst Bloch* (New York: Routledge, 1996), 9–45. On Einstein, see Sibylle Penkert, *Carl Einstein: Beiträge zu einer Monographie* (Göttingen: Vandenhoeck und Ruprecht, 1969).

25. Carl Einstein, *1929–1940,* vol. 3 of *Werke:,* ed. Marion Schmid and Liliane Meffre (Berlin: Medusa, 1985), 459–62. Cited hereafter as E.

26. Alfred Baeumler, "Antrittsvorlesung in Berlin" (May 10, 1933) in *Männerbund und Wissenschaft* (Berlin: Junker und Dünnhaupt, 1934), 123–38. *Männerbund und Wissenschaft* hereafter cited as *MW*.

27. Klaus H. Kiefer, *Diskurswandel im Werk Carl Einsteins* (Tübingen: Niemeyer, 1994), 519.

28. Alfred Baeumler, *Männerbund und Wissenschaft* (Berlin: Junker und Dünnhaupt, 1934), 114.

29. Ernst Bloch, *Heritage of Our Times,* trans. Neville and Stephen Plaice (Berkeley: University of California Press, 1991), 108–10.

30. George Mosse, *The Crisis of German Ideology: Intellectual Origins of the Third Reich* (New York: Grosset and Dunlap, 1964), 8–10.

31. For a more elaborate discussion of Einstein's theories on myth and sacrifice, see David Pan, *Primitive Renaissance: Rethinking German Expressionism* (Lincoln: University of Nebraska Press, 2001).

32. See Allan Megill, *Prophets of Extremity: Nietzsche, Heidegger, Foucault, Derrida* (Berkeley: University of California Press, 1985), 65–82.

33. Compare Martin Michael Ross, "'Die staatgründende Tat' — Alfred Baeumler und die Politisierung der Ästhetik," in *"Die besten Geister der Nation,"* ed. Ilse Korotin, 66. Because he rejects any attempt to recover art as a mediator of experience, Ross's critique of Baeumler's aesthetic theories as a politicization of aesthetics is too general to be of any use for an analysis of the aesthetic issues involved here. In his description of the dangers of a "unified aesthetics" ("Einheitsästhetik"), he identifies such diverse figures as Immanuel Kant, Friedrich Schiller, Friedrich Schelling, and Martin Gropius as supporters of such an aesthetic and fails to differentiate between their theories and that of Baeumler. Brunträger provides a much more useful description of how Baeumler's ideas on myth diverge from Nietzsche's aesthetic account. Brunträger, *Der Ironiker,* 94–95.

34. Nietzsche's best example of this process is his reading of the Prometheus myth, which condenses the human experience of technology into a parable about the limits of progress (*BT* 48–50).

35. See, e.g., Nietzsche's description of the lyric poet (*BT* 28–33).

36. "The artist has already given up his subjectivity in the Dionysiac process; the image which now shows him his unity with the heart of the world is a dream scene which gives sensuous expression to the primal contradiction and pain, along with its primal lust for and pleasure in semblance" (*BT* 30).

37. Alfred Baeumler, *Alfred Rosenberg und der Mythus des 20. Jahrhunderts* (München: Hoheneichen, 1943), 70.

38. Alfred Baeumler, *Studien zur deutschen Geistesgeschichte* (1930; Berlin: Junker und Dünnhaupt, 1937), 258.

39. Rosenberg, *Der Mythus des 20. Jahrhunderts*, 34–44.

40. Baeumler, *Alfred Rosenberg*, 47.

41. Baeumler, *Studien*, 258.

42. As Brunträger demonstrates, Mann's understanding of myth was strongly influenced by Baeumler's. Just as Baeumler maintains a separation between an original cultic substance without language and a philosophical appropriation of the ritual, Mann distinguishes mythic substance that is constant from a manifestation that is open to intellectual manipulation. Yet, Mann's view of myth diverges from Baeumler's conception at a crucial point when Mann sides with Nietzsche against Baeumler in recognizing a connection between myth and psychology. Brunträger, *Der Ironiker*, 116–24.

43. Rosenberg, *Der Mythus des 20. Jahrhunderts*, 42–45.

44. Baeumler, *Studien*, 258.

45. Bloch, *Heritage*, 108–10.

46. Ibid., 113.

47. Ibid., 113–14.

48. Jürgen Habermas, *The Philosophical Discourse of Modernity: Twelve Lectures*, trans. Frederick Lawrence (Cambridge, Mass.: MIT Press, 1987), 124.

49. Manfred Frank, *Der kommende Gott: Vorlesungen über die Neue Mythologie, I. Teil* (Frankfurt am Main: Suhrkamp, 1982), 167. Cited hereafter as *KG*.

Chapter 3

1. Georges Bataille, *The Accursed Share: An Essay on General Economy*, vol. 1, *Consumption*, trans. Robert Hurley (New York: Zone Books, 1988), 23. Cited hereafter as *AS1*.

2. Georges Bataille, *The Accursed Share: An Essay on General Economy*, vol. 2, *The History of Eroticism*, and vol. 3, *Sovereignty*, trans. Robert Hurley (New York: Zone Books, 1991), 220.

3. George Wilhelm Friedrich Hegel, *Phenomenology of Spirit*, trans. Arnold V. Miller (New York: Oxford University Press, 1977), 111. Cited hereafter as *PS*.

4. Bataille, *The Accursed Share*, vol. 3, *Sovereignty*, 222.

5. Susan Buck-Morss, "Hegel and Haiti," *Critical Inquiry* 26, no. 4 (Summer 2000): 842–49.

6. Georges Bataille, *Theory of Religion*, trans. Robert Hurley (New York: Zone Books, 1989), 43.
7. See Georges Bataille, *Story of the Eye*, trans. Joachim Neugroschel (New York: Urizen Books, 1977) and Georges Bataille, *The Trial of Gilles de Rais*, trans. Richard Robinson (Los Angeles: Amok Books, 1991), 15.
8. Carl Einstein, *Werke*, vol. 1: *1908–1918*, ed. Rolf-Peter Baacke with Jens Kwasny (Berlin: Medusa, 1980), 202.
9. Einstein, *Werke*, 1:203.
10. René Girard, *Violence and the Sacred*, trans. Patrick Gregory (Baltimore: Johns Hopkins University Press, 1977), 10. Cited hereafter as *VS*.
11. René Girard, *Things Hidden Since the Foundation of the World*, trans. Stephen Bann and Michael Metteer (London: Athlone Press, 1987), 26. Cited hereafter as *TH*.
12. Walter Burkert, *Homo Necans: The Anthropology of Ancient Greek Sacrificial Ritual and Myth*, trans. Peter Bing (Berkeley: University of California Press, 1983), 22. Cited hereafter as *HN*.
13. See Jack Miles, *God: A Biography* (New York: Vintage, 1996), for a discussion of how Judeo-Christian rituals function as covenants.
14. Charles Peirce, *Peirce on Signs: Writings on Semiotic* (Chapel Hill: University of North Carolina Press, 1991), 23–33.
15. Konrad Lorenz, *On Aggression*, trans. Marjorie Kerr Wilson (New York: Harcourt Brace Jovanovich, 1974), 184–85.
16. Terence Deacon, *The Symbolic Species* (New York: Norton, 1997), 403–5. Napoleon A. Chagnon, *Yanomamö: The Fierce People*, 3rd ed. (New York: CBS College Publishing, 1983), 1–3, 146–69.
17. Lorenz, *On Aggression*, 160–212.

Chapter 4
1. Walter Burkert, *Wilder Ursprung: Opferritual und Mythos bei den Griechen* (Berlin: Wagenbach, 1990), 30.
2. Walter Burkert, *Anthropologie des religiösen Opfers: Die Sakralisierung der Gewalt* (Munich: Siemens Stiftung, 1984), 21–25. Karl Meuli, *Gesammelte Schriften*, 2 vols. (Basel: Schwabe, 1975), 2:935–48.
3. Rudolf Hess, "Eröffnungsrede," *Offizieller Bericht: Der Parteitag Grossdeutschland vom 5.-12. September 1938* (Munich: Franz Eher, 1938), 40.
4. Yvonne Karow, *Deutsches Opfer: Kultische Selbstauslöschung auf den Reichsparteitagen der NSDAP* (Berlin: Akademie, 1997), 16.
5. Ibid., 17.
6. Michael Ley, *Holokaust als Menschenopfer: vom Christentum zur politischen Religion des Nationalsozialismus* (Münster: LIT Verlag, 2002), 12–13.
7. Karow, *Deutsches Opfer*, 17, and Ley, *Holokaust*, 7.
8. Giorgio Agamben, *Homo Sacer: Sovereign Power and Bare Life*, trans. Daniel Heller-Roazen (Stanford, Calif.: Stanford University Press, 1998), 85. Cited hereafter as *HS*.

9. Carl Schmitt, *Political Theology: Four Chapters on the Concept of Sovereignty*, trans. George Schwab (Chicago: University of Chicago Press, 2006).

10. For a more extended discussion and critique of Agamben's approach to violence and culture, see David Pan, "Against Biopolitics: Walter Benjamin, Giorgio Agamben, and Carl Schmitt on Political Sovereignty and Symbolic Order," *German Quarterly* 82, no. 1 (Winter 2009): 42–62.

11. Claudia Koonz, *The Nazi Conscience* (Cambridge, Mass.: Belknap Press, 2003), 6.

12. Adolf Hitler, "Grundsätzliche Betrachtungen über die Kunst," *Bausteine zum deutschen Nationaltheater* 1, no. 3 (Munich: Franz Eher, 1933): 66. Cited hereafter as AH.

13. Dr. H. B., "Die erste Woche," *Deutsche Bodensee-Zeitung* 16 (97), no. 210 (September 9, 1939): 1.

14. Tim Klein, "Vorrede," in *Das Buch vom Opfer*, ed. Tim Klein and Hermann Rinn (Munich: Verlag Georg D. W. Callwey, 1934), 6.

15. *Neue deutsche Biographie*, vol. 11, ed. Bayerische Akademie der Wissenschaften (Munich: Dunker und Humblot: 1977), s.v. "Tim Klein."

16. Hannah Arendt, *The Origins of Totalitarianism* (New York: Harcourt, Brace and World, 1966), 323–24. Cited hereafter as OT.

17. Ernest Gellner, *Nations and Nationalism*, 2nd ed. (Ithaca, N.Y.: Cornell University Press, 2008), 52–56.

18. Georg Bollenbeck, "German Kultur, the Bildungsbürgertum, and Its Susceptibility to National Socialism," *German Quarterly* 73, no. 1 (Winter 2000): 67–83.

19. Ibid., 75–79.

20. Karl Christoph Lingelbach, *Erziehung und Erziehungstheorien im nationalsozialistischen Deutschland* (Frankfurt am Main: Dipa-Verlag, 1987), 28–29. Adolf Hitler, *Mein Kampf*, 2 vols. (Munich: Franz Eher, 1939), 2:400; my translation.

21. Hitler, *Mein Kampf*, 2:425–26; cited in Lingelbach, *Erziehung*, 32.

22. Ibid., 2:420; cited in Lingelbach, *Erziehung*, 29–30.

23. Leske, *Philosophen im dritten Reich*, 203–4. Sluga, *Heidegger's Crisis*, 126–31, 223–30.

24. Lingelbach, *Erziehung*, 82–85.

25. Moses Mendelssohn, "On the question: what does 'to enlighten' mean?" (1784), *Philosophical Writings*, ed. and trans. Daniel O. Dahlstrom (Cambridge, UK: Cambridge University Press, 1997), 313. "Über die Frage: was heisst aufklären?" (1784), *Schriften über Religion und Aufklärung* (Darmstadt: Wissenschaftliche Buchgesellschaft, 1989), 461.

26. Ibid., 462–63.

27. Rudolf Vierhaus, "Bildung," in *Geschichtliche Grundbegriffe: Historisches Lexikon zur politisch-sozialen Sprache in Deutschland*, vol. 1, ed. Otto Brunner, Werner Conze, and Reinhart Koselleck (Stuttgart: Ernst Klett, 1972), 515–18, 526–28.

28. Mendelssohn, "On the question: what does 'to enlighten' mean?" 316. Mendelssohn, "Über die Frage: was heisst aufklären?" 465.

29. Johann Gottlieb Fichte, *Addresses to the German Nation*, trans. R. F. Jones and G. H. Turnbull, ed. George Armstrong Kelly (1808; New York: Harper and Row, 1968), 12. Cited hereafter as JF.
30. Sluga, *Heidegger's Crisis*, 149.
31. Alfred Baeumler, *Bildung und Gemeinschaft* (Berlin: Junker und Dünnhaupt, 1942), 185. Cited hereafter as *BG*.
32. Koonz, *Nazi Conscience*, 3.
33. On this point see David Sorkin, "Wilhelm von Humboldt: The Theory and Practice of Self-Formation (Bildung), 1791–1810," *Journal of the History of Ideas* 44, no. 1 (Jan.–Mar. 1983): 55–73. Although Sorkin argues that, in contrast to Fichte, Humboldt suppressed his civic notion of *Bildung* in order to avoid the nationalist consequences he saw, Sorkin concludes: "While Humboldt had not departed from his liberalism, his educational reform did in the end become a basis for the capitulation of the intelligentsia to the state" (73). In contrast to Sorkin, the argument here will be that Humboldt's maintenance of a distance between *Bildung* and the state was at the core of his nationalism.
34. Wilhelm von Humboldt, *On Language: On the Diversity of Human Language Construction and its Influence on the Mental Development of the Human Species,* ed. Michael Losonsky, trans. Peter Heath (Cambridge: Cambridge University Press, 1999), 43.
35. Wilhelm von Humboldt, *The Limits of State Action,* ed. J.W. Burrow (Cambridge: Cambridge University Press, 1969), 16.
36. Humboldt, *On Language*, 42.
37. Ibid.
38. Ibid., 31–32.
39. Ibid., 35.
40. Humboldt, *The Limits*, 23–24.
41. Humboldt, *On Language*, 44–45.
42. Adolf Hitler, "Der Führer spricht zu den politischen Leitern," *Der Kongress zu Nürnberg vom 5. bis 10. September 1934: Offizieller Bericht über den Verlauf des Reichsparteitages mit sämtlichen Reden* (Munich: Franz Eher, 1934), 162.
43. Ibid.
44. Ibid., 161.
45. Humboldt, *The Limits*, 23–24.
46. Adolf Hitler, "Der Führer bei der HJ," *Der Kongress zu Nürnberg.*
47. Adolf Hitler, "Die Schlussrede des Führers," *Der Kongress zu Nürnberg.*
48. Karow, *Deutsches Opfer*, 18; Lingelbach, *Erziehung*, 32–33.
49. Arnold Schoenberg, *A Survivor from Warsaw,* Op. 46, for narrator, men's chorus, and orchestra (1947; Hillsdale, N.Y.: Boelke-Bomart, 1949).
50. Theodor Adorno, "Arnold Schoenberg 1875–1951," *Prisms* (Cambridge, Mass.: MIT Press, 1981), 172. Christian Martin Schmidt, "Schönbergs Kantate 'Ein Überlebender aus Warschau,' Op. 46," *Archiv für Musikwissenschaft* 33 (1976): 277. David Lieberman, "Schoenberg Rewrites His Will: A Survivor from Warsaw, Op. 46," in *Political and Religious Ideas in the Works of Arnold*

Schoenberg, ed. Charlotte M. Cross and Russell A. Berman (New York: Garland, 2000), 217.

51. I diverge here from Lieberman, "Schoenberg Rewrites," 216.

Conclusion

1. See Richard Evans, "Sein wahres Gesicht," trans. Stephan Klapdor, *Süddeutsche Zeitung*, January 23, 2009, and Karl Heinz Bohrer, "Die Entlarvung des 20. Juli; Man darf Stauffenberg nicht als einen Helden unserer heutigen Zeit sehen — eine Antwort auf die Thesen des Historikers Richard J. Evans," *Süddeutsche Zeitung*, January 30, 2009.

INDEX

Accursed Share, The (Bataille, Georges), 82–91
action, 61, 111, 130, 149, 151
Adorno, Theodor: on aesthetics, 5–6, 40–41; *Aesthetic Theory*, 19–29; on aesthetic truth, 13–16, 39, 47, 79; beauty, 21–22, 47–48; on critique of art, 37–40; *Dialectic of Enlightenment*, 13–18, 31, 45, 51–52; on dissonance, 23; on enlightenment, 53; on expression, 18, 23, 32–33, 41–42, 71; form, 71; on Kant, 23; on myth, 16–20, 34, 48, 53; on nature, 20; on non-identity, 6, 21; on reconciliation, 20–23, 90 (*see also* reconciliation); on reification, 28, 91; on sacrifice, 4, 37, 40, 43, 102; on semblance, 18, 71; on sublime, 17, 21, 24; on utopia as transcendence, 26–28, 30, 32, 39; on utopia vs. sacrifice, 4–5, 21, 81, 90; on victims, 93
aesthetics: in Adorno, 5–6, 40–41; ethics and, 10, 26, 57, 68; as expression, 18; inner form, 18; as mimesis, 7, 19 (*see also* mimesis); of myth, 18–19, 34, 36, 40, 45–48, 57, 58–62, 71, 75, 77, 79, 82; in Nietzsche, 18–20; of reception, 39, 40, 43, 57, 58–62, 64, 68, 77, 80; of sacrifice, 40–43, 104–11, 147; as semblance, 18; subject and, 9; as truth, 13–16, 47, 57, 70, 150
aesthetic truth. *See* aesthetics: as truth
affinity, 135–36
African art, 54, 55
Agamben, Giorgio, 4: biopolitics, 115–16; on father principle, 122; on *homo sacer*, 100, 114–16
aggression, 3–4, 45, 81, 93–95, 101, 103, 108, 134
Alfred Rosenberg und der Mythus des 20. Jahrhunderts (Baeumler, Alfred), 66

alienation, 17
anarchism, 56
animal: human vs., 118, 121–22; sacrifice, 113
anti-Semitism, 66, 114–21. *See also* Jews; racism
Apollo, 18–19, 40–42, 49–50, 68; as semblance, 71–72, 75
Arendt, Hannah: on nationalism, 124–25, 131–34; on Nazism as movement, 12, 137; *Origins of Totalitarianism*, 124
art: as play, 71; as sacred, 75–76
Aryan, 66, 114
Asiatic culture, 66
aura, 53
Aztec sacrifice, 83–84, 90–91

Bachofen, Johann Jakob, 49–50, 55
Baeumler, Alfred, 48–51, 54–55; *Alfred Rosenberg und der Mythus des 20. Jahrhunderts*, 66; on education, 126–31, 135, 139–42; liberalism of, 50–52; on materiality, 7; on mother principle, 49–50; on myth, 49–50, 53, 58–62
bare life. *See* body: as bare life; *homo sacer*
Bataille, Georges: *Accursed Share, The*, 82–91; on destruction, 4; *Documents*, 82; Einstein, Carl and, 82; on ethics, 6; on Rais, Gilles de, 91; on reification, 83, 88–90; on sacrifice, 83–86, 103; on sovereignty of individual, 86–89; *Story of the Eye, The*, 91; on violence, 81
Baum, Herbert, 150
beauty: Adorno on, 21–22, 47–48; Kant on, 21–22
Bebuquin (Einstein, Carl), 54
Benjamin, Walter, 53, 81
Berlin, University of, 54

163

Beyond the Pleasure Principle (Freud), 81
Bildung. See education
Bildungsbürgertum, 125
biological reality, 149: Baeumler, Alfred on, 62–63, 65, 79–80; Bataille, Georges on, 82–84; Frank, Manfred on, 72, 79–80; Nazis on, 116–20
biopolitics, 115–16
Birth of Tragedy, The (Nietzsche), 18, 23
Bloch, Ernst, 53–58; *Geist der Utopie,* 53; *Heritage of Our Time,* 55; on myth, 68–69
blood as reality, 58, 62, 63–66, 72
body: as bare life, 4, 115, 121–24, 144; subordination of, 146. See also *homo sacer*
Bohrer, Karl Heinz, 151
Bollenbeck, Georg, 125
Braque, Georges, 58
Brentano, Clemens, 131
Brunträger, Hubert, 50
Buddhism, Tibetan, 90
Burke, Edmund, 125
Burkert, Walter, 81, 101–11, 113

camp: concentration, 115; extermination, 144
caprice, 89–91
chaos, 65–66, 82, 90, 145
Chinese language, 134
Christianity, 93, 97–98, 118, 149, 150
chthonic, 67
church, 132, 135, 144. *See also* religion; *Civilization and Its Discontents* (Freud), 81
collective interest, 43
comfort, 138
communicative rationality, 15, 30–31, 50, 70, 74, 76
communism, 54, 117, 150. *See also* Marxism
community, 31, 33–34, 43, 100, 127, 149, 150; national, 114, 117, 128, 140–43
concentration camp. *See under* camp
concept. *See* reason
consumerism, 83–84
consumption, 91, 113
Creuzer, Friedrich, 50

critique of art, 37–40
Critique of Judgment, The (Kant), 21–26
cult. *See* ritual: cultic
culture as mediator, 114, 122–24, 146, 149. *See also* symbolic order

Deacon, Terrence, 107–8
dead spirits, 62, 65
death, 86, 90; as drive, 81; of German soldiers, 113–14, 116; mechanical, 113; nonsacrificial, 113; ritualized, 113–14; sacrificial, 100, 113–14
decision, 9; as founding moment, 10, 43, 106–7, 110–11; sovereign, 115
Declaration of Independence, 125
delusion about sacrifice, 96–98
de Rais, Gilles. *See* Rais, Gilles de
destruction: in Bataille, 4, 82–85, 89–92; as consecration, 8; as freedom, 85; in Nietzsche, 19
development. *See* subject: development of
Dialectic of Enlightenment (Horkheimer and Adorno), 13–18, 31, 45, 51–52
Dilthey, Wilhelm, 53
Dionysus, 18–19, 23, 33, 40–42, 60, 66–68; as expression, 71–72
disinterestedness, 40, 67, 79, 86
dissonance, 23
domination: of nature, 6, 18, 28, 30, 36, 52, 80, 88–89; by reason, 6, 16, 28, 30, 45, 51–52, 65, 70, 74; as sacrifice, 14; by subject, over object, 20. *See also* hierarchy; subject: subordination of

economy, general, 84
education, 115, 123–24, 126–28, 130, 139–43, 146; as *Bildung* for nation, 11, 128–37; as *Bildung* in Nazism, 124–27, 137, 138–41; as *Erziehung,* 128, 140–42; Nazism and, 49, 125–27
Einstein, Carl, 53–55; on aesthetic experience, 57–58, 68–69; and Bataille, Georges, 82; *Bebuquin,* 54; *Documents,* 82; *Georges Braque,* 55; *Kunst des 20. Jahrhunderts,* 55; on myth, 70; *Negerplastik,* 54; on sacred, 65; on sacrifice, 81
enemy, 117, 120, 126, 142–43, 150

Index   165

energy as reality of existence, 82–84
enlightenment, 51, 52, 53, 67, 128, 141
epic, 50, 60–62
Erwartung (Schoenberg), 145
Erziehung. See education
ethics, 4–5; and aesthetics, 26, 32, 41–43, 46–47, 57, 68; Christian, 6; as decision, 10; and horror, 29–30; individualist, 6; Nazi, 9, 151; politics and, 150; reason and, 31, 42, 45, 149; sacrificial structure of, 9–10, 35, 107, 118, 149–51; sublime and, 7, 29–30
Eurocentrism, 79
exception, state of, 115
excess, 83–84
experience, 15–17, 32, 39, 45, 70, 71, 75, 80; aesthetic, 42–43, 57, 59, 61; of sacred, 57, 60
expert culture, 15, 74
expression, 18, 23, 32–33, 41–42, 71, 75
Expressionism, 53–54, 56
extermination camp. *See under* camp

family, 127, 132, 135, 140–42, 144
fascism, 51–52, 56, 67, 72, 77
father principle, 49–50, 66–67, 122–23
fear: as absolute, 86–87; of nature, 25, 32, 35; in ritual, 104; in sublime, 24–25, 29–30
Fichte, Johann Gottlieb, 11, 128–30, 133, 142
folk culture, 54, 56–57, 68–69
form, 50, 59–60, 65–67; as aesthetic, 71
Frank, Manfred, 50, 55, 67, 69–77; *Lectures on the New Mythology*, 70–77
freedom: as destruction, 85; of expression, 58–59, 64–65, 68, 147; from nature as constraint, 24–25, 38; as self-activity of individual, 130–35; slavery vs., 88; as sovereignty of individual, 86, 88–89
Freud, Sigmund, 4, 81; *Beyond the Pleasure Principle,* 81; *Civilization and Its Discontents,* 81, 93; *Totem and Taboo,* 81

generality: of aesthetic judgment, 34; of sacrifice, 4–5, 10. *See also* universalism

Geist der Utopie (Bloch, Ernst), 53
genius, 133, 134
Georges Braque (Einstein, Carl), 55
German idealism, 11, 128–29, 134
Girard, René, 4, 6, 81, 93–101, 102; *Things Hidden Since the Foundation of the World,* 97–98; *Violence and the Sacred,* 93–97
goals. *See* values
greatness, 138
guilt, 95–96, 104

Habermas, Jürgen, 14–17, 31, 50, 69–70
Hegel, Georg Wilhelm Friedrich, 47, 86
Heritage of Our Time (Bloch, Ernst), 55
Hermes, 3
heroes: Baeumler on, 62, 64; in Nazism, 12, 113–14, 139
Hess, Rudolf, 114, 116
hierarchy, 131, 134–35, 137. *See also* domination
history: in art, 20, 23; universal, 134–36; as violence, 27
Hitler, Adolf, 11, 49, 150; on education, 126; on Jews, 114, 117–20, 126; on rationality, 47; on sacrifice, 117–20, 138–39
Hitler Youth, 138
Hohendahl, Peter Uwe, 15, 37
Holocaust, 3, 114, 117
homo sacer, 4, 12, 100, 114–16, 122
Horkheimer, Max: *Dialectic of Enlightenment,* 13–18, 31, 45, 51–52; on myth, 16; on sacrifice, 4, 81, 102
horror, 29–30, 62
household, 137, 141–42
Hubert, Henri, 8, 9
Huhn, Tom, 24
humanism, 49, 128–31. *See also* universal humanity
human rights, 125
human vs. animal, 118–20
Humboldt, Wilhelm von, 11, 130–39
hunting, 100, 107

idealism, 49, 118–19, 139; *See also* German idealism
ideals. *See* values
ideology, 4, 115, 116; myth as, 46–48, 65, 67, 73–74, 76, 79

imagination, 29
immanence, 20, 32
imperialism, 119, 121, 124
index as sign, 107–11
individual. *See* subject
individual development. *See* subject: development of
individualism, 124–37
individual rights, 125
innocence of sacrificial victims, 95, 97–99
intimacy, 89–90. *See also* nonidentical
irrationalism, 53, 54
Islam, 90

Jameson, Frederic, 20–21
Jews, 12, 114–21, 143, 144–47. *See also* anti-Semitism; Judaism; racism
Judaism, 12, 41–42
judgment: 38–40, 45, 48, 67, 69, 70, 77, 80, 150, 151
Jünger, Ernst, 53

Kant, Immanuel: on aesthetic judgment, 37; on beauty, 21–22; *Critique of Judgment*, 21–26; on freedom, 25; on sacrifice, 40–43; on sublime, 7, 22, 24–26, 29, 40–43, 82
Kiefer, Klaus, 55
Klages, Ludwig, 53
Klein, Tim, 121–22
Koonz, Claudia, 9, 130
Koopmann, Helmut, 49
Kunst des 20. Jahrhunderts (Einstein, Carl), 55

labor, 87–89
Lacou-Labarthe, Philippe, 46–47
language, 129, 132, 134, 136. *See also* word as opposed to reality
Lebensphilosophie, 53
Lectures on the New Mythology (Frank, Manfred), 70–77
Leipzig, University of, 54
liberal democracy, 115
liberalism 48, 50–52, 56, 77, 80, 131, 140, 151
Liebknecht, Karl, 55
Lingelbach, Karl Christoph, 126
Lukács, Georg, 53, 81

Luxembourg, Rosa, 55
Lyotard, Jean-François, 29–30

magic, 16, 51, 72
manipulation, 52
Mann, Thomas, 48–49, 53; "German Address: An Appeal to Reason," 49; *German Listeners!*, 49; liberalism of, 50–52; "On the German Republic," 48; *Pariser Rechenschaft*, 52; "Reflections of an Unpolitical Man," 48
Männerbund, 142–43
Marshall Plan, 83, 90
martyrdom, 3, 149
Marxism, 54, 56, 69. *See also* communism
materialism, 46, 50–51, 58–67, 73, 77, 87, 118–20, 121, 142
maternal. *See* mother principle
Mauss, Marcel, 8, 9
memory, 146
Mendelssohn, Moses, 128
men's association, 142–43
mimesis, 14; conflictual, 94–97; as form, 41–42; of history, 20, 79–80; myth and, 51–52; of nature, 21, 28, 31, 79–80; reason and, 7; of subjectivity, 33; of violence, 93–94
mimetic violence, 93–94
Mosse, George, 56
mother principle, 49–50, 66–67
myth: as aesthetic, 18–19, 34, 36, 40, 45–48, 57, 58–62, 71, 75, 77, 79, 82; as archaic, 50; as chaos, 50; as Dionysian, 72; as ideology, 46–48, 65, 67, 73–74, 76, 79; as materiality, 48, 58–62, 64; mimesis and, 51–52; as new mythology, 70, 74; in Nietzsche, 58, 62, 71; reason and, 49, 51, 74; as religion, 59; science vs., 16–17; suppression of, 52–53, 65, 67, 150; violence of, 36, 53
Myth of the 20th Century, The (Rosenberg), 49, 67–68

Nancy, Jean-Luc, 46–47
narrative, 8, 45, 60–61, 73, 104–7, 110–11, 149
national community, 140–43

Index

nationalism, 49, 77; German, 8, 11, 114, 118–20, 124–43, 150–51
nation-state, 124–25, 130, 133–35
nature: as abyss, 30–31; beauty of, 21–22; as contradiction, 19–23, 25; as horror, 32; as nonidentical, 89; power of, 32, 35, 40, 51–52, 81, 88; as reconciliation, 20–21, 23, 35, 90; as violence, 6, 14, 23, 36, 81
Nazi Party Congress, 114, 137–39
Nazism: education under, 49, 125–27; enlightenment and, 51, 52; folk culture and, 56; ideology of, 115; individualism and, 11; as movement, 12, 136, 137; myth and, 46–49, 51–52, 68, 150; nation and, 11, 135; particularity of, 115; racism in, 12, 46, 118–19, 124, 126–27, 130, 143; sacrifice in, 113–20, 126–27, 137–39, 142–43, 149, 150; violence of, 12, 144–47
negation, 86–87
negativity, 40–42, 76, 87
Negerplastik (Einstein, Carl), 54
new mythology, 70, 74
Nicholsen, Shierry, 34, 37–38
Nietzsche, Friedrich, 7; on aesthetics, 18–20; on Apollo (*see* Apollo); *Birth of Tragedy, The*, 18–19, 23, 58; on Dionysus (*see* Dionysus); on dissonance, 23; influence of, 54; *Lebensphilosophie* and, 53; on myth, 58, 62, 71; on primordial unity, 19, 23, 33–34, 60
noncontemporaneity, 56, 68–69
nonidentical: Adorno on, 6, 21–22, 41, 76; Bataille on, 89–90
nonsacrifice, 97–98, 113–14, 119–21, 144

Old Testament, 41
Origins of Totalitarianism (Arendt), 124

particularity: of art, 39; of community, 8, 33–34, 43, 123–24, 134–35, 147, 150; of experience, 16; of nation, 132, 136; of Nazism, 115; of sacrifice, 4–5, 10, 82, 98, 107; of subject, 79–80, 143, 144
paternal. *See* father principle

pedagogy. *See* education
Peirce, Charles, 107–8
performance, 60, 108, 110
performativity, 108, 110, 149
personality, 130–31
philosopher as leader, 64–68, 76
philosophy: and art, 37–40, 47, 70; and myth, 64, 67; as truth, 70, 76
Plataeans, 104–5
Plato, *Protagoras*, 3
pleasure, 91
political idea, 142–43
political repression, 68
popular culture. *See* folk culture
poststructuralism, 50
potlatch, 83
power of life and death, 122–23
primitive culture, 3, 35, 50, 54, 55
primordial unity, 19, 23, 33–34, 60
progress, 5, 35, 81, 131, 133–37, 147
promise, 5, 105, 108–11, 114, 151. *See also* ritual: as promise
Protagoras (Plato), 3

racism, 51, 58, 61, 63–64, 130–32, 134; Nazism and, 12, 46, 118–19, 124, 126–27, 130, 143
Rais, Gilles de, 91
rationality. *See* reason
reality, 6, 47–48; as principle, 81. *See also* biological reality; supernatural
reason, 48, 128, 131–32: communicative, 15, 30–31, 50, 70, 74, 76; as domination, 6, 16, 28, 30, 45, 51–52, 65, 70, 74; ethics and, 31, 42, 45, 149; limits of, 38; mimesis and, 7; myth and, 49, 51, 74
reception, aesthetic, 39, 40, 43, 57, 58–62, 64, 68, 77, 80
reconciliation, 20–21, 23, 35, 90
Reichsparteitag. *See* Nazi party congress
reification: in Adorno, 28, 89–90, 91; in Bataille, 83, 88–90, 91; in Hegel, 88. *See also* utility
relativism, 149–50
religion, 41–42, 77, 140, 142; art and, 58; as enthusiasm, 42; myth and, 59, 66; as ritual, 72, 76
representation, 18–19, 33, 40–42, 71–72, 147, 149

resistance to violence, 12, 144–47, 150–51
Rights of Man, 125
Rilke, Rainer Maria, *Sonnets to Orpheus*, 75
ritual, 43, 49; cultic, 50, 59–62, 64–65, 70–72, 77; as destruction, 83; as materialist, 67, 103–4; myth and, 53, 56–57; Nazi, 114; as performative, 108, 110; as promise, 105, 108–11, 149; religious, 72, 76; sacrifice and, 94–96; as theatrical, 103–4; tradition and, 39, 57
romanticism, 50, 131
Rosenberg, Alfred, 53, 66; *Myth of the Twentieth Century, The*, 49, 67–68
Rousseau, Jean-Jacques, 133

sacred, 57, 60–62, 73; as *homo sacer*, 116
sacrifice: aesthetics of, 40–43, 104–11, 147; animal, 113; anti-Semitism and, 114–20; arbitrary, 97–98; Bataille, Georges on, 83–86, 103; Christian, 93, 97–98; as cultural marking, 114, 116, 122, 149 (*see also* sacrifice: symbolic order); death and, 100, 113–14; delusion about, 96–98; as destruction, 82–85, 92; as domination, 14; education and, 115, 126–27, 139–43; ethics and, 9–10, 35, 107, 118, 149–50; generality of, 4–5, 10; of German soldiers, 113–14, 116; for greatness, 138; guilt and, 95–96, 104; hunting and, 100, 107; as ideology, 4, 116; innocence and, 95, 97–99; irrational, 97–98; as martyrdom, 149; narrative of, 104–7, 110–11; for nation, 114, 116, 117, 120, 126–27, 138–40, 143; Nazi, 113–20, 126–27, 137–39, 142–43, 149, 150; necessity of, 81, 120–21; nonsacrifice and, 97–98, 113–14, 119–21, 144; particularity of, 4–5, 10, 82, 98, 107; as resistance, 144–47, 149; ritual and, 94–96; scapegoat and, 4, 12, 94–95, 99–101, 117, 120; self-sacrifice, 3, 40–43, 90, 98, 101–2, 118, 149; sovereignty and, 86, 90; as

subject formation, 80, 119, 141–43, 144, 147; sublime as, 40–43, 82, 111; as substitution, 85; as symbolic order, 80, 91–92, 96, 103–4, 104–6, 107–11, 114, 146, 149–50; universal structure of, 96; utility and, 4, 85; values as result of, 43, 101–2, 107, 149–51; violence and, 79–80, 81–82, 93–95, 103–4, 149
sacrificial crisis, 95–96, 110
Sanskrit language, 134
scapegoat, 4, 12, 94–101, 117, 120
Schelling, Friedrich, 50, 53, 70
Schmitt, Carl, 115
Schoenberg, Arnold: *Erwartung*, 145; *Survivor from Warsaw, A*, 12, 144–47
Scholl, Hans, 150
Scholl, Sophie, 150
secularization, 17
self-activity: of individual, 131–33, 136, 147; of nation, 137–39
self-sacrifice, 40–43, 90, 98, 101–2, 118, 149
semblance, 18, 71, 75
Shema Yisroel, 145–46
sign: as index, 107–11; as symbol, 58, 72–73, 107–11
Simmel, Georg, 53, 54
slavery, 88
Sluga, Hans, 129
socialism, 80
Sonnets to Orpheus (Rilke), 75
sovereignty: father principle and, 122–23; individual, 86–89, 91, 146–47; political, 114–15, 120; as power to kill, 122–23; sacrifice and, 86, 90; values and, 122–23
Spanish Civil War, 55
specificity. *See* particularity
Stalinism, 54
state of exception, 115
state power, 135, 137, 145
Stauffenberg, Claus von, 150–51
Stern, J. P., 7, 47–48
Story of the Eye, The (Bataille, Georges), 91
subject: aesthetics and, 9; in community, 8, 14; development of, 131–37, 139–41, 147; dissolution of, 144–45;

Index   169

freedom of, 128–31; nation and, 11; Nazi, 11; object and, 20, 88–89; particularity of, 79–80, 143, 144; as sovereign, 87, 89, 91, 146–47; subjectivity of, 59–61; sublime and, 7; subordination of, 80, 119, 141–43, 144, 147; universality of, 33–34, 79
sublime, 14; Adorno on, 17, 21, 24; as horror, 29–30; Kant on, 7, 22, 24–26, 29, 40–43; Lyotard on, 29; as sacrifice, 40–43, 82, 111
subordination. *See* subject: subordination of
sun as source of life, 82, 84
supernatural, 61–62, 72, 79–80, 149
Survivor from Warsaw, A (Schoenberg), 12, 144–47
symbol: as real, 58, 63–64; as sign, 58, 72–73, 107–11
symbolic order: as myth, 58; as reification, 89–90; sacrifice as, 80, 91–92, 96, 103–4, 104–6, 107–11, 114, 146, 149–50 (*see also* culture as mediator)

Things Hidden Since the Foundation of the World (Girard, René), 97–98
Tibetan Buddhism, 90
totalitarianism, 115, 124–25, 131, 134–35, 137
totality, 32, 45
total mobilization, 117
Totem and Taboo (Freud), 81
tradition: as aesthetically based authority, 56–57, 64, 108; as culturally specific, 122; individual freedom vs. 60, 123–24, 130–2, 136, 147; rationality vs., 39, 43, 48, 68, 127, 134; as stagnant, 140, 143
tragedy, 18, 50, 60–62, 65, 113
transcendence, 28–30, 32, 38–40, 86
truth, 47
Tübingen, University of, 50
twelve-tone row, 145–46
20th Century Art (Einstein, Carl), 55

universal history, 134–36
universal humanity, 134–35, 147. *See also* humanism
universalism, 121, 129–30, 134–35, 147, 149. *See also* generality
U.S. Constitution, 125
utility, 4, 83, 84–85, 88–89. *See also* reification
utopia, 75–76, 90, 114. *See also under* Adorno

values: Baeumler on, 130, 142; Bataille on, 84–85, 90, 92; Kant on, 35; sacrifice as constitutive of, 43, 101–2, 107, 149–51
value spheres, 15–16, 31
violence: acquisitive, 94–95; culture and, 5; in history 27; as ineradicable, 81; mimetic, 93–94; of myth, 36; as nature, 6, 14, 23, 36, 81; in Nazism, 12, 144–47; as real, 7, 47, 82, 84, 86–87, 89–90, 103; reciprocal, 95; resistance to, 12, 144–47; sacrifice and, 79–80, 81–82, 93–95, 103–4, 149; as sovereignty, 89; sublime and, 23
Violence and the Sacred (Girard, René), 93–97
vitae necisque potestas. See power of life and death
völkisch movement, 56
voluntarism, 130
von Humboldt, Wilhelm. *See* Humboldt, Wilhelm von
von Stauffenberg, Claus. *See* Stauffenberg, Claus von

Weber, Max, 15
Weimar Republic, 48
Wellmer, Albrecht, 30–32
Western culture, 66
will, 130, 149, 151
Wölfflin, Heinrich, 54
word as opposed to reality, 61, 63–64, 130. *See also* symbol; symbolic order
work. *See* labor
World War I, 113, 139

Yanomamö Indians, 108–10

Zeus, 3
Zuidervaart, Lambert, 22

ABOUT THE AUTHOR

David Pan is a professor of German at the University of California, Irvine.